The Stranger Is Our Own

REFLECTIONS ON THE JOURNEY
OF PUERTO RICAN MIGRANTS

Joseph P. Fitzpatrick, S.J.
1913-1995

The Stranger Is Our Own

REFLECTIONS ON THE JOURNEY OF PUERTO RICAN MIGRANTS

Joseph P. Fitzpatrick, S.J.

Sheed & Ward
Kansas City

Sheed & Ward™ is a service of The National Catholic Reporter
Publishing Company.

Library of Congress Cataloguing-in-Publication Data
Fitzpatrick, Joseph P.
     The stranger is our own : reflections on the journey of Puerto
Rican migrants / Joseph P. Fitzpatrick.
          p.   cm.
     Includes bibliographical reference.
     ISBN 1-55612-905-X (alk. paper)
     1. Puerto Ricans—New York (State)—New York—Social conditions.
2. Church work with immigrants—New York (State)—New York.
3. Church work with immigrants—Catholic Church. 4. New York
(N.Y.)—Ethnic relations. 5. New York (N.Y.)—Emigration and
immigration. 6. Puerto Rico—Emigration and immigration.
I. Title.
F128.9.P85F58   1996
305.868'729507471—dc21   96-46596
                                                                          CIP

Published by: Sheed & Ward
                      115 E. Armour Blvd.
                      P.O. Box 419492
                      Kansas City, MO 64141-6492

To order, call: (800) 333-7373

Contents

Preface

FOR MORE THAN HALF OF THE 82 YEARS OF HIS LIFE, JOSEPH P. FITZPATRICK, S.J., ministered to the Puerto Ricans and studied their migration to the United States mainland. The first part of this book is a personal memoir which puts forth his view of the migration, as he and the newcomers moved along on what he refers to as a "bittersweet journey." The second part of the book consists of a series of articles, papers, and talks by Father Fitzpatrick. Each work he selected reflects a particular stage in the migration, his relationship to it, and his analysis of it. Both parts emphasize the cultural dimension in behavior and his call for intercultural understanding. Long before diversity and multiculturalism became popular, he championed them.

In a homily entitled "The Stranger Is Our Own," Father Fitzpatrick summarized his perspective on migration in general.[1]

> "Yahweh said to Abram, 'Leave your country, your family, your father's house, for the land I will show you. I will make you a great nation: I will bless you, and make your name so famous that it will be used as a blessing.'" (*Genesis* 12:1)
>
> God's plan for the salvation of the human family began with a migration; at every stage of God's intervention, it is marked by a migration; where migration takes place, we can be sure that the finger of God is writing the crooked lines that make up the straight phrases of the salvation of His children from sin and evil and death. The symbol of human liberation in God's revelation, in liturgy, in poetry, and sacred song is the migration of the Hebrews into Egypt and the miracle of their escape in the forty-year migration through the desert to the Promised Land. It was the migration of the Hebrews into the Diaspora, those little Hebrew communities in Greek and Roman, Egyptian and

---

1. Homily prepared for the Inauguration of Charles Keely as the occupant of the Donald Herzberg Chair of International Migration, at Georgetown University, January 28, 1988.

Syrian cities, that served as the beachheads of the establishment of Christianity in the Greek and Roman world. It was the turbulent migration of the Huns and the Vandals and others into Southern Europe that slowly transformed the Roman Empire into the great Christian civilization of the Middle Ages; it was the migration of European Catholics from the farms of Ireland and Germany, later from Italy and Central Europe that brought the Catholic Church to the United States. And now, migrations from Central and South America, from Asia, from the Caribbean, are bringing Catholics of the next century in large numbers to our nation. "A blessing" [is how] the American bishops defined it in their pastoral letter on the Hispanic Presence. That is what God said to Abram: "Your migration will be a source of blessing." When God's children are on the move, you can be certain God is with them.

When the Lord struck His covenant with His people, He reminded the Israelites of their experience and set down the rules that were to guide His people in relation to strangers (to immigrants, to refugees): "If strangers live with you in your land, do not molest them; you must count them as your own countrymen and love them as yourselves for you were once strangers yourselves in Egypt. I am Yahweh your God." (*Leviticus* 19:33-34) "When you gather the harvest of your land, you are not to harvest to the very end of the field. You are not to harvest the gleanings of the harvest. You must leave them for the poor and the stranger. I am Yahweh your God." (*Leviticus* 19:9-10)

You must count the strangers as your own countrymen, and love them as yourselves. What a vision! What a commandment! How sadly forgotten and how seldom we are guided by God's wisdom in our response to the strangers in our midst....[Yet] the final judgment on our lives, our final destiny is linked to this. "Come blest of my Father. When I was homeless you took me in ... when you did this to the least of my brethren, you did it to me." (*Matthew* 25)

What does it all mean? ... What did the painful migration of forty years through the desert mean? We did not have the sophisticated categories of sociology then to analyze it. But the Lord told us what it meant: "If you obey my voice and hold fast to my covenant, you of all the nations shall be mine." (*Exodus* 19:5) You will see the blessings of the Promised Land for which this migration is preparing you.

What did the migration mean that brought the wild tribes to the walls of Rome? Augustine thought it was the end of the world; he could not imagine the City of God outside the context of the

Roman world. If only he could have seen medieval Paris or Cologne, or Chartres. What did the migration mean that brought the suffering Irish to our shores in converted lumber and fish boats? Half of them on some of the boats died in passage. A British doctor came over on one of the boats to see how they survived. "If you placed a wooden cross on the Atlantic Ocean for every Irish person who died in passage," he said, "you could pave the Atlantic Ocean with a wooden highway from Cobh to Boston and New York." The doctor could not foresee the remarkable Church the Irish immigrants helped to establish in the new nation. "I am Yahweh, your God, and I am with you." What do the crippled boats from Vietnam mean, and the pirates, and refugee camps; or dangerous trips across the Mexican border, paying a life's savings to a "Coyote" to reach Los Angeles? "I am Yahweh, your God, and I am with you."

We do not see in clear detail how this unfolds. But the record of history makes it clear. It is with migrations that the finger of God writes the history of liberation and salvation.

And so as we begin to seek the help of the human sciences to gain what insight we can into the experience of migration, we ask God to give us the vision and the grace to make [the covenant] clear to His people. . . . To do this in a complicated world, however, needs more than prayer and sacrifice; it needs all the human knowledge and wisdom we can muster to help us understand the reasons for the migration, the experience of migrants who suffer as all migrants and immigrants have suffered, to give us the insight into the process of their adjustment to a new land, and the process whereby we seek to accept them as our own. For this effort of science and scholarship and policy, we ask the blessing of the Lord . . . [on scholars and students, as well as on the] immigrants and refugees who . . . will be accepted as our own.

A consummate priest, Father Fitzpatrick brought compassion and empathy, morality and ethics to the debate about the migrants and their place in our society; a consummate scholar and teacher, Professor Fitzpatrick gathered empirical data and developed an analytical framework, shaped by his doctoral studies at Harvard University, and brought them to the attention of the secular and religious institutions with which the migrants came into contact. His influence lives on in the generations of his former undergraduate and, especially, graduate students who continue to study, serve, and work with migrants in the United States, Latin America and many other parts of the world; indefatigable community activist and seeker of social justice, Padre José – as he was known in the

Puerto Rican community – assumed a leadership position early in the migration. He influenced not only the Catholic Church's response to the migrants and their pastoral needs, but also New York City's response to their secular and material needs. This book provides a glimpse into his life, the lives of many Puerto Ricans, and the ways in which they were intertwined for so long. In so doing, it also begins to make clear his role in the Catholic Church and in sociology.

Madeline E. Moran
March 1995

Part I

Personal Reflections

THE JOURNEY OF THE PUERTO RICANS TO THE U.S. MAINLAND BEGAN LATE last century, but the major part has taken place since World War II. It has been my own good fortune to walk this latter part of the journey with them. It has been a bittersweet journey, one of many tribulations, but one that has been marked more often by excitement and the abundant joy of sharing the experience of a newly arriving people, struggling with the challenge of trying to find themselves as they seek to find their place in the larger experience of the United States. I have often been asked: How did I ever become involved with the Puerto Ricans, and what has this meant to me? Where do I think the migration is going, and what do I think it has meant to them? A complete answer to these questions would require volumes. The best I can do here is to sketch out certain highlights of the journey, theirs, and mine, and sometimes ours. I hope that this may be of some help to the Puerto Rican people, giving them one person's insight into who they are and have been. Perhaps it may reassure them to know that, despite the problems and the failures along the way, they have been part of a profound experience not only theirs but also of all Americans.

When I first began to read of the influx of Puerto Ricans, especially to New York City in the late 1940s, I saw it through my own youthful sociologist's eyes as yet another coming of immigrant people to the United States. The long experience of New York City with newcomers was merely continuing. As my journey with them began and progressed, I was to see things differently. Many of the characteristics of the new-comers were the same, indeed, as those of previous groups. But I realized more and more that important differences were present in the Puerto Rican experience and they shed light on those that were taking place in the United States at the same time. Puerto Ricans were a new kind of people coming to a new kind of nation. Puerto Ricans were also a different kind of Catholic coming to a different kind of Catholic Church.

Therefore, I set out in this little book to try to answer those who had questioned me and, in doing so, to inquire into one facet of our changing nation and our changing church.

I try as well as I can to describe my own journey from the first naive judgement that Puerto Ricans would make the journey just as everyone else had made it, to a new and clearer perception of the new and strange world to which they had to adjust, and the new and strange ways by which they would seek to achieve that adjustment. I shall make some cautious comments about where I think the journey is going; more important will be my comments on what the Puerto Ricans have suffered and what they have achieved along the way. In my own response to the Puerto Rican experience, I have given numerous lectures, conferences, and workshops and I have written many things, some published, some unpublished. Some of these reflect my own perceptions at various moments of the journey. I shall include some of these in Part II of this book. The narrative will provide the setting for these statements. But the articles speak for themselves of what I was thinking of the Puerto Rican experience at those various moments, and what I was trying to get others to think as well.

This is neither a revision of my book, *Puerto Rican Americans: The Meaning of Migration to the Mainland*[1] nor is it a sequel (see p. 64). It is a series of reflective essays and research articles which identify where I was in the journey with the Puerto Ricans at successive moments in time.

My first recollection of Puerto Rico is amusing. My brother Vincent's religious community, The Missionary Servants of the Most Holy Trinity, had just taken over a Catholic high school in Puerto Rico, and he was telling me enthusiastically of the report of their Superior when he returned. I naively asked him: "Did your Superior stop at Hawaii on the way back?" That was the extent of my awareness of Puerto Rico in the mid-1930s. I thought it was near the Philippines.

My second contact with Puerto Ricans was much more immediate and surely sadder. It took place in December 1944. I was spending a period of training as a young priest in a New York hospital, a public hospital which cared predominantly for the very poor. I do not wish to identify the hospital; it no longer exists. I was still hopelessly naive. I kept coming across names like Hernandez and Gomez, and I thought they were Italian, probably because the priest we always called about

---

1. Joseph P. Fitzpatrick. *Puerto Rican Americans: The Meaning of Migration to the Mainland*, Englewood Cliffs, N.J.: Prentice Hall, 1st ed. 1971, 2nd ed. 1987.

these deaths was a Father Grande at Milagrosa Parish, then the national parish for Puerto Ricans in the City.[2] I thought the name, Grande, was Italian. However, one afternoon I was called to minister to a woman and the nurse identified her as Puerto Rican. Her child was to be delivered by Caesarean section. I was called to administer to her the "Sacrament of the Sick," a series of prayers and anointing for the health and well being of the patient. Let us call her, Mrs. Gonzalez.

Despite the eventual tragedy of it, I look back at that anointing with some astonishment. I knew no Spanish, but we carried around a little polyglot booklet with essential words in various languages for the administration of the Sacraments to the Sick in the hospital. Here I was, trying to hear the woman's Confession and administer the Sacrament of the Sick in Spanish. Knowing what I do now about Puerto Ricans, I suspect Mrs. Gonzalez did not have the faintest idea what Confession was nor what the Sacrament of the Sick was. But she patiently accepted my ministry and responded with what I came to appreciate in Puerto Ricans, a warm and affectionate gesture of thanks. She may not have known what I was doing, but at least I was "Un Padre" giving her some attention, and she appreciated it. The time was about 3 p.m. About 11 p.m. I was called out of bed to go to the operating room to minister to a critical case. The patient was listed as "Catholic" on her chart. I rushed up to the operating room and, to my amazement, I was told the patient was Mrs. Gonzalez. The doctor had delivered the baby by Caesarean; but the mother went into shock. The equipment for blood transfusions had broken and the operating room personnel were frantically trying to get a replacement. In any event, here at 11 p.m., hours after the Caesarean, the doctors were fighting to save her life. I began to say the prayers for the dying but while I was still praying, she died.

The following morning as I was going into breakfast, I met the pediatrician who had taken the baby to the nursery. I said to him: "That was very sad about Mrs. Gonzalez last night, wasn't it?" In amazement he said: "What was very sad?" I said, "But don't you know she died?" The pediatrician was shocked. "I can't believe it," he said, "it was a beautiful operation; the baby is wonderful. What could have happened?" I described to him what I knew of the death. After breakfast, as I left the dining hall, a forlorn looking man was standing outside the

---

2. A national or language parish is a parish without geographical boundaries, staffed by Spanish-speaking priests that minister especially to Puerto Rican people. The model for this was the Italian, Polish, German, etc., parishes which proved so effective for the immigrants from Europe. Later on this policy was to be changed under Cardinal Spellman (see p. 15).

maternity ward. I suspected who he was and I asked him, "Are you Mr. Gonzalez?" He answered, with tears in his eyes, "Yes, I am." He spoke enough English to communicate with me. I extended my sympathies. I told him I had ministered to his wife before she went to the operation, and that I was with her during her final moments when she died; that I had said all the prayers for the dying and, after her death, said the prayers for the dead. Again, as his wife did, he expressed his thanks with great emotion and affection. That afternoon as I was returning to my residence after lunch, I saw the nurse who was head of the maternity department, the one who had called me in the first place. She was a large, strong looking, Irish woman who had been on that service for many years. The gossip of the hospital was that she knew more than any of the doctors and was the one who taught them as they came, one after another, for their training. I said to her, "That was very sad about Mrs. Gonzalez last night." The doctor, a resident surgeon who had performed the Caesarean, was over in front of the doctors' residence fixing his car. The nurse looked at me with an icy stare and remarked: "Father, you don't know how sad that really was. There was no need for that Caesarean yesterday. Do you see that doctor over there? He did the operation. We have had more Caesareans in the year he has been here than we had in the previous ten. He got on the phone and badgered the Chief of Service until he was given approval for the Caesarean. He is getting lots of practice. But Mrs. Gonzalez is dead." This was the beginning of my insight that there were people called Puerto Ricans in New York and that they often suffered as helpless victims. That was 1944. It was to be a number of years before the spark would become a flame and I would find myself one of the prominent advocates for the Puerto Rican newcomers.

WOODSTOCK COLLEGE AND HARVARD:
THE BEGINNING OF THE VISION

My initial awareness of the Spanish-speaking world was really related to Latin America as it was described to me by Father William Gibbons, S.J., a classmate of mine during our theological studies at Woodstock College in Maryland, 1940-1944. Gibbons, on his own initiative and by his own reading, had developed an extraordinary knowledge of Latin America. Later, for a number of years, he was to publish an annual report, *Basic Ecclesiastical Statistics of Latin America*. In many of our conversations, he talked about Latin America and I became aware of its increasing importance to the future of the Church (one-third of all

Baptized Catholics in the world), and to the future of the United States. Population growth was diminishing in the United States; the highest rates of population growth in the world were in Latin America. Before I left Woodstock College in 1944, I was well aware of the significance of Latin America, and very much concerned about my future relationship to it as a priest.

However, the experience that was to prepare me for the Puerto Ricans occurred at Harvard University where I studied for my doctorate degree, 1945-48. This proved in one way to be an unusual redirection of my life. My interests up to this time had been in the field of Labor Relations. I had been Director of the Xavier Labor School in New York City, a center of adult education for workers who faced the problem of union organizing during the late 1930s. I went to Harvard to get a degree in Industrial Sociology and my dissertation, *White Collar Worker on Wall Street*, was a study of labor/management relations in the stock exchanges and brokerage houses. While I was at Harvard, I took two courses with the eminent historian of American Immigration, Professor Oscar Handlin. One was "Boston's Immigrants, 1780-1840," really a history of the Irish immigration to Boston. The other course, "The Boston Community, 1840-1880," was a history of the rise of the Irish immigrants to political control of the City of Boston. These were fascinating courses and I was almost converted to devote myself to studies of immigration history. The striking thing about these courses was this: Handlin, a Jew, taught me what it meant to be Irish. I had very little knowledge of the Irish immigration, even though all my grandparents were Irish immigrants. My father's parents had died before I was born, but my mother's parents lived with us for a number of years; they never spoke much about Ireland or the immigrant experience. It was through my courses with Handlin that I became aware of my background, of the culture from which I came, of the history of the immigrant experience of my grandparents. Although my degree was in industrial sociology, nevertheless I returned to New York with an extensive knowledge of immigrant experience and an enthusiasm about it.

FORDHAM UNIVERSITY: 1949 TO PRESENT

I returned to Fordham in November 1948, and began teaching in January 1949. I established an Institute of Labor/Management Relations which enjoyed considerable success for a number of years. More importantly, I arrived in New York when the migration of Puerto Ricans was reaching new highs. As a sociologist I was well aware of the migration and of its significance even before I came to Fordham. It was frequently discussed at Harvard. Shortly after arriving at Fordham, I was asked to collaborate on a study of Puerto Rican newcomers, specifically, I was to write the section on the participation of Puerto Ricans in the labor unions. This brought me into face-to-face, live contact with Puerto Rican newcomers for the first time. I was appalled. I had thought that, by this time, New York and New Yorkers would know how to deal with newcomers; the City had been receiving newcomers for two hundred years. Not so. Here were the Puerto Ricans going through many of the same problems that earlier immigrants had faced, only with a different cast of characters. Instead of white, Anglo-Saxon Protestants mistreating the Catholic Irish, now it was establishment-Irish, Jews, Italians, Germans, etc., mistreating Puerto Ricans. Dislike, misunderstanding, complete ignorance of Puerto Rican culture, and a forgetfulness of what they had suffered themselves, bias and prejudice; all of it was there, and the Puerto Ricans were in the middle of it. The vision of Mrs. Gonzalez came alive again in my memory. It seemed to me that somebody should be saying something about this. Nobody seemed to be doing it, at least, nobody that I was aware of. I decided to begin to talk. At this moment in the 1950s I saw the Puerto Rican exprience in two perspectives: 1) Their need for advocates, someone to explain to New Yorkers who they were, what they were like, what their cultural background was as well as their experience in New York. And to explain to the Puerto Ricans what was involved in their adjustment to New York City. 2) The religious dimension of their experience, and the need to alert the priests, bishops and Catholic people to the significance of the presence of Puerto Ricans in our midst.

FRIENDS WHOM I MET EARLY IN THE JOURNEY

Very early I began to become acquainted with many of the Puerto Ricans, prominent or poor, who talked to me about the journey and walked with me along it. Many of them were women who played an important leadership role in the Puerto Rican community during the 'fifties and early 'sixties.

One of the outstanding women was Encarnación Padilla de Armas. Encarnación had come from a distinguished family in Puerto Rico. After an unfortunate and failed marriage in Cuba, she came to New York with her young son, Ramon Bosch, and starting with humble labor, began the task of surviving in this complicated City. She later married Antonio Armas, a Spaniard and journalist who was living in New York. However, she soon became the Spanish-speaking organizer for the Liberal

Party, a position she held during the 1950s. She had remarkable political insights and was sophisticated as an organizer. She was a powerful public speaker and campaigner who could bring any audience quickly to its feet. I always told her that she wound up working for the wrong party. Had she tied in with the Democratic Party of the City, I am convinced she would soon have risen to highly placed appointed or elected positions. She certainly had the ability to warrant this. But the Liberal Party was rather small, and had little or no association with the Catholic community of New York to which the Puerto Rican community, at least by religious background, belonged.

Encarnación was my first great teacher about Puerto Rican culture and experience. She was thoroughly acquainted with every level of the community, from the poorest to the most influential and affluent. She also wrote a column for the Puerto Rican press. She was a devout Catholic, often critical of the lack of response of the Catholic Church to the spiritual and religious needs of the Puerto Ricans. It was her recurring criticism that urged me to speak and write frequently about Catholic responsibilities to the Puerto Rican newcomers.

In 1961, when Ivan Illich[3] inaugurated his Center of Intercultural Documentation in Cuernavaca, Mexico, a training center for persons preparing to work among the Spanish-speaking either here or in Latin America, he convinced Encarnación to become the administrator of the center, a difficult task in which she served well. Later in the 1960s she worked for the Catholic Committee for the Spanish-speaking of the Southwest. When the Secretariat for the Spanish-speaking was established at the U.S. Catholic Conference in Washington, she became a member of that staff. After returning to New York in the 1970s, she organized the Agrupación de Viejos Hispanos de Nueva York (The Organization of Spanish-Speaking Elderly in New York), a remarkable group that even today can turn out two thousand people for an annual meeting.

She died in August 1992. In her older years, she was often referred to affectionately as "La Madrina" (The Godmother) of the Puerto Rican community.

Among the other women I met who were community leaders was Luisa Quintero, a columnist for *La Prensa* and later for *El Diario y La Prensa*. Luisa knew everything that was going on. She must have attended every meeting that took place in the City. She was a very influential woman and a vociferous advocate for Puerto Rican causes.

---

3. See p. 16 and following for a lengthy description of Ivan Illich.

Antonia Pantoja was the founder of Aspira, the remarkable organization of students' clubs (Aspira Clubs) which prepare high school students for college. "Toni" was also one of the founders of the Puerto Rican Forum, an organization of Puerto Ricans seeking to promote the betterment of their community. She also promoted the Puerto Rican Community Development Project, a well conceived plan which never came alive (see p. 58). Toni was a militant leader with great vision. She later helped to found Universidad Boricua, originally a college without walls for Puerto Ricans, but later a four-year college which is still a major institution in New York City. Toni returned to Puerto Rico in the early 'seventies where she continues to be active in various kinds of community organizing. Matilde de Silva, a charming, gentle, and humorous woman who spent many years with the Office of the Commonwealth of Puerto Rico, promoted educational training programs for teachers by arranging trips for them to Puerto Rico. Blanca Cedeño was a member of the New York City Housing Authority, and more recently has been Chairperson of the Board for Universidad Boricua. Marta Valle was the first Puerto Rican woman appointed to a commissionership in New York City. She was Commissioner of the New York City Youth Board. Sister Isolina Ferré was director of the Doctor White Community Settlement in Brooklyn and represented the Puerto Rican community on the Council Against Poverty (see p. 38). These and so many others in politics, in labor unions, in community activities, in religious activities, were outstanding Puerto Rican leaders who spent hours and days explaining to me the background of Puerto Rican culture and the experience of Puerto Ricans in New York. They had organized the Agrupación Femenina Puertorriqueña during the 1950s and they were involved in most of the active organizations at that time. Someday, someone should write a history of these extraordinary women and the leadership they exercised in the community in the early and difficult days.

Later they founded the Consejo de Organizaciones Puertorriqueñas y Hispano-Americanas de Nueva York. The Consejo was one of the early efforts at a coordinating organization in New York City. Now there are numerous Consejos, the most important one being the Puerto Rican Coalition, a national level organization with offices in the Washington, D.C., area.

I gave the address at the Consejo's inauguration of new officers in 1961 and it was typical of the kind of lectures I would give to them on other occasions.[4] I stressed two things: the importance of retaining the

---

4. See Part II: "The Newcomer Becomes Our Own."

best of their cultural background and of trying to communicate some of its benefits to the larger society of the United States. I stressed the importance of retaining a strong sense of their own identity and a deep sense of unity among their own people. The terms "assimilation" and "integration" appear in my text. That was before these terms became rejected by Puerto Rican writers who thought "assimilation" meant the absorption of their people into the society of the United States, and the loss of their culture and identity. There has been much confusion in the use of the terms. I have always used them with a strong emphasis on the pluralism of American society, the importance of Puerto Ricans retaining their cultural values and their sense of identity while, at the same time, they participate as respected equals in the mainstream of American society. On the other hand, there has been resistance in the American community against cultural pluralism, resistance to bilingual education and bicultural programs. For example, the "English only" campaign criticizes the continuing use of Spanish and advocates a declaration of English as the national language. Actually the movement is much more a rejection of foreign language and culture than a genuine dedication to American ideals. No group of newcomers has struggled more than the Hispanics for the retention of their language and culture while they master the use of English and seek to become part of the mainstream of American life. I sought to emphasize in my inaugural address my own awareness of the deep desire of Puerto Ricans to be themselves while they took their rightful place in American life.

One of my early contacts with Puerto Ricans on a humble level was through a young man, Frankie Droz, who at that time worked in the cafeteria at Fordham. Learning that he was Puerto Rican, I began to talk with him about his experiences. We became good friends. He invited me to his home and asked me to baptize his latest baby — which I did. This brought me into close contact with a working-class Puerto Rican family for the first time. Frankie was what many Puerto Ricans had described to me as a *jíbaro*, a man from the mountains of Puerto Rico. The *jíbaro* was a man of great personal dignity, very honorable, trustworthy, and faithful. I found all these qualities in Frankie. The visit to his family was impressive. He had four or five children by that time but his home, poor though it was, and in a very poor section of the South Bronx, showed how well a family like Frankie's could convert such an environment into a comfortable home. When he brought me to visit his mother, the scene was different. She was living in a one-family frame house that had been converted into seven furnished rooms, with one kitchen and one bathroom for all seven families. The owner must have been making exorbitant profits from the building which had been built to house one family. Still and all, there was a great dignity about the elderly woman, and she was happy to be close to her son and his family. I saw first-hand the exploitation in housing that Puerto Ricans had to face. I was able on many occasions to use my influence to get Puerto Rican families into public housing projects.

Frankie taught me a great deal about the experience of Puerto Ricans like himself. He was a creative man. Many years later when my Puerto Rican friends gave me a celebration in Central Park (see p. 63), Frankie wrote a poem about me and sent it to be read by the Master of Ceremonies. He left Fordham to take a much better job as a maintenance man in a large building downtown. I kept in touch with him for many years, but in the 'seventies we lost track of one another. I thank him for all he taught me about a working-class Puerto Rican family.

THE FIRST PUBLIC ADDRESS

I was invited to give the Communion breakfast talk at the Golden Jubilee Celebration of the Vera Cruz (Holy Cross) Council of the Knights of Columbus on May 18, 1952. This was my first public address about the Puerto Ricans.[5] I welcomed the opportunity. I reminded the Irish and Italian members of their own history as immigrants. I quoted from newspapers and magazines to illustrate the prejudice of New Yorkers against the Irish especially, and made a special plea that they would not allow that unfortunate history to repeat itself. I reminded them that their organization was named after a great Italian who discovered America when he was sailing for the Queen of Spain; also that the title of their Council, Vera Cruz, was in the language the Puerto Ricans spoke. Since most Puerto Ricans were Catholics, I pointed out the special responsibility we all had to welcome them as our own. The reaction of the audience was enthusiastic, although there were a few criticisms about my quotes about the New York Irish.

Luisa Quintero (see p. 9), the well-known columnist at that time for *El Diario de Nueva York* published a long interview with me in Spanish in *ECOS* (July 5, 1952), a weekly magazine which covered community events. Shortly after, *El Diario de Nueva York* printed the piece in Spanish and published an editorial, "Gracias al Padre Fitzpatrick." *El Mundo* in Puerto Rico gave it front page coverage and published an editorial also.

---

5. See Part II: "Puerto Ricans in New York: The Great Challenge to the Charity of Catholics."

Overnight I found myself a hero of the Puerto Ricans. However, what really made me famous (or infamous) was the article that Arthur Mulligan wrote in *The Daily News*, August 17, 1952. As my correspondence with Arthur Mulligan indicates, his piece set off a storm of angry letters which I still have in my folder. It was clear that the Puerto Ricans had few advocates. As newcomers, they were not in a position to be their own advocates and few, if any, others were speaking on their behalf. Thus the reaction to my talk. I was one of the few, publicly pleading their cause. I received numerous requests for the talk and the response from those who received it was enthusiastic. Unfortunately, it was never published in a prominent English-speaking periodical.

FIRST VISIT TO PUERTO RICO: JUNE-JULY 1952

One other important consequence followed the Vera Cruz Council talk. Present at the breakfast was Frank Goering, who had business interests in Puerto Rico. He spoke to me after the breakfast and I asked him to try to get his business friends in Puerto Rico to donate some money for scholarships for the Puerto Ricans up here. He said that rather than doing that, he would send me to Puerto Rico to promote some of that myself. This would also help me to know the background of the island better. As a result, I went to Puerto Rico for the first time in June 1952, for one month. This was a remarkable experience for me. I met many of the priests ministering to Puerto Ricans in the parishes in all parts of the Island. Father Gregorio of the Capuchin Fathers as well as Father Venard Kanfush and Father Leo Morgan were to remain devoted friends. I had some excellent visits with Bishop James Davis, Archbishop of San Juan. I travelled to many important places throughout the island and I had excellent contacts with the people in the government, especially the people involved in the Economic Development Program. I had long conversations with Teodoro Moscoso, then the director of the Economic Development Program, as well as Fernando Berdecia and Petra America Colon in the Department of Labor. I attended a conference given by Jaime Benitez, president of the University of Puerto Rico, and was able to speak with him afterwards. I was able to visit many of the developments sponsored by the Department of Agriculture. Dairy farming was just beginning on the island and there was experimentation with cows and bulls that could withstand the tropical heat of Puerto Rico. I also had contacts with some of the Labor Union people. It was an intensive month. On the last day of my visit, July 24, 1952, Puerto Rico celebrated the inauguration of its new constitution as a Free Associated State.

The visit gave me an extensive knowledge of the Island and many of its cultural features that was to enable me to prepare much more effective lectures than I could have prepared without it. It also gave me increased credibility; I could say I had been to Puerto Rico and had some first-hand experience with the people and their culture. When I returned, I wrote a report for myself about the visit and sent a copy to Bishop James Davis. The report, too long for incorporation here, called attention to two things: 1) the need to develop better communication between the Island and New York in order to create support systems for the migrants before they leave and after they arrive in New York; and 2) my surprise that there was so little contact between the Church and the people involved in the economic development of the Island. There was a system of cooperatives that had been developed by a priest from Nova Scotia, Father McDonald. Even he seemed to be remote from the bishops and priests. I also met a young diocesan priest, Antulio Parilla, who was living in a very poor parish in Barrio Obrero and was involved in cooperatives. He was later to become a Jesuit priest and then a bishop. I met many of the important persons involved in the economic development and I suggested in my report that it would be helpful to the Church to collaborate more frequently with and have closer contact with these developments. The report was to have some interesting consequences. (See section on Ivan Illich, p. 16.)

WORLD SODALITY DAY, MAY 10, 1953

The next significant address was the sermon I delivered at World Sodality Day, on the Fordham Campus, May 10, 1953.[6] World Sodality Day was an important Catholic event in those years. Throughout the world, Catholic college students who were members of a students' religious association called "The Sodality" gathered for a celebration in honor of Mary, the Mother of Jesus. The New York area celebration took place on the large quadrangle, Edwards Parade, at Fordham University. Students from the Catholic colleges of the area gathered for hymns and prayers, a crowning of the Blessed Virgin with a wreath of flowers, the Rosary, then a religious ceremony called "Benediction" and a sermon. The Cardinal always presided. An unforeseen, but related, event occurred that day that makes it memorable for other reasons.

The Spring of 1953 was very cold and rainy. The night before the celebration, the weather changed and the temperature went above 90

---

6. See Part II: "A Plea for Christian Unity."

degrees on Sunday afternoon, May 10th. The young women from neighboring colleges who were standing out on the field in their caps and gowns for about an hour before the beginning of the ceremony (there were no chairs), began to faint in the heat. Their companions started to carry them off by the dozens. There was no First Aid available. The only thing that saved the day was the Nurses' Sodality from Fordham Hospital, at that time a hospital contiguous to the campus. The nurses intervened and were very helpful in assisting the 100 or so young women who fainted that afternoon. I said to the Monsignor who was conducting the ceremony: "Surely you are not going to have a sermon in view of this!" His response: "But Father, His Eminence is here; we must have the sermon." So on I went, and as I tried to deliver my eloquent words, I kept watching them carrying the young women off the field. All the newspapers the following day had front-page coverage. *The Daily News* had a full page picture of it with the caption, "Hundreds Felled at Church Rite." It was a day that will not be forgotten. The sermon, "A Plea for Christian Unity," included a section about the challenge of the Puerto Rican presence to the Catholics of New York, to which the media paid scant attention.

However, I learned later that during the talk, Cardinal Spellman turned to the Monsignor next to him and remarked: "What is Fitzpatrick talking about? Don't we have that problem taken care of?" The Monsignor answered: "Evidently Fitzpatrick doesn't think so." A short while later, His Eminence was present at another talk given by one of his own priests who followed a theme similar to mine. Shortly after, Cardinal Spellman called a number of us to his office. It was the first time I saw His Eminence in action as an administrator. I was impressed, indeed. There were about twenty of us around the table. The Cardinal said: "You are telling me that we have not taken care of the ministry to the Puerto Ricans who have been coming in large numbers. All right, we will go around the table. I want you to tell me: What am I doing that I should not be doing? What am I not doing that I should be doing?" And he went around the table to each of us. It was quite a challenge to us to come up with suggestions on the spur of the moment, but the discussion went well. When it ended, His Eminence (he had a little book in his hand in which he jotted notes) said: "All right, what you have told me is helpful. First, we should establish an Office for the Puerto Rican Apostolate. Monsignor Connolly (Monsignor Joseph Connolly, a New York Archdiocesan priest), you will establish that office immediately and direct it. Secondly, you tell me that my plan of sending two priests to Puerto Rico for a whole year is not enough. Very well, I will send half the Ordination class from the Archdiocesan Seminary to Georgetown for Spanish language training. We will start that this summer. Finally, you tell me we need a religious festival to give the Puerto Ricans a sense of identity, a continuity of their traditions here in New York. Monsignor Connolly, you will arrange to have a special celebration of the feast of Saint John the Baptist on June 24th." Then he thanked all of us. I was stunned. Every aspect of the Cardinal's new policy of pastoral care for Puerto Ricans was put into place. The meeting was evidence of Cardinal Spellman's concern for the Puerto Rican newcomers. He was prepared to do anything possible to respond to their spiritual needs. It seems to me that he has never received the credit he deserves for this attention to the Puerto Ricans.

IVAN ILLICH

In the spring of 1953, I was sitting in my office in Keating Hall when Father William Lynch, S.J., then editor of *Thought*, the Fordham University quarterly, came into my office. He said: "There is a young priest in my office and he would like to meet you. His name is John Illich." (See also p. 9.) And so I met the man who was to have a profound influence on me and on the Church during my generation. I walked into Father Lynch's office and I was immediately struck by the appearance of the man: tall, exuding energy and tension, and intense in conversation. "I followed you all over Puerto Rico," he said, "and I read the report you left with Bishop Davis. You are the one person I wanted to meet when I came back." Illich, a native of Yugoslavia, had come to New York and had been accepted into the Archdiocese of New York. He was assigned to Incarnation Parish in northern Manhattan, a parish which was becoming Puerto Rican. Illich wanted to learn more about these newcomers, where they were coming from and why. He spent a month in Puerto Rico, learned Spanish (he is a remarkable linguist) and visited every part of the Island. He then described for me his whirlwind month in Puerto Rico. It was far different from mine during which I was accompanied from door-to-door of prominent people, introductions arranged ahead of time. Illich walked over miles of rural roads, took to horseback, visited towns in remote mountains and crowded urban barrios. In his conversation with me, he began to comment on the customs and culture of the people. For a person who was neither an anthropologist nor sociologist, his perception of the culture and lifestyle of the Puerto Ricans was remarkable. I said to myself, "This is a man I want to keep in touch with." We talked for almost two hours, during which I learned many things I had not known about aspects of Puerto Rican life. After he left, Father Lynch asked me, "What is your impression?" I don't know what it was that prompted me to say it; I knew nothing at that moment of Illich's background. I replied, "Bill, he reminds me of some of my brilliant Jewish intellectual friends. I wonder if there is something Jewish about him!" Years later, I was to meet his mother and learn that she came from Sephardic Jewish ancestry. She had become a Catholic to marry Illich's father and she remained a devout Catholic until her death.

Illich had been assigned to Incarnation parish by Cardinal Spellman. When he arrived at the parish, he introduced himself to the pastor: "I am Ivan Illich." "Yes, I know," said the pastor. "But from now on we will call you Johnny." Illich thought that this was part of American life and custom and he accepted the anglicizing of his name. I was introduced to him as John Illich, and for some years this was the way he was known. It was not until he went to Puerto Rico in 1956 that he realized how foolish the name change was and what poor insight on the part of the pastor it reflected. He reverted to his original name of Ivan. Let me briefly describe a few things here which revealed the genius of the man, his creativeness, and the impact he was to have on the Archdiocese and the Church. He had captured with remarkable perception, the culture and life-style of the Puerto Ricans and he realized that, if their faith was to be saved and developed in this strange new world of New York, we would have to create an environment in which they were completely at home, *en su casa* as they would say. This meant ministry to them in their own language, but also in the style which characterized their religious belief and practice in Puerto Rico. Illich began to emphasize this with Cardinal Spellman, with his pastor at Incarnation parish, and with all of us who were collaborating with him in the ministry to Puerto Ricans.

EL CUARTITO DE LA SANTISIMA VIRGEN
(The Little Room of the Most Holy Virgin)

Illich realized that, to be of assistance to Puerto Rican people, the relationship had to be family-like and very personal. He rented a ground-floor apartment in a large building where many Puerto Rican families lived. He had made many friends among young men and women in the city. He encouraged a group of the young women to fix up the apartment with pictures and items reminiscent of Puerto Rico, and just be there to allow the children and mothers to come by, to mind the children when mothers went shopping; in brief, to create a familiar, neighborhood place where the people could gather with no formality, but which was carefully organized by the young women. They could teach the children English and many other things including their faith. It was a remarkable example of receiving the Puerto Ricans as our own, in a situation where they were very much at home among their own. After Illich left Incarnation parish and went to Puerto Rico (November 1956), the interest faded and eventually *El Cuartito* disappeared.

THE SLIDE-SHOW

Both he and I were concerned about the large number of migrant farm workers who were coming to the Mainland during the summer to work on the farms. The Puerto Rican Government (The Free Associated State) had established an arrangement whereby Puerto Rican workers could be recruited for temporary farm work on the United States Mainland, and would return home after the harvest. It was fortunate that the Mainland harvest season coincided with the "dead season" in the sugar cane fields of Puerto Rico. It was the only situation of its kind in the United States where farm workers were protected by a contract which guaranteed their work, wages and living conditions. I had visited the camps in New Jersey and I was not impressed by the quality of the living conditions. But it provided income and much more protection than other American migrant farm workers had. The Puerto Rican farm workers seemed satisfied. We wanted in some way to assist them, to help them understand life on the Mainland, and to provide some support for them both in their social and religious life. Illich conceived of an arrangement of slides depicting experiences of the farm workers, and a cassette which would provide an explanation for the workers of the experiences depicted in the slides. We worked very hard on this. I wrote the text for the cassette. Illich was to have professionals do the slides. We had some of the best people in Puerto Rico and New York involved in it. I do not know what happened. At the last moment, it never came off. I have always regretted this since it would have been a very effective approach to a ministry to the farm workers. It was a brilliant Illich idea which, for some reason, was aborted.

THE FIRST OUTDOOR SAN JUAN FIESTA

As indicated above, the San Juan Fiesta, a religious celebration in honor of the patron of Puerto Rico, which had begun in 1953, was continued for the next two years in St. Patrick's Cathedral. Illich said that this was ridiculous and that a fiesta like this should be held outside with processions and civic celebrations. He convinced Monsignor Connolly to hold the 1956 Fiesta outdoors on the Fordham University Campus. This was to prove to be quite an event. Illich planned a procession from one point of the campus to the other, followed by a Mass celebrated by Cardinal Spellman with a sermon by the Cardinal in Spanish. This was to be followed by a civic celebration at another part of the campus.

Three days before the event, the police captain of the local precinct called us to a meeting asking how many persons we expected so that he would know how many policemen he should assign to the detail. Monsignor Connolly, who was a timid man, said he thought we might have three thousand. He had asked the maintenance staff to place three thousand chairs widely around the field to give the impression that there were more people. Illich said there would be many more, but would not venture a number. Then the captain asked me. I had been listening to the spot announcements on the Spanish radio stations, and knew that Illich was going through the Puerto Rican neighborhoods with a sound truck, inviting everyone to come to the Fiesta. I said I would not be surprised if there were thirty thousand people at the event. The captain responded: "Let me cut the figure in half and plan on fifteen thousand people."

Actually thirty thousand people attended. On the morning of the Fiesta, I arose about five a.m. and when I looked out of my window, there were streams of people already coming to the Fiesta which was not scheduled to begin until ten o'clock. Everything went well in the religious celebration and we moved over to another field for the civic celebration.

The civic events began with the breaking of a *piñata*, a *papier-maché* container shaped into the form of an animal, filled with gifts. A dignitary is blindfolded and seeks to break the *piñata* by striking it with a bat while the children swing it back and forth. When the batter breaks the *piñata*, the gifts fall out and all the children rush to get them. It is a central part of Puerto Rican fiestas. Robert F. Wagner, then mayor of New York, was blindfolded and asked to break the *piñata*. Various dignitaries — Mayor Wagner, Doña Felisa Rincón de Gautier, mayor of San Juan, Cardinal Spellman — knew what to expect when a *piñata* is broken. But no one had thought to explain this process to the New York Police Department! When Mayor Wagner struck the *piñata* and broke it, everyone naturally ran to get the gifts. Unfortunately, the police thought a riot was breaking out. They surrounded the Cardinal, the Mayors, and other dignitaries and led them off the field, thinking they were protecting them. Other policemen rushed in to break up the crowd scrambling for the gifts. It was certainly the strangest *piñata*-breaking in history.

The following day, a Sunday, all the newspapers had front page coverage: "Cardinal Mobbed at Church Rites," "Police Protect Cardinal from Puerto Rican Rioters," etc. I was very angry. I met the chairman of Fordham's Communications Department, an experienced journalist, and I said to him, "Some job your colleagues did about yesterday's Fiesta. Here was a great religious and civic celebration and all they highlight is a so-called riot." He answered me, "Father, you should thank God that it happened. If it had not occurred, maybe a few papers would have given you a few lines. But this morning, every paper from Maine to California has a front-page story about thirty thousand Puerto Ricans celebrating with His Eminence. You can't buy that kind of publicity even with millions of dollars!"

Actually the day *was* a great success. It was my own judgement that this was the first time that the Puerto Rican community felt completely at home in New York City. This was a fiesta as Puerto Ricans understood it. It also established the Church and the Cardinal as significant figures in the experience of Puerto Ricans.

The following year the Fiesta was moved to the stadium on Randall's Island. It was much too big an event for the Fordham Campus. The Fiesta has continued until today. However, it has deteriorated in recent years. Numbers have diminished; the support of the parish priests is missing; and the committee will have to evaluate it and determine what changes are necessary to revive it as a significant event.

The Fiesta Committee established a practice of honoring a man or woman for special service to the Puerto Rican community: the Man or Woman of the Year Award. At the celebration of the twenty-fifth year, in 1979, I was one of the few who had been at all the celebrations. The Committee decided to honor me that year by naming me "The Puerto Rican Man of the Year."

THE 1950s

Meantime the Puerto Ricans continued to come into the City in large numbers. Between 1950 and 1960, the Puerto Rican population of New York City increased from 245,880 to 612,574, an increase of one hundred and fifty percent. Every institution of the City was feeling the pressure of their increasing numbers. I began to get calls and letters telling me that Puerto Ricans were appearing increasingly at social agencies, schools, parishes, hospitals, and police precincts. Could I help the persons in these agencies to understand the Puerto Ricans; explain how to deal with them, or how to help them? It was a very sincere appeal of people anxious to be of service to the newcomers. I began to try to respond to the appeal. I organized workshops, conducted conferences, wrote articles which sought to explain to New Yorkers the background of the Puerto Ricans and their experience in adjusting to New York. At the same time, I tried to explain to Puerto Ricans what life in New York was like and what the experience of previous newcomers had been. Understandably, the Puerto Ricans thought they were the first ones to face the misunderstanding, discrimination and hostility. I tried to give them some of the history of earlier immigrants to prepare them for the culture shock they were facing. The various articles in the second part of this book give an indication of how I went about this. I felt very much drawn into a vacuum of a desire for information and explanation. I responded to this and by the mid-fifties, I was so deeply involved in it that I found it impossible to continue my Labor/Management Seminars. My life was being given a new direction.

THE FIRST CONFERENCE ON THE SPIRITUAL CARE OF PUERTO RICAN MIGRANTS, APRIL 11-16, 1955, SAN JUAN AND PONCE, PUERTO RICO

Both Illich and I were concerned about establishing more effective links between the Island and the Mainland. Through his influence with Cardinal Spellman, the first Conference came into being: a meeting of priests who were experienced in ministry to Puerto Ricans in Puerto Rico, with priests who were seeking to minister to them on the Mainland. There was a Redemptorist priest in Puerto Rico, Father Thomas Gildea, C.SS.R., who was very much concerned about the migration. He was setting up an organization, "Ayuda Católica," at the San Juan Airport where Church workers would meet the migrants coming to New York, find out where they were going, and inform the pastors about those migrants who expected to settle in the area of the parish. The hope was that the New York priests would be able to establish contact with the migrants, welcome them to the parishes and thus help them to be faithful to their Catholic faith.

Together with Father Gildea, Illich and I set out to organize the Conference. I was teaching a full-time schedule in the graduate and undergraduate programs at Fordham; I was also involved in my Institute of Labor/Management Relations, and Illich was an active parish priest. But we put the Conference together with a great effort, and Father Gildea took care of local arrangements very well, including a modern simultaneous translation set-up. Cardinal Spellman financed the event and made it possible for the Mainland priests to attend. Preliminary papers were prepared and circulated; presentations were given; and the discussions were excellent. We had the opportunity to visit various places in San Juan and Ponce. It was the first serious discussion by both groups of priests with each other, the beginning of a dialogue we hoped would continue.

The Proceedings were published in a book entitled *Spiritual Care of Puerto Rican Migrants.*[7] The Dedication by Cardinal Spellman was really a statement of policy to guide the pastoral care of the Puerto Ricans who were coming to the Archdiocese. This statement which had been inspired by myself and Ivan Illich is a clear indication of the policy we were recommending to the New York Archdiocese and the other dioceses of the United States to which Puerto Ricans were coming.

There was one unanticipated consequence to the Conference. Father William Ferree, a young priest of the Marist Congregation, and Rector of the Catholic University of Puerto Rico, met Illich and saw him in action. Ferree was another brilliant young priest with fine qualities of leadership somewhat similar to those of Illich. Father Ferree suggested to Bishop McManus, Bishop of Ponce and Chancellor of the Catholic University, that he ask Cardinal Spellman to assign Illich to the Catholic University as its Vice Rector. Thus the effort was set in motion to get Illich to Puerto Rico in November, 1956. One other unanticipated event occurred. In October 1956, Father Ferree was elected by his Congregation to a prominent position in Rome. He was replaced by another member of his Congregation, Father Thomas Stanley, who having none of the brilliance of Ferree, found life very turbulent with a genius like Illich as second-in-command. Illich sought the counsel of many of his friends about going to Puerto Rico. We had already begun to realize how important he was in New York, but three considerations tended to swing the balance in favor of his going. Many of us were aware of the fact that South America would become increasingly important for the United States and the Church. We saw the possibility of Puerto Rico being a bridge between both lands. It was culturally and historically "Latin" – it shared a basic style of life with the South American nations. Secondly,

---

7. *Spiritual Care of Puerto Rican Migrants*, edited by William Ferree, Ivan Illich and Joseph P. Fitzpatrick, S.J., New York Archdiocese, Office of the Chancery, 1955 (dedication by Cardinal Spellman.) A second printing was published by Illich at CIDOC, Cuernavaca, Mexico, in 1970. Finally, Arno Press, New York City, a New York Times Company, reissued it as part of the Arno Publication Series in 1980.

it would be a place where persons from North America and South America could meet, discuss common concerns, and serve as an excellent channel of communication in both directions. Finally, using his base in Puerto Rico, Illich could guide the response of the Church in the United States to the Puerto Ricans. Actually this was not to be. We discovered that many Latin Americans saw Puerto Rico as a "mini-Gringo-land," since it was an American possession, and they were not disposed to seeing it as a bridge between the two areas.

While Illich was still in New York, in the Spring of 1955, he introduced me to another person who was to have a great influence on my life, Dorothy M. Dohen. *Integrity*, a popular Catholic monthly magazine, had been started by a woman named Carol Jackson, and sought to be an expression of the ideas and ideals of Catholics who were dedicated to what was then called the "Lay Apostolate" – remarkable young men and women who sought to serve God in a dedicated life in the world as lay persons. Dorothy Dohen was one of them. She became the editor of *Integrity* and, under her guidance, it became a bright and influential magazine of Catholic lay leaders. Illich, typically, sought out every Catholic he could find who provided intellectual leadership for the Church. He had sought out Father Lynch, editor of *Thought*, and he had sought out Dorothy Dohen.

One afternoon, when I was visiting Illich, Dorothy appeared at the rectory and Illich introduced us. I did not know at the time that this was the beginning of a friendship that was to affect her life as it would my own. She later became a graduate student under my direction at Fordham and then a colleague as a professor in the Department of Sociology and Anthropology. Quite beyond that, she was a woman of remarkable spiritual life, saintly in many ways, and my friendship with her was to be the source of unusual spiritual insight and grace.

During our brief visit, Dorothy asked me to do an article on the Puerto Ricans. Under Illich's influence she had decided to edit a special issue of *Integrity* on the Puerto Ricans. I prepared the article and it appeared in July 1955, under the title: "Catholic Responsibilities and New York's Puerto Ricans."[8] This was a popular article suitable for a magazine like *Integrity*. It was important as my first publication about the Puerto Ricans, and it brought the issue of their migration to a much wider audience. The article would now be a library item, accessible to a nationwide audience.

---

8. See Part II: "Catholic Responsibilities and New York's Puerto Ricans," *Integrity*, July 1955, pp. 12-21.

Meantime, Father William Lynch, editor of *Thought*, really launched me into publication. In September 1951, he published a lecture I had given about "Catholic Responsibilities in Sociology."[9] It gave me the confidence to publish more. Robert Merton, the well-known professor of sociology at Columbia University, also read it and asked me to expand it into a book. Unfortunately and much to my regret, I never did that.

In 1955, Father Lynch asked to write something on the Puerto Rican migration. I put together, "The Integration of Puerto Ricans,"[10] a sociological analysis of the migration and a theoretical piece about the problem of Puerto Ricans maintaining a continuing identity, which focused on the importance of the community or "barrio" in providing stability while they moved from a position of strength into a place in American society. I was to build on this piece over the years and it became an important theoretical basis for my book, *Puerto Rican Americans*. It was my first serious sociological article about the migration and brought me to the attention of my sociological colleagues throughout the country as an important scholar in the field of inter-ethnic and minority relations.

By late 1955, I was writing more frequently. I wrote an article for *America*[11] which provided another aspect of the vision of our work with Puerto Ricans and Hispanics in the United States. Long before I arrived in New York, I had become aware of the Latin world, and I had come to realize that it was to play a very important role in the future of the United States and its Catholic Church. When I came to New York and began working with Puerto Ricans, I began to see their migration as part of the upward movement of millions of people from Mexico, Central and South America and the Caribbean Islands. Thus I began to see the larger picture of the presence of Hispanics in the United States. It became clear to me that the future of the Catholic Church would be profoundly affected by this migration. I presented this in the context of the Mexican and Puerto Rican presence and began to see that, in the Providence of God, their presence could serve as a strategic bridge between the United States and Latin America. It was this perspective that prompted us to recommend Illich's transfer to Puerto Rico. We saw him as the ideal person to help create the bridge.

---

9. "Catholic Responsibilities in Sociology," *Thought*, September 1951.

10. See Part II: "The Integration of Puerto Ricans," *Thought*, Autumn 1955.

11. See Part II: "Mexicans and Puerto Ricans Build a Bridge," *America*, December 31, 1955.

THE INSTITUTE OF INTERCULTURAL COMMUNICATION

The Conference of 1955 had convinced all of us of the need for a more permanent link between Puerto Rico and the Puerto Ricans in New York. When Illich was reassigned to Puerto Rico in the Fall of 1956, one of his first objectives was the establishment of a center in Puerto Rico for the training of priests, sisters, brothers, and lay persons who were preparing to work with Puerto Ricans in New York. Illich began to plan for a center where they could gain a basic knowledge of the language, and be introduced to Puerto Rican culture and the problems of migration to the Mainland. In 1957, with the financial support and encouragement of Cardinal Spellman, Illich established the Institute of Intercultural Communication at the Catholic University in Ponce, Puerto Rico. The participants arrived during the summer and spent six weeks in intensive training in the language. Meantime, I gave the course on the background of Puerto Rican culture and on the problems of migration to the Mainland. Invited lecturers spoke about various aspects of Puerto Rican social, political and religious life. Following the course, the priests spent another month living and working in a Puerto Rican parish. The other participants had the opportunity to travel around the Island and become familiar with its people. The Institute was probably the single most important aspect of the response of the New York Archdiocese to the migration of the Puerto Ricans. Some of the young priests, sisters, brothers, and lay persons who were trained at the Institute became outstanding pastors, teachers and important figures in the ministry to the Puerto Ricans. Many of them are still very active. A satellite center was set up at one of the Catholic high schools of New York City where mini-courses in language and culture were given on Saturdays for persons who could not get to the Island. The Institute continued until 1972, and in its fifteen years of existence played a major role in the response of the Archdiocese of New York, and other dioceses, to the Puerto Ricans. A substantial number, in fact an entire generation, of priests, religious personnel and lay persons were formed in the perspective of Illich and others, that ministry to Puerto Ricans must be offered in their own language and in a style of religious belief and practice in which they were "at home." There was no effort to try to pressure the Puerto Ricans to adopt American ways without delay.

In 1958 Illich invited Cardinal Spellman to Puerto Rico. He had arranged visits not only with all important Catholic leaders, but with the Governor, Luis Muñoz Marin, and the well known mayor of San Juan, Doña Felisa Rincón de Gautier, and many other prominent persons on the Island. It highlighted to all the involvement of the Cardinal in the experience of the Puerto Ricans in New York. Illich arranged to have the Cardinal enter Ponce in a motorcade with thousands cheering from the sidewalks. It was something of a triumphal entry of the Cardinal into this prominent city on the south coast of Puerto Rico where the Institute functioned. The Cardinal's Spanish was minimal, but he insisted that Illich prepare a talk for him in Spanish, to be delivered at the dedication of a new building at the Catholic University. At one moment of the speech there was a loud round of applause. Illich who had been carrying chairs from the classrooms out to the many standees at the celebration asked me, "What did the Cardinal say?" I told him, "The Cardinal has just made you a Monsignor."

During the second year of the Institute, religious sisters came for the first time. When they were departing at the end of the session, an interesting conflict of culture took place. The Puerto Rican chef named "Eddie," a large, jovial man whom everybody liked, told the sisters he would prepare a *despedida* (a farewell) in truly Puerto Rican style. They would have *lechón asado* (suckling pig) for their farewell dinner. Unfortunately, a few days before the *despedida*, Eddie bought the pigs on the hoof and had them tied on the lawn outside the dining area. Over the two last days, the sisters took a real liking to the pigs, even saw them as their little friends. As they were returning from class on the day of the *despedida*, Eddie was slaughtering the pigs near the path where the sisters passed. It almost ruined the *despedida*. The sisters could not eat the suckling pigs, they were so sorry that these little creatures, to whom they had taken a liking, had been killed. Eddie was disappointed, but his only remark to me was: "Padre, you did not teach them enough about our culture."

By the mid-1950s, I was becoming more familiar with the Puerto Ricans' experience in New York City. My principal concern at this moment was the response of the Catholic Church to their presence. The 1955 Conference was the beginning of a series on Puerto Rican and Hispanic newcomers. In June 1957, we convened a meeting of New York priests to follow up the conference in Puerto Rico and to examine more carefully the situation in the New York Archdiocese. I had prepared the data for the conference. We estimated that there were close to 500,000 Puerto Ricans in New York City at that time, and we identified 175 priests in the New York Archdiocese who could speak Spanish. The outline of the conference indicated that we were well aware of the issues and were planning an effective response. All presentations were made by active and experienced parish priests and touched on the issues of contact with the newly arriving Puerto Ricans, their spiritual formation, the adaptation of ministry and liturgy to their traditions, and serious attention to strengthening family life and preparing youth to meet the challenge of adjustment to American life. The conference also dealt with educational issues, organizations of Puerto Ricans and community organizations to enable them to develop strength and stability in their neighborhoods. Monsignor James Wilson, coordinator of Spanish Catholic Action, conducted the conference and it was sponsored by Cardinal Spellman who spoke at the luncheon.

It is interesting to reflect on these conferences from the viewpoint of 1994. There was enormous enthusiasm in the 1950s. Many of the young diocesan priests had been trained for work with the Puerto Ricans. The Puerto Rican population was much smaller; the great majority were first generation migrants. There was a clarity to the issues and a confidence among the clergy that we were beginning to get the situation in hand. A second conference followed in October 1957, this time on a national basis. It was a meeting of priests who were directors of the Hispanic apostolate in their respective dioceses. Forty priests attended, representing twenty-two dioceses. Monsignor Wilson presided again but Father Leo Mahon, who had organized a remarkable program for Puerto Ricans in Chicago, played a major role. Father Mahon had organized the Caballeros de San Juan (Knights of San Juan) as a religiously inspired community action group among Puerto Rican men. This enjoyed impressive success and became a model which others hoped to initiate in their dioceses. Behind Father Mahon's program was his theory that religious development takes place best where some level of social stability prevails. The Caballeros provided this stability as well as self-confidence.

Finally, the director of the Bishops' Committee for the Spanish-Speaking of the Southwest, Father William O'Connor, explained the activities of this regional committee in coordinating the Apostolate to the Hispanics in the sixteen dioceses of that area. This prompted a long discussion of the advisability of a National Committee. After some years this recommendation was accepted; a Secretariat for Hispanics was established in the U.S. Catholic Conference, with centers in six regions of the United States where large numbers of Hispanics were located. This conference brought us face-to-face with the complications of Hispanic ministry nationwide. The great differences between Mexicans in the Southwest and Puerto Ricans in the Northeast became clear, and the complexities of coordinating both became *very* clear. This was before the influx of refugees from Cuba and later from Central America as well as immigrants from the Dominican Republic and South America. The enthusiasm of the response to Puerto Ricans in New York was tempered by the realization that, in the long run and on a nationwide basis, the task was to be more demanding and more frustrating than we thought. My writings for conferences such as these were largely resource papers, compilations of demographic or ecclesiastic statistics. I was very much involved in the planning of these conferences and in the efforts to implement their recommendations.

Meantime, Father Thomas Gildea was active with his "Ayuda Católica" at the San Juan airport (see p. 21). The program experienced two difficulties: the Ayuda reached only a small percentage of the migrants, and the mainland pastors did not have the time or the staff to contact the newcomers and introduce them to parish life. As the numbers of travellers back and forth to Puerto Rico increased and the problem of contacting migrants either in Puerto Rico or on the Mainland became more complex, the Ayuda became less effective and was discontinued. For example, its staff contacted 15,000 persons in 1957, less than one-third of the 50,000 migrants that year. It was an imaginative program at its beginning and reflects the effort that Catholics were making to respond to the Puerto Rican newcomers.

ILLICH AND SPELLMAN

It is evident from the above that Cardinal Spellman played a key role in the development of ministry to the Puerto Ricans. He supported it by personnel, by institutional changes and especially with money. However, the "grey eminence" behind the Cardinal was Ivan Illich, and numerous writers have been puzzled by the relationship between two men apparently so disparate. There is no doubt that Illich had extraordinary influence with the Cardinal. When Illich came to New York, he came with glowing credentials from people in Rome. Cardinal Spellman immediately sensed the importance of this. But beyond this, on two occasions, the details of which I never knew, Illich intervened to save the Cardinal embarrassment by events which had happened in the Archdiocese. Illich, with his consummate diplomacy, straightened things out before the Cardinal would have become involved. Thus, from the very beginning, the Cardinal knew that Illich had extraordinary gifts which could be helpful to him. At the same time, Illich knew that Spellman's involvement in the Hispanic apostolate was critical. Spellman's confidence in him enabled Illich to bring ideas and suggestions to him and to get support for his proposals for the Hispanic apostolate. What became clear later on was that Spellman became Illich's great protector.

In 1960 a political problem developed in Puerto Rico in which both Spellman and Illich became involved. The Catholic Bishops of Puerto Rico, Bishop Davis of San Juan and Bishop McManus of Ponce, became critical of the political policies of the ruling party of Luis Muñoz Marin, the Partido Popular or Popular Party. Their criticism stemmed from the birth-control programs of the government, and the government's disapproval of a released-time program for public school children to enable them to have religious instructions. In their indignation, the Bishops established a political party, the Partido Acción Cristiana, and ran candidates for the government against Muñoz Marin's party. The Bishops went so far as to suggest that Catholics could not in conscience vote in favor of the policies of the Popular Party. Illich, by this time, had become a close friend and counsellor of Muñoz Marin and of many prominent people in the Popular Party. It was clear that many of them were consulting him for guidance. The situation caused consternation on the Mainland where John F. Kennedy, a Catholic, was running for President, and the action of the Puerto Rican Bishops seemed to confirm the criticism of Protestants against a Catholic as president, that, if elected, the Church would tell him what to do.

In the midst of what became a hostile fracas, Bishop Davis was elevated to the rank of Archbishop and celebrated the event with a dinner to which he invited Muñoz Marin, as Governor. Bishop McManus forbade any of his priests (including Illich) to attend because Muñoz Marin had been invited. Then word was announced that Cardinal Spellman was coming to the dinner and that he was to hold a brief meeting at the airport with Governor Muñoz Marin. The publicity for Muñoz in the midst of the campaign against the Catholic Party created a sensation in Puerto Rico. Because of Spellman's presence, Illich attended the dinner. (There was many a rumor, never completely confirmed, that Illich had arranged the whole thing.) As a result, Bishop McManus dismissed Illich from Puerto Rico. The Catholic Party lost disastrously.

Illich, with Spellman's support and approval, established another training center in Cuernavaca, Mexico, where he also became a very controversial figure because of his teaching, which some conservatives considered unorthodox.[12] Enormous pressure was put on the Vatican by conservative leaders in Mexico to get him out of their country. Nothing happened while Spellman was alive. The day after Spellman's bur-

---

12. For example: "The Seamy Side of Charity." *America*, January 21, 1967, pp. 88-91, a severe criticism of Catholic missionary methods in South America, and *De-Schooling Society*, New York: Harper & Row, 1967, a criticism of contemporary education recommending radical reforms.

ial, instructions came from Rome to the administrator of the New York Archdiocese to call Illich back to New York immediately. Actually Illich never came back. Rome eventually made an effort to prevent bishops and religious superiors from sending their subjects to Illich's center in Cuernavaca, and they eventually called Illich to Rome to answer numerous questions about his orthodoxy. Illich resigned voluntarily from all exercise of priestly ministry. Although he has never officially resigned from the priesthood, nor has he been "laicized" by Rome, he continues to write and teach and lecture as a layman.

MONSIGNOR ROBERT J. FOX

One of Illich's best-known disciples was a young priest of the New York Archdiocese, Monsignor Robert J. Fox. He was to become one of the key figures in the response of the Catholic Church in New York to the Puerto Ricans. Fox appeared suddenly and shot across the horizon like a meteor. No one who met him would ever be the same again. I met Fox during the second year of the Institute of Intercultural Communication in Ponce. I have written a memoir about him which was published in a memorial volume, *Fox-Sight,*[13] and my statement is reproduced among the readings. Fox became the third director of the Office for the Hispanic Apostolate, succeeding Monsignor Wilson. With Fox a whole new world developed.

Monsignor Fox was a street priest. He had little interest in organizations and funded projects and conventional ministries. He insisted in simply "being with the people on the streets" celebrating every aspect of their lives, enabling them to see, even in the garbage on the sidewalk, something that could speak of beauty and human dignity. He wanted to live with the Puerto Ricans so that they could see that, even in what the middle class called deprivation, Puerto Ricans could find a meaning to their lives that could be celebrated. About the best way of describing Fox's role in the Puerto Rican apostolate would be: "He taught us how to celebrate."

The first thing Fox did was to gather together hundreds of nuns, seminarians, and interested lay people and bring them to the streets, simply to be with Puerto Rican children and parents in a celebration of their lives. They danced and sang; they traced marvelous designs, press-

---

13. See Part II: "Commentary," in Bea McMahon (ed.). *Fox-Sight: Telling the Vision of Robert J. Fox.* Huntington, IN: Our Sunday Visitor Publishing Division, 1989, pp. 160-163.

ing paper on sewer covers; they painted reproductions of every tiny aspect of street life on sheets they would hang up for display. For those brief moments of "Summer in the City" the Church was alive in the streets with the Puerto Rican people. This was an unconventional apostolate, but it will never be forgotten.

Fox then organized some families in East Harlem to buy some burned out buildings and re-build them for themselves. His objective was not to convert them into construction teams and property owners; his objective was to bring them to a consciousness of their own abilities, to become aware of themselves in the context of their creative activity. He coined the term, later to be widely used, "sweat equity" – the personal involvement of one's life in building something. This was another method of linking the life of the Church (or rather the life of Church people) with the Puerto Ricans in their streets and homes. If Puerto Ricans learned anything from this, they learned that the Church meant life, fully lived. Sister Isolina Ferre was to modify the concept somewhat in Ponce with her famous key words: "The Glory of God is man and woman fully alive in a community that is fully alive."

During the riots of 1967, New York was fearful of outbreaks like those in Newark and Detroit. When a Puerto Rican was killed in East Harlem, it looked as if the moment had arrived. The police were advising people to stay off the streets. Fox did the opposite. He gathered thousands of people in East Harlem, and with crucifix, vestments and incense and candles, they processed through the streets of East Harlem calling the people to walk with them, pray with them and sing with them. There was no riot. The "barrio" remained calm and Mayor Lindsay gave great praise to Fox for converting a potential riot into a celebration.

Fox was unhappy that the San Juan Fiesta had turned into a civic fiesta with much carousing, drinking and gambling. He tried to correct this by holding the religious part of the Fiesta at midnight. He surrounded it with symbols of celebration similar to "Summer in the City." Unfortunately, the Puerto Ricans, with their conventional attitudes toward religious ceremonies, did not understand and many were critical of it.

Sometime later Fox was replaced as director of the Spanish Apostolate. He then dedicated himself to the development of small leadership training programs for Puerto Ricans in the parishes. I collaborated with him in this by raising funds to bring Paulo Freire, the great Brazilian educator, to New York as our consultant. Fox was using the Freire method of adult education in his training programs, and the presence of Freire was a significant event in our response to the Puerto Ricans. Freire later returned to the United States to teach at Harvard. Still later he became educational consultant to the World Council of Churches. Fox and I gave him his start outside of South America.

Fox, in his later days, developed a program of celebration called "Full Circle Associates." His creative influence was nationwide. He died at the young age of 54. His funeral was the celebration of celebrations at the Church of Saint Paul in East Harlem. His influence is never reported in statistics or institutions, but his spirit gave remarkable life to the work of the Church with Puerto Ricans, and among those who knew him, it still continues.

THE PAROCHIAL SCHOOL AND CHANGING NEIGHBORHOODS

I was invited to a conference in Chicago in November 1956, by Father Leo Mahon, a very creative priest of the Chicago Archdiocese, on the role of parochial schools in relation to Puerto Rican newcomers (see p. 27).

I was asked to speak about the problem created for the schools by rapidly changing neighborhoods. Although this was a Chicago event, the substance of my talk was a description of Manhattan and the Bronx, and the problem that rapidly changing neighborhoods created for both parochial and public schools. It was a recognition that the effective education of Puerto Rican children involved much more than what happened in the classroom. It was seriously affected by conditions in the community. One theme of the conference was expressed as follows:

> We are aware that 'teaching' the Puerto Ricans is only part of
> the teacher's dilemma. The teacher ought to understand what
> a community in chaos is and what adequate social structure
> means.

Thus the focus of the conference was on the neighborhood situation in which the child lives.

However there was one impressive event in the conference that had nothing to do with neighborhoods. Six small Puerto Rican children, about seven or eight years of age who had just arrived from Puerto Rico and who spoke no English, were brought to the stage by a Sister Joan for a demonstration of her method of teaching English to these children. It was an incredible performance. Before the hour was finished, the children were speaking with each other about simple human experiences in English. It was a proof that, despite the neighborhood situation, a skillful teacher can educate children well.

In any event, I delivered the talk, "The Changing Neighborhood and the Parochial School," which appears in the second part of the book.[14] I became very sensitive to the neighborhood problem and the importance of establishing stable Puerto Rican neighborhoods if the lives of the migrants were not to be disrupted. In the talk I presented in concrete terms what I had presented in theory in the article, "The Integration of Puerto Ricans" (see p. 24; also Part II). I began to use the phrase for which I became well known: "One integrates from a position of strength, never from a position of weakness." I emphasized the need for a strong and stable community of immigrants or migrants. Without this stability, the danger of disorganization is great. I gave abundant detail about the rapidly changing neighborhoods of New York City and how difficult it was for Puerto Ricans to maintain community strength and stability in these circumstances.

Shortly after the Chicago talk, work began on the Cross Bronx Expressway, and I was to witness one of the most convulsive changes in New York City's life. The Expressway destroyed about six stable neighborhoods in the Bronx. Thousands of older residents of European background left the area, and thousands of Hispanics, largely Puerto Rican, moved in. A good example of the effect of this change on the public schools was P.S. 6. When I first visited it in 1958, there were 900 children in the school, mostly Jewish, German and Irish. The principal, a remarkable woman, had asked me to come over because the first two Puerto Rican children had just entered the school and she was anxious to know how to deal with them and their parents. It was one of the best schools in the city at that time. Ten years later, in 1969, there were 1900 children in the school, most of whom were Hispanic or black. Half of the teachers were substitutes, and the principal would join the parents and community leaders when they demonstrated at city hall for better facilities.

There was much confusion in the school and one of our collaborating psychiatrists who was working with a team of Fordham University researchers remarked: "Any child who does not become disturbed in that school must be abnormal." This was what I called convulsive change, so precipitous that it was almost impossible to control it. Yet this was the situation that large numbers of Puerto Rican families had to face as they struggled to adjust to life in New York City. For years I had been writing and lecturing on the importance of the stable immigrant community and I would continue to speak about it. For this reason I was to become an advocate of the community development plan of the Puerto

---

14. See Part II: "The Changing Neighborhood and the Parochial School," address to the Committee for the Spanish-Speaking of Chicago, November 1, 1956.

Rican Forum (see p. 57) and was disappointed when it never became an actuality.

There was an interesting development after the Chicago talk. Leonard Covello, one of the great teachers of those days, heard about it and wrote for a copy. He then wrote me a letter in which he confirmed my own ideas:

> For quite some time I have been interested and concerned about the "integration" of our Puerto Rican people, and any new people who come here speaking a foreign language and having a different culture. As you know, the word is being used loosely in the public press by speakers, teachers, etc. We know that too rapid integration or assimilation has often meant disintegration, accompanied by painful and deplorable consequences. We certainly do need to clear our thinking about this process and make sure that we know exactly what we are talking about, when we use such words as assimilation, integration, etc.

I was happy that this was the occasion of my meeting Leonard Covello, an Italian, who, at the time was the remarkable principal of Benjamin Franklin High School in East Harlem. In the early days of the migration, he was one of the outstanding educators in the adaptation of the schools to the needs of Puerto Rican students. Many of his students became leaders of the Puerto Rican community. I was to become a close friend of Dr. Covello and I came to respect him very much. His death some years later was a great loss to the City and the Puerto Rican community.

THE PUERTO RICAN STUDY: 1953-1957

In 1953, I was invited to serve on an advisory panel for a very large study of the education of Puerto Ricans in New York City, funded by the Ford Foundation. It was called, *The Puerto Rican Study: 1953-1957* and was one of the first major surveys of Puerto Ricans in New York. In the four years of the study, many experiments were tried on the types of learning experience which would be most suitable and helpful to Puerto Ricans. A great deal of material was generated for the use of teachers in the public schools and, finally, twenty-three recommendations were made which reflected a great deal of insight into the experience of Puerto Ricans in New York City schools. I am always surprised to see how frequently these recommendations are repeated in so many studies of education that have occurred since. We still have not succeeded in applying them effectively to the education of Puerto Ricans.

The experience with *The Puerto Rican Study* was extremely important for me. It was my first association with a large public agency that was dealing with the migration. In the course of our work I came to meet some outstanding people in New York City who were related to the Puerto Rican experience. Dr. Jay Cayce Morrison, who was the Director of the Study, was a significant person at the time and I came to know him well. On many other occasions after the study was finished, I had the opportunity to appear with him at conferences and workshops. I also got to know Joseph Monserrat, who became a very close friend of mine. Joe was a young Puerto Rican who had come to the United States Mainland as a child and had finished his education under Leonard Covello at Benjamin Franklin High School. Joe was later to become the director of the Office of the Commonwealth of Puerto Rico in New York City. But at this time, he was a young man involved in community activities and I was happy to make his acquaintance since we would collaborate on many occasions in our efforts to assist the Puerto Rican community in New York. Another acquaintance I met at that time was Clarence Senior. Senior had worked in Puerto Rico and later came to New York and was appointed director of the Office of the Commonwealth of Puerto Rico in New York. Senior was not a Puerto Rican but he was well acquainted with all aspects of Puerto Rican experience both on the Island and here on the Mainland. Likewise, I was to see a great deal of him and collaborate on many projects after *The Puerto Rican Study*. There were many other people, such as Dan Dodson, who was a professor at New York University; Mary Finocchiaro; and Virginia Massimine, both from the Board of Education, with whom I was to collaborate on many occasions in later years. When the study was finished in 1957, there was a feeling of satisfaction that we had made a great deal of progress in providing a framework for the education of Puerto Rican children in New York City schools. Actually, here in 1994, one of the major problems for the Puerto Ricans in New York is still the failure of so many of the schools to provide an adequate education for them. The *Study* emphasized the need for a continuing inquiry into the experience of Puerto Ricans and an evaluation of their progress so that difficulties could be corrected where they existed. There was a great emphasis on serving the individual pupil, keeping the individual student's needs in mind and trying to adjust a program to his or her particular needs.

The *Study* focused on the need to recognize the diversity in the Spanish-speaking community. Surprisingly enough, many of us who are studying the Puerto Rican experience, are still making this recommendation in our latest research. In fact in the early years, the Board of

Education reported Puerto Ricans separately in their annual census. They eliminated this some years ago and now the Board reports only the aggregated figure for the total Hispanic population, which is not very useful for planning purposes. *The Puerto Rican Study* requested a "unity of purpose and practice in teaching non-English speaking pupils." However, this has never really been achieved. It is evident that schools and districts differ greatly in the type of program that they prepare for Puerto Rican students. Most of all there was a request for a continuing and important interrelationship with the parents of non-English speaking pupils in all matters pertaining to the children's welfare. Whatever efforts may have been made to fulfill this recommendation, the schools still have a long way to go before they have established an effective relationship with the parents. Emphasis was placed on adequate staffing by Spanish-speaking personnel. A great deal of progress has been made in this area. However, in specialized areas, such as psychological counselling, the number of bilingual staff is still inadequate. Nonetheless, *The Puerto Rican Study* was a giant step forward in the effort of the Board of Education to relate effectively to the educational needs of Puerto Rican children. For me it was a very important experience. For the first time I felt that I was making a contribution to one of the major agencies of the City of New York in its effort to serve the Puerto Ricans. I was to find myself in this position on many occasions later, but this was one of the most interesting and informative experiences I had in the mid-'fifties.

THE LINCOLN CENTER RELOCATION

At this early moment of my associations with the Puerto Ricans, another problem arose from an unexpected direction. The area now known as Lincoln Center, much of it a poor, deteriorated area where many Puerto Ricans lived, was designated as a Title I[15] redevelopment area. One of the stipulations of this project was that 25% of the redevelopment had to be occupied by a non-for-profit educational or health facility. Through the intervention of Robert Moses, who was one of the promoters of the Project, Fordham was chosen as the educational institution. Moses was a close friend of Father Laurence J. McGinley, S.J., then President of Fordham University. McGinley had earlier sought the assistance of

---

15. Title I Redevelopment Project was a slum-clearance, urban redevelopment project in which the City purchased the area by right of eminent domain, relocated the residents to other housing, and rebuilt the area as middle class housing or recreational or business facilities. One-third of the cost was paid by the City; two-thirds by the Federal Government Title I funds.

Moses to find another campus for the downtown schools of the University. The Fordham campus was located at 302 Broadway in an area designated for later development of government buildings in Federal Plaza. When plans began for the development of Lincoln Center, Moses remembered Fordham's need of a new downtown campus and was able to arrange to have Fordham chosen as the educational participant in the project. Although the city and federal government paid the costs of relocation, the University had the responsibility of carrying it out. Thus, Fordham found itself in the difficult position of relocating large numbers of families, many of whom were Puerto Ricans. This issue became very controversial. Many of the human rights advocates, and some of the neighborhood organizations, protested strongly against the relocation and against the Title I project. A lawyer, Mr. Harris Present, represented the Puerto Rican groups that had protested. I was later to become a good friend of Present. In the early 'sixties he became the lawyer for the Puerto Rican Family Institute on whose Board of Directors I served. But at this time he was challenging Fordham University and the other developers about the relocation.

I did not take a public position about this. I was aware of the controversy since I was a member of Fordham's faculty and I was living in the same residence as Father William Mulcahy, S.J., the priest who had responsibility for the relocation. For one thing, I did not see much hope of stopping the project. Fordham was a minor part of a massive project involving the Metropolitan Opera House, the New York State Theatre, the Avery Fisher Hall for the Philharmonic, the Vivian Beaumont Theatre, the Julliard School of Music, and thousands of units of middle-class housing. Secondly, I felt that every effort was being made to conduct the relocation fairly, and to ensure that the relocated families found suitable and better housing than they had. Thus, I remained quiet although I was aware of the problems this created for the Puerto Rican and other families involved. It made me aware of the many other similar situations which had taken place with earlier immigrants, such as the building of Grand Central Station and Rockefeller Center. I did not know any of the Puerto Rican families involved nor did I follow them to their new residences. I always regretted this. If I had had the time and resources, it would have been an excellent and valuable piece of research.

AFL-CIO CONFERENCE, 1960

On January 15, 1960, the AFL-CIO Community Services were conducting an annual conference on social issues around which the Unions had many interests. This year they dedicated it to a study of the Puerto Rican experience. The keynote address was given by Sister Isolina Ferré, a member of the religious community, Missionary Servants of the Blessed Trinity.[16] She prepared an excellent talk about the characteristics of Puerto Rican culture, which was later quoted frequently and parts of which appeared in her subsequent talks and publications. I had met Sister Isolina Ferré in Puerto Rico in 1952 when I first visited the Island. But I came to know her better in 1958 when she served as a teacher in the Institute of Intercultural Communication in Ponce, Puerto Rico. As indicated earlier, the Institute had been founded by Ivan Illich in 1957 for the training of priests, religious personnel, and lay people for ministry to Puerto Ricans on the Mainland. Sister was to become one of my outstanding teachers about the culture and experience of the Puerto Ricans. She gave courses on the folk religious practices of the Puerto Rican people, which provided remarkable insight into the religious attitudes and practices of the poor on the Island.

She came from one of the most prominent families in Puerto Rico. Her brother, Luis Ferré, served as Governor from 1968-1972. In her service with the Missionary Servants of the Blessed Trinity she had been assigned to the poorest sections of Appalachia, Cape Cod, and New York City. When I met her, she was actively serving the poor in Cabo Rojo, a small city in the southwestern part of Puerto Rico. In 1958 she was reassigned to the Navy Yard section of Brooklyn where she lived in a turbulent area populated by African Americans and newly arrived Puerto Ricans. At this same time she became the director of the Doctor White Community Settlement, a Catholic settlement house in that area. While faced with the task of assisting the Puerto Ricans and African Americans, she occasionally found herself intervening to prevent fights between them. She developed a marching band, the Riversiders, who became well known for their performances in many of the City's parades. She mastered the skills of political action and community organization. And, when the "War On Poverty" was declared by President Lyndon Johnson, Sister Isolina was named to represent the Puerto Rican community on the Council Against Poverty, which was formed in New York City in 1965 by Mayor John Lindsay.[17] At the same time, her own local

---

16. At that time, before the nuns returned to their family names, she was known by her religious name, Sister Thomas Marie.

17. When President Lyndon B. Johnson established the War On Poverty, block grants of money were given to each city to be dispersed to selected anti-poverty programs by a Council Against Poverty, composed of representatives of many segments of the community who were either elected by

community elected her to represent them. In 1958, Sister began her studies at Fordham University for an M.A. in sociology, a degree which she earned in 1960.

After ten years on the turbulent streets of Brooklyn, Sister returned to Puerto Rico where she has created a remarkable community project, originally called "Youth and Community Alerted" and now renamed, "Centro Sister Isolina." (See p. 67.)

Her talk at the AFL-CIO meeting was one of her first public statements, many of which were to make her one of the most respected spokespersons of the Puerto Rican community. The organizing committee of the Conference felt that more was needed as a background to Sister's talk. She was also anxious to have me on the program in some way, since it was her first major address in New York and she was quite apprehensive. It was agreed that I would write a background paper about Puerto Rican family life and organized social services.[18] The paper was distributed to all participants and was surprisingly well received. The Union circulated thousands of copies and it was published in a little brochure together with Sister's talk and some other features of the program. I incorporated much of it into my chapter on "The Puerto Rican Family" in my book, *Puerto Rican Americans.* It was my first statement about the topic which was to engage my attention for many years to come.

THE 1960s

The journey through the 'sixties was to be a mixture of favorable and unfavorable developments. The migration of Puerto Ricans slowed down, but fairly large numbers continued to come. The Puerto Rican population in New York City increased from 612,574 in 1960 to 860,584 in 1970, an increase of about 40%. Many of the new Puerto Ricans had been born here; the second generation in 1970 numbered 344,412, or more than one-third of the New York Puerto Rican population. However, the 1960s were to see the influx of large numbers of other Hispanics, particu-

---

their constituencies, or appointed by the Mayor. Her talk at the AFL-CIO Conference brought her to the attention of a city-wide audience and began to establish her as a leader, not only in the Brooklyn Navy Yard section, but among the Puerto Ricans in the entire city.

18. See Part II: "Background Paper on Puerto Rican Culture and Organized Social Services," AFL-CIO Community Services, National Advisory Conference on "Labor and the Puerto Rican Community – Working Together for Better Social Services," New York, January 15, 1960.

larly Cubans and Dominicans. Thus the diverse Hispanic population emerged quickly during this period and was to change the environment to which the Puerto Ricans were responding.

The development of organizations was to continue as the Puerto Rican community matured and its experience with the New York environment increased. Puerto Ricans became active in the War On Poverty, and their number of elected and appointed officials increased. It was also the period of the Vietnam War and the peace demonstrations. The Young Lords appeared and made their presence felt. They were an organization of militant young men and women, probably inspired by the Black Panthers. And student demonstrations became an expected part of life.

However, it was the period when the drug scene developed rapidly and struck the Puerto Ricans heavily, and violence appeared frequently to trouble their lives. But they journeyed onward with confidence and hope, and by the 1970s were recognized as a major segment of the New York population.

THE APPEARANCE OF VIOLENCE

Nineteen fifty-nine was a "red hot summer" in New York in terms of delinquency. They were the days when gangs and gang warfare were still common. The heroin craze had not yet affected the youth; they were still tough and strong and militant. These were the last days of "West Side Story." Soon the heroin was to debilitate many of them, render them stupefied, then the fighting ceased, to be replaced by over-doses and heroin deaths that made the deaths from gang fights look trivial. Violence took a new form, of robbery and mugging, the desperate effort of addicts to get money for their drugs. The Puerto Rican community was caught in the middle of it.

In the summer of 1959 on the lower East Side, a Puerto Rican gang, headed by Julio Rosario, was feuding with a black gang. In the fighting an innocent bystander, Theresa Gee, a young black, was killed in the Puerto Rican crossfire. The black gang, obviously enraged, retaliated against the Puerto Ricans and, in the conflict, Julio Rosario was mortally wounded. A Jesuit priest, a friend of mine, was attending him. As he lay dying he kept mumbling: "Tell the guys they can count on me. Tell them, I'll be there."

Shortly after this, there was another murder of an Irish boy by a Puerto Rican in Washington Heights. But the incident that set the City aghast was the case of "Dracula and the Umbrella Man." On August 31,

1959, two boys from Holy Cross parish on West 42nd Street, Robert Young and Anthony Korzensky, were walking home from a theater and were attacked in the park between 45th and 46th Streets by a group of Puerto Ricans called "The Draculas." In the conflict, Salvador Agron (Dracula or The Cape Man: he always wore a nurse's cape) killed the two boys. He was assisted by Tony Hernandez (The Umbrella Man: he always carried an umbrella). Both youths were arrested. The reaction of the City was wild. The pastor of Holy Cross Church preached vigorously about the need to control these wild youths; a Congressman in Brooklyn wanted to introduce legislation to forbid Puerto Ricans to come to New York; editorials by the dozens commented on the brutality of the Puerto Rican youths, and the demand for reprisals and punishment was loud and clear. No one was saying a word in support of the Puerto Ricans.

Early in September I returned to New York. I was deeply concerned about the level of hostility and the manifestations of public anger against the Puerto Ricans because of the murders committed by Agron. I learned that a Jesuit priest at the Fordham Business School was planning some public lectures, so I asked him to sign me up for the first, to take place on October 8th. The lecture was an event. The hall was packed! The press was there in large numbers and I delivered the talk which created a sensation. It was the first important statement in support of the Puerto Ricans. It was covered in the New York press the following day; the following week my picture was in *Time* magazine with a story. The word was out.

Two things happened: I became the hero of the Puerto Rican community and I was featured in *El Diario*, the Puerto Rican newspaper; I received numerous calls and letters from Puerto Ricans and many non-Puerto Ricans who were grateful to me for the talk. There was the other reaction from hostile New Yorkers. I have a file filled with hate letters accusing me of everything from being a Puerto Rican lover to lacking a sense of responsibility for the safety of the citizens of New York. The 1959 talk, "Delinquency and the Puerto Ricans," was later retitled, published and widely circulated.[19] It has been quoted many times by elected officials, both Puerto Rican and non-Puerto Rican. I really think it put the problem of delinquency in perspective. The scholarly community, as well as many of the persons involved in the juvenile justice system, had great praise for it. I simply pointed out that delinquency

---

19. See Part II, "New York City and Its Puerto Rican 'Problem,'" *Catholic Mind*, January/February 1960.

was not something the Puerto Ricans brought with them; it was something that happened to them in New York as it had happened to many other immigrants who had come to the City in the nineteenth and early twentieth centuries. It was a consequence of the uprooting from a traditional culture, where norms of behavior were consistent and enforced by the community. When Puerto Rican youths came to New York they found themselves in a world where things that were all right in Puerto Rico were wrong in New York and *vice versa*. It was unthinkable at that time in Puerto Rico for a high school girl to go to a dance without a chaperone, but in New York, she was ridiculed if she appeared with one. Growing up in this world of ambiguity, the youths had no consistent norms by which to guide their behavior and, in this strange and often hostile environment, the Puerto Rican community found it difficult to enforce consistent norms. The result was often delinquent behavior.

In this context, the established community did what it has always done, it blamed all the evils of the City on the newcomers – in this case the Puerto Ricans. They were an obvious and easy target, unable to protect themselves. It was important to define the problem correctly and do everything possible to help the Puerto Rican youths and their families to cope with the cultural transition as effectively as possible.

Salvador Agron and Tony Hernandez were tried, convicted and sentenced for their crime. At that time New York State had a policy of capital punishment. Agron was sentenced to death in the electric chair. The reaction of the Puerto Rican community was extraordinary. Capital punishment does not exist in the Latin countries and they were appalled that a boy so young (at sixteen, he would have been the youngest ever to be executed), would be sentenced to die. A tremendous appeal to Governor Nelson Rockefeller was raised and on New Year's Day, 1961, the Governor commuted Agron's sentence to life imprisonment. In 1977, he was released on parole. He violated parole and was returned to prison but was released again and later died.

By the early 'sixties, I had become very much involved in the problem of delinquency among Puerto Ricans. When I gave the talk in 1959, "Delinquency and the Puerto Ricans," I was speaking from a common sense perspective and a sensitivity to culture. But I began to notice that the officially published reports on delinquency showed a rate of Puerto Rican delinquency, much higher than their proportion of the population. A colleague of mine, Professor John Martin, was a specialist in criminology and I began to discuss the issue with him. Furthermore, I began to receive calls and letters from social workers expressing their concern about the behavior of some of the judges in the juvenile court. For example, one judge refused to place a delinquent youth on probation in the custody of his parents because the parents were not married. They were living in a "consensual union," a situation quite common in the Caribbean area in which a man and woman live together for many years, possibly for life, and raise their children responsibly.[20] The social worker in the case had investigated the family and found the parents to be serious and responsible. But the judge perceived the case as if it were similar to a man and woman living together in an Irish Catholic culture. I was asked to intervene with the judge and explain to him the nature of consensual unions, especially the fact that, in many cases, the parents were as serious and responsible as legally married couples, sometimes more so.

This led me to look into the problem of delinquency more carefully. I began to suspect that the important cultural factor in behavior was being overlooked. In many cases, what was being judged as delinquent behavior in New York, was not seen as delinquent in Puerto Rico, and what was considered delinquent in Puerto Rico was permitted as appropriate in New York.

About this time, I was asked to participate in the evaluation of the program of a correctional institution for Catholic boys, Lincoln Hall in Lincolndale, New York. It was directed by the Christian Brothers, most of whom were of Irish background. John Martin and I asked the Brothers to give us two cases, one of which they considered their best success, and another which they considered their worst failure. When we looked at the two cases, it was interesting to us that the best success was an Irish American boy; the worst failure was a Puerto Rican. Strangely enough, the offense of the Irish American boy had been much more serious than that of the Puerto Rican. When I read through the Puerto Rican case, I was surprised that his behavior was analyzed entirely with psychological and psychiatric concepts. There was nothing in the case about the cultural background of the boy, about the characteristics of the social environment where he lived, about the companions he played with, or details of the situation in which the offense occurred. It was clear to me that the behavior of the boy could not be adequately assessed until these aspects of the case were introduced into the analysis.

---

20. In the Roman Law, some features of which still prevailed in Puerto Rico, there was no such thing as "common law marriage." People lived together consensually, but their children were defined as "natural children," not as illegitimate children.

In 1964 together with my colleague, John Martin, I published a book, *Delinquent Behavior: A Redefinition of the Problem*,[21] in an effort to introduce the cultural and social factors into the analysis of delinquent behavior. Professional personnel in the field of corrections were identifying delinquency as a personality defect, to be corrected by psychological counselling or psychiatric treatment. We showed that this was inadequate and frequently led to serious misdiagnoses. For example, the Puerto Rican boy (let us call him Pedro) was diagnosed as a "sociopath," a boy with a weak ego because he had grown up without a father. The facts that at age twelve he had joined a gang of boys who were fourteen and that he wore a mustache and goatee were interpreted as an effort on his part to look older than he was. When I made contact with his gang, I discovered that, far from having a weak ego, Pedro was the defender of the barrio, a fearless fighter who was recruited by the fourteen-year-olds to join them. "When Pedro is here" they said, "we are safe." The boys asked me if I wanted to meet Pedro's father. I said I did. When they introduced me to him, he was wearing a mustache and goatee exactly the same as what Pedro wore in imitation of his father. There were many other features about his life which were missing in the psychological reports but which were essential if the behavior of Pedro was to be understood.

The book was very successful. From the viewpoint of the Puerto Ricans it protected them from being diagnosed and adjudicated on the basis of norms that prevailed in New York, but not in Puerto Rico. In other words, the method we proposed meant finding out what the behavior meant to the boy before you judged according to our Mainland standards. We insisted that the social and cultural background of the boy as well as the situation in which the delinquent incident occurred, must be introduced into the analysis in order to make an adequate judgment of the behavior of a delinquent youth. We later followed this book with a second,[22] which elaborated upon the details of our approach.

THE DRUG SCENE

Involvement in delinquency issues led me directly into the study of drug abuse. Drug abuse struck the Puerto Rican community early; it was

---

21. *Delinquent Behavior: A Redefinition of the Problem.* New York: Random House, 1964.

22. With John M. Martin and Robert E. Gould, M.D. *The Analysis of Delinquent Behavior: A Structural Approach.* New York: Random House, 1969.

already widespread during the 1950s. Dan Wakefield's famous chapter, "Trip to the Moon," in his book, *Island in the City*,[23] was a vivid report on the presence of drugs in East Harlem. Professor Isidor Chein, of New York University, did his first study of drugs in New York City in 1955.[24] He found that 75% of the drug users were concentrated in 15% of the City's census tracts, and these were the poorest areas where residents had the lowest level of education, lowest income, poorest housing. Many of the tracts had large concentrations of Puerto Ricans. But it did not require studies to convince the people in East Harlem that drug use was prevalent. They saw it on the street corners every day.

My first contact with it was through one of the great figures in the neighborhood at that time, the Reverend Norman Eddy, pastor of the East Harlem Protestant Parish. Eddy was deeply involved in the life of the people in the community. A very spiritual man of great compassion, but with a great deal of common sense, he started trying to bring peace among some of the fighting gangs of the area. He made space available for a club where the youths could come, no questions asked, and participate in activities. Slowly Eddy was able to bring some of them to a situation where the youths themselves became the peacemakers.

The Reverend Eddy soon became involved in the effort to prevent or correct drug abuse, and the Parish became one of the more effective centers. His objective was not so much religious conversion, as an effort to bring the youths to a deeper sense of self-respect and self-dignity, and to move them along to a productive adulthood. The Parish was one of the main community resources during the 'fifties and 'sixties. However, despite his heroic efforts, the drug problem escalated and was to become a plague among the Puerto Ricans. A detailed description of it is found in my book, *Puerto Rican Americans*.

My relation to the drug scene was to remain indirect. In 1965, Mayor John Lindsay invited to New York, Efren Ramirez, a Puerto Rican psychologist who had developed a method of rehabilitation of drug addicts in Puerto Rico. Through the influence of Ramirez, federal funds were obtained to start a number of rehabilitation centers in New York City. My task, together with colleagues at Fordham University, was to evaluate these projects for the federal government. Between 1965-1970, this occupied much of our time.

---

23. Dan Wakefield, *Island in the City*. Boston: Houghton-Mifflin, 1959.

24. Reported in Isidor Chein *et al. The Road to H.* New York: Basic Books, 1964, Chap. 2.

However, it was not until 1975 that I became involved in a major research project on "Puerto Rican Addicts and non-Addicts." This was a federally funded study of fifty Puerto Rican addicts and fifty non-addicts. Working with me on the project were my colleagues, Drs. John M. Martin, James Brown, and Morton Levine. The results of the study were published in a book edited by Ronald Glick and Joan Moore, *Drugs in Hispanic Communities.*[25]

My purpose here is not to review my experience with drug rehabilitation programs, or the results of our research, but to say something about the impact of drugs on the Puerto Rican community. It has been a devastating blow and has created, for Puerto Ricans, problems of adjustment to American society which earlier immigrants did not face since drugs were not available to them.

Ramirez used a confrontational approach. He was convinced that drug addiction was part of a process of running away from reality. His method was to compel individuals to face their reality, and the reality of the world around them. This he did by challenging them in a circular gathering until they broke down and admitted their weakness, their flight from reality and their need to face up to themselves.

Ramirez always claimed he had success in this method. But, our experience in evaluating the program was that it often resulted in clients, especially Puerto Ricans, leaving the program. They found it too personally humiliating. Meantime, a reformed Puerto Rican addict in the Bronx organized a program called SERA (Hispanic Association for a Drug Free Society), designed specifically for Puerto Ricans. It was bilingual, but aimed to keep the addict at home, among his peers. The addict would come to the program every day. This was not confrontational as was the program of Ramirez, but it enjoyed considerable success. However, the original founder slipped back into addiction and the program was taken over by others. Although it increased in size and later became a recipient of large amounts of federal money, the new directors became involved in corrupt practices and the program was terminated.

An effort was made by Manuel Diaz to revive it under the name of PROMESA. Eventually it was taken over by a very able Puerto Rican, Felix Velasquez, who has developed it into one of the largest rehabilitation programs in the City. It flourishes now in the Bronx and is becoming more and more involved in the South Bronx where it is active in housing and community development.

---

25. *Drugs In Hispanic Communities.* New Brunswick, N.J.: Rutgers University Press, 1990.

Addiction has been an embarrassing trial for the Puerto Rican community. In the year 1969 alone in New York City, 119 Puerto Ricans died of drug abuse. Between 1969-1971, among Puerto Ricans aged fifteen to forty-four, 340 persons died of drug abuse, 12.3 percent of all Puerto Rican deaths. It was the second greatest killer among this population. Perhaps more tragic, the most frequent cause of death was homicide. Great efforts were made to prevent addiction and correct it, but the federal and local governments have had little success in curbing the flow of drugs to the streets. PROMESA as well as other rehabilitation programs, such as Odyssey House, Phoenix House, and many others in which Puerto Ricans constitute a large part of the client population, have been very successful in bringing the addicts back to a productive life, but the effort cannot keep up with the challenge. Now, to complicate the situation further and add to the embarrassment of the community is the plague of AIDS which, in the Puerto Rican community, is closely related to the problem of addiction.

THE CUBAN REFUGEES

In 1960 the Hispanic presence in New York took on a new character. Cubans, who were fleeing from the Revolution under Fidel Castro, began coming to the United States in large numbers. Castro's Revolution against the government of Fulgencio Batista was finally successful in 1959. When it became clear, one year later, that Castro intended to establish a Communist nation, thousands of middle- and upper-class persons fled from the Island. Since they came, not as immigrants, but as refugees from a Communist nation, they were given considerable assistance in the United States, and began to settle in Miami especially, but also in the northeast in New York and northern New Jersey.

Thus another people, quite distinct from Puerto Ricans, were here as newcomers. In contrast to the Puerto Ricans who were mostly poor and working-class, the Cubans were middle- and upper-class. They were also predominantly white. The Puerto Ricans found it necessary to adjust not only to Americans of European background; they now had to adjust to the presence of Cubans. Cubans, because of their perceived racial and class backgrounds, found it easier to adjust to the mainstream of American life. They were able to move more easily into jobs requiring more skill.

A student of mine, Eleanor Rogg, did a study of the Cubans in west New York, New Jersey, a city with the largest concentration of Cubans in the Northeast.[26] They became the most active group of parishioners at Saint Joseph's parish, and began to distinguish themselves in the public schools. They started their own businesses, at the time mostly neighborhood shops and stores. But it was obvious that they were advancing into middle-class American society much more rapidly than the Puerto Ricans. The second study by Dr. Rogg describes a well established community, determined to stay in the United States, and prospering.[27]

A second wave of Cubans, called the Mariel Cubans, came in 1980. These came in a wild, disorganized flight in small boats from the Port of Mariel. Many of them were poor, black, and from the working-class. To their numbers, Castro added a number of criminals from his jails, and patients from his mental hospitals. The task of receiving them was marked by endless confusion. But finally they were received and resettled; the effort has been made since to return the criminals and patients to Cuba. The presence of the Cubans marked the beginning of the large scale multi-Hispanic population of New York City, and the need of the Puerto Ricans to adjust to a Spanish-speaking world of great variety and to Hispanic cultures very different from their own.

It was clear to me early in the 1960s that New York was moving into a new multicultural situation, and one which would be more complex than the simple adjustment of Puerto Ricans to the Irish or Germans. This would be a new challenge requiring a new response.

THE PUERTO RICAN FAMILY INSTITUTE

The Puerto Rican Family Institute was founded in 1962 by Agostín Gonzalez, a Puerto Rican social worker, together with a few Puerto Rican social worker volunteers. In 1963 he formed a Board of Directors and asked me to serve on it. I have been on the Board ever since. Gonzalez was a small, harmless looking person who gave the appearance of hardly knowing what was going on, but he was shrewd with a great deal of imagination and courage. The Institute, a symbol of the maturity of the Puerto Rican community, has become the most important city-wide agency for Hispanics in the City of New York.

---

26. Eleanor Meyer Rogg and Rosemary Santana Cooney. *Adaptation and Adjustment of Cubans*. New York: Hispanic Research Center, Fordham University, 1960.

27. Eleanor Meyer Rogg. *The Assimilation of Cuban Exiles*. New York: Aberdeen Press, 1974.

Gonzalez had a creative concept in mind. He wanted to perpetuate the institution of *compadrazgo* in New York. *Compadrazgo* is a form of ritual kinship which is deeply rooted in Puerto Rican culture. The sponsors at Baptism and Confirmation become the *compadres* (the co-parents), with the parents of the child. The best man and maid of honor become the *compadres* of the married couple. It is a serious relationship that binds the *compadres* together in a network of rights and responsibilities. One *compadre* is expected to come to the assistance of the other whenever asked and in whatever circumstances. One can reprimand another in circumstances where even a brother or sister would be reluctant to intervene.

Gonzalez had noticed that many Puerto Rican families were suffering in the transition to New York. He also noticed that many retained a remarkable strength and resiliency in their adaptation to life in the City. Gonzalez wanted to identify the weak families and sought to link them with a very strong family in the same area and in the same social class. Thus the strong could be a support for the weak and help it to weather the storms of the transition to New York. This he started to do with his small team of volunteer social workers.

When President Lyndon B. Johnson established the War On Poverty in 1963, federal money became available for agencies like the Institute, and Gonzalez succeeded in getting a grant to support it. This enabled him to serve full-time as its executive director and to hire a small staff of full-time workers. It also made the role of the Board of Directors more important. He moved to a rented facility on West 14th Street and expanded the work of the Institute. The number of families it was serving increased. He later developed a "Placement Prevention Program," a team of experienced social workers who would intervene to support a family that sought to place its children in foster homes or institutions. The team would work with the family to find solutions to their problems and enable them to keep the children at home. The Institute later developed a program to divert Hispanic youth from the juvenile justice system and to keep them at home and in their neighborhood; it developed a mental health clinic for troubled children and families.

My service on the Board brought me into contact with Puerto Rican social workers and Puerto Rican families, both strong and weak. At this time, in the early 'sixties, the number of out-of-wedlock children among the Puerto Ricans was relatively small, as was the number of female-headed families. These two problems were to escalate sharply during the 'seventies and 'eighties despite the efforts of the Institute. In the early 'sixties the Puerto Rican family was still a strong institution and the Institute sought to keep it that way. It flourished during the 1960s and 1970s and represented a strong Puerto Rican presence in the City.

In the early 1970s, the remigration of families to Puerto Rico had increased. Gonzalez noticed that many of them who had adapted well to the culture of New York City, now faced an uprooting in reverse. They were no longer prepared for family life in Puerto Rico. Therefore, he established an office in Rio Piedras, one of the large sections of San Juan, where a trained staff sought to help returning families adjust to life back in Puerto Rico.

Gonzalez unfortunately was killed in an automobile accident in Mexico in 1984. But he had put together a highly competent staff that has kept the Institute going as an important institution of the Puerto Rican and Hispanic communities. Maria Elena Girone, the executive director, and her assistant, Elvira Gonzalez, have continued its strong development. It now has its own building on 15th Street and satellite offices in every borough except Staten Island.

THE QUESTION OF LANGUAGE AMONG PUERTO RICANS

Of the many continuing questions about the Puerto Ricans, few have been as hotly debated as that of English. It is a question as serious in Puerto Rico as here on the Mainland. After Puerto Rico became a possession of the United States and when citizenship was granted unilaterally in 1918, an educational policy was adopted that required that English be the language of instruction in non-language courses in the public schools of the Island.[28] This was a short-sighted policy of political leaders and educators who presumed that Puerto Rico would eventually become a State of the Union. Therefore, it would be essential that the Islanders know English; and the best way to accomplish this would be to have Puerto Rican students have all their instruction in English. Another reason was given: that this would enable Puerto Ricans to become "Americans" more quickly. The result was disastrous and has been reported and analyzed in many books and articles about language learning in Puerto Rico. Probably the harshest criticism was the cynical remark, but very true: "Puerto Ricans were becoming illiterate in both

---

28. Ismael Rodriguez Bou, "Significant Factors in the Development of Education in Puerto Rico," in *Status of Puerto Rico: Selected Background Studies*. Washington, D.C.: United States/Puerto Rican Commission on the Status of Puerto Rico, 1966.

languages." The policy was changed officially in 1948 when the first elected Puerto Rican Governor, Luis Muñoz Marin, took office. He changed the language of non-language instruction back to Spanish. English was taught at all levels for one hour a day. This enabled the Puerto Ricans to preserve their Spanish language tradition, but it did not result in a command of English among the students. The debate still goes on (1994) and no successful resolution of the language question in Puerto Rico has been achieved. The issue flowed over to the Mainland where it became a question of the teaching of English as a second language. Serious efforts were made at an early date to develop an effective policy of language instruction for Puerto Ricans in New York. *The Puerto Rican Study*, (see p. 34 above) sought to identify a method of instruction that would be effective for Puerto Ricans, not only in English, but in other subjects as well. In the Congressional Hearings about the Bilingual Education Act,[29] the debate centered on the question as to whether bilingual programs funded by the Act would be "transitional," that is, an effective way of teaching English that would be terminated once the child had achieved a mastery of English; or whether they would be designed to preserve the mastery of Spanish while the child learned English, so that the child would be perfectly bilingual. The "transitional" school prevailed and the programs funded by the Bilingual Education Act are designed to use Spanish simply as an instrument in the mastery of English. Finally there is the continuing mythology that Puerto Rican students do not learn English. They may not gain a mastery of it, but English is certainly the ordinary language of communication of second generation children. The 1990 Census reported that 85% of the second generation were proficient in English. More recently the "English-only" movement has been gaining support. Some states have already passed State Constitutional Amendments defining English as the official language of the State. The movement seeks an amendment to the Federal Constitution to the same effect.

In view of the earlier controversy, a Conference on "The Puerto Rican Child in His Cultural Context," was convened in Barranquitas, Puerto Rico, November 18-20, 1965. The focus of the Conference was largely on language, but the context, as the title stated, was the cultural environment of the Puerto Rican child. I presented a paper at the Conference that specified the importance of language maintenance as an

---

29. Bilingual Education: Hearings Before the Special Committee on Bilingual Education. Committee on Labor and Public Welfare, United States Senate, 19th Congress, First Session. Washington, D.C.: U.S. Government Printing Office, 1967.

essential factor in the continuing sense of identity of Puerto Ricans.[30] The paper is interesting in that it reflects so many features of Puerto Rican experience in the mid-1960s. It discussed the language issue as a complex socio-political issue involving much more than the ability to read, write and speak. It refers to the non-determining plebiscite conducted in Puerto Rico in 1965 in which the maintenance of language was emphasized. It also makes reference to the challenge to psychological and psychiatric approaches to Puerto Rican issues which neglected the social context of language and language learning; it cites Mobilization for Youth, a massive program funded largely by the Anti-Poverty Program, which sought to create legitimate channels of upward mobility for marginal, Puerto Rican youth. It refers to the growing emphasis on culture as a factor in the behavior of delinquent Puerto Rican youth. It notes that although the percentage of Puerto Rican delinquents was much higher than the percentage in the population as a whole, the element of culture was almost entirely missing from the assessment of delinquent behavior (see p. 43). It is clear from the paper that I was concerned about the maintenance of language among Puerto Ricans, and its importance for their continuing sense of identity as well as its significance in their effective adjustment to American society.

OSCAR LEWIS AND THE PUERTO RICAN FAMILY

I met Oscar Lewis in November 1965, at the Conference in Barranquitas. He was finishing his study of Puerto Ricans in the culture of poverty in La Perla, a very poor section of San Juan, Puerto Rico. This was published the following year as *La Vida: A Puerto Rican Family in the Culture of Poverty, San Juan and New York*.[31] He presented a paper at the Barranquitas Conference; one chapter of the book he was preparing. I was impressed by Lewis' ability to capture the intimate, day-to-day, concrete details of the life of the Puerto Ricans he was describing. In his book on Mexicans, *Five Families*,[32] Lewis had presented his theory of the culture

30. See Part II: "The Role of Language as a Factor of Strength for the Puerto Rican Community." Special presentation on "The Puerto Rican Child — His Cultural Context," Barranquitas, Puerto Rico, Nov. 18, 1965. This paper was later published. See: "Función del Lenguaje Como Factor de Cohesión en la Comunidad Puertorriqueña." Educación #19 (Abril 1966), Departamento de Instrucción Publica, Hato Rey, Puerto Rico.

31. *La Vida: A Puerto Rican Family in the Culture of Poverty, San Juan and New York*. New York: Random House, 1966.

32. *Five Families*. New York: Basic Books, 1959.

of poverty for the first time.[33] In the preface to *La Vida*, he elaborated on this description in the context of the Ríos Family, the name he gave to the family he had studied in La Perla.

The publication of *La Vida* was a crushing blow to the Puerto Ricans in New York. Lewis tried to make it clear that the family he had studied was a carefully selected family of slum residents with a history of prostitution; he had not intended it to be a description of typical Puerto Rican families in general, nor even of poor Puerto Rican families in particular. However, his disclaimer was included in the fifty-five page introduction, much of which dealt with anthropological concepts and research methods, as well as statistical data. Little of Lewis' explanation was understood by, or of interest to, most readers. The fact was that the Ríos family most definitely was *not* representative of any group outside the culture of poverty. However, that qualification was largely missed in the public reaction to the book. It became a best-seller, and the public generally formed their impression of Puerto Ricans from the description presented in the book. The book appeared in the mid-sixties when the Puerto Ricans were struggling desperately against distorted and unfavorable images of themselves that were current in the Mainland American press. What hurt the Puerto Ricans most, however, was that this book touched the most sensitive nerve – their pride in their family life. As one of my Puerto Rican friends said to me: "When I am talking with an American these days, I feel inside me that he is thinking of me in terms of Lewis' book, *La Vida*, and that makes me angry as hell." I was familiar with La Perla, the poor section where the study was located and which he names "La Esmeralda." Whenever I visited Puerto Rico, I always spent some time with the Capuchin priests of the parish of San Francisco in Old San Juan. One of them, Father Venard Kanfush, was the pastor of La Perla (see p. 13). He was also one of the best-known priests in San Juan, known and loved by the poor, the wealthy, the entertainers, the alcoholics, by everyone. La Perla was off limits for U.S. servicemen, but Father Venard (called Father Ponce in the book) could go down there any time, day or night, and he was respected and secure. One of my criminologist friends, while visiting Puerto Rico, wanted to see La Perla and Father Venard took us through it at 1 a.m. when most ordinary citizens would not go near the place.

---

33. "The culture of poverty," as defined by Lewis, is a life-style developed by some extremely poor people. It reflects their adaptation and reaction to their marginal position in capitalistic societies. As such, it is not peculiar to Puerto Ricans on the Island or on the Mainland.

When Lewis had finished his manuscript, he sent me a copy. By this time we had become good friends as well as professional colleagues and so he asked me for my reactions. I sent him a long letter with comments which I largely incorporated in my published article-length review of his book.[34] He called me to discuss my remarks. He appreciated them, he said, but the one thing that pained him most was my remark, "Oscar, when Father Venard reads this book, I am afraid he will feel deeply hurt." Lewis held Father Venard in high esteem; Father had been very helpful to him in his study of La Perla, and the last thing he would want to have done was to disappoint Father Venard. I expressed my fears that the book would be misinterpreted by the "best-seller" readers, the vast majority of whom were neither social scientists nor social workers. I felt strongly that what made the book attractive to many readers were the vivid details of the sex life of the Ríos family. I tried in the review to place *La Vida* where it belonged: in the context of other social scientific studies of Puerto Rican families. I have great respect for what Lewis was trying to do in his book, and I always had my students read it, but not until they had a broad background in Puerto Rican culture and family life. What always has amazed me in Puerto Rico is the great variety of family types on the Island. Sidney Mintz's *Worker in the Cane*,[35] for example, is a remarkably sensitive and most respectful portrayal of families living in consensual unions, couples living together without civil or religious marriage; *Esperanza*, by Carlos Buitrago Ortiz[36] is as different from *La Vida* as night from day. It portrays the family life of devout Puerto Ricans in a town of strong Catholic belief and practice. There are many others.

Puerto Rican families have developed serious difficulties in New York City, but they are not the ones that would have been anticipated by *La Vida*. Problem families are by no means the complete picture of Puerto Rican life in New York. The study of second generation families by Lloyd Rogler and Rosemary Santana Cooney, *Puerto Rican Families in New York City: Intergenerational Processes*[37] presents a different picture (see p. 75).

---

34. See Part II: "Oscar Lewis and the Puerto Rican Family," *America*, Dec. 10, 1966.

35. *Worker in the Cane*. New Haven: Yale University Press, 1960.

36. *Esperanza*. Tucson: University of Arizona Press, 1972.

37. *Puerto Rican Families in New York City: Intergenerational Processes*. Maplewood, N.J.: Waterfront Press, 1984.

Lewis called me when he was on his way to Cuba to study the families living under Fidel Castro's regime. He wanted to test his hypothesis that, in a socialist society, the culture of poverty would not exist. He came back to New York in December 1970, on his way to Puerto Rico for a rest before continuing his study in Cuba. While in New York he called me. We talked a while about his experiences and his hopes for the Cuban studies when they were to be published. He wanted to know about my own book which I was preparing on the Puerto Rican experience in New York. I enjoyed talking with him and hearing of his work. The following day I picked up the morning paper to read that he had died suddenly the previous night, shortly after we had talked together. His studies were completed and published by his wife, Ruth L. Lewis, and a research associate, Susan M. Rigdon: *Four Men* (1977), *Four Women* (1977), and *Neighbors* (1978).

THE DOMINICANS

After 1965, immigrants from the Dominican Republic began to arrive in large numbers, further complicating the multi-cultural situation of the Spanish-speaking in New York. Under Rafael Trujillo's dictatorship, 1930-1961, emigration from the Dominican Republic was restricted. After his assassination in 1961, restrictions were lifted and immigrants began to come to the United States. In 1965 alone close to 10,000 immigrants came from the Dominican Republic. The 1990 census counted 300,000 in New York City. The interesting aspect of the Dominican immigration is that, when they moved into the Washington Heights areas of Manhattan, the Puerto Ricans who had been there in large numbers, moved out. This was only the first indication of the antagonism between the two groups. Later there were to be conflicts about competition in drug trafficking. However, in 1991, very large numbers of Dominicans and Puerto Ricans were marrying each other, a sign that old time antagonisms were not affecting intermarriage. In the meantime, Dominicans have moved to many areas of the Bronx, Manhattan and Brooklyn where they share Hispanic neighborhoods with Puerto Ricans and others.

THE CATHOLIC SCHOOL

During all the years of my association with the Puerto Rican community, the problem of schooling always appeared as one of the most critical. We saw gangs and poverty and discrimination in the fifties; we saw drugs and poverty and discrimination in the 'sixties, but always, foremost in the minds of most Puerto Rican people, was their unfortunate experience in the schools. The Ford Foundation Study, (1953-57), was an extensive study of the problem along with recommendations to remedy it. (See p. 34) Conference after conference followed *The Puerto Rican Study*, and repeatedly the same recommendations were presented, with little evidence that they were being seriously implemented. In my book, *Puerto Rican Americans*, I include a long chapter on the educational experience of Puerto Ricans. The 1990 dropout rate from high school was close to 50% of the Puerto Rican students. This indicated the schools' continuing failure. None of the efforts designed to correct this seems to have been successful.

I had been involved since the early 'fifties in workshops, conferences, and consultations, about the education of Puerto Ricans. Lack of Spanish-speaking competence on many levels was a major problem, not so much for communication with the children as for communication with their parents. But more important was the failure of the schools (both Catholic and public) to create a learning environment in which the Puerto Rican child felt completely at home. There was the problem of recognizing the pressure of the family for another wage-earner. There was the failure to develop a curriculum and methods that made clear to the students the relevance of their schooling for their future economic success. The problems were numerous and widely recognized. But, for the most part, the system was not working. I was aware of some schools, both Catholic and public, where good things seemed to be happening. The role of the principal in these cases appeared to be the critical factor.

A 1985 report of the Board of Education[38] acknowledged that the dropout problem was as bad as ever.

The Hispanic Policy Development Project published a remarkable study of Hispanics in the schools throughout the nation, *Make Something Happen*.[39] Even at this date (1994) the problem remains. It remains to be seen whether these and other reports will have any effect.

An example of the thrust of my efforts appears in the address which I gave at a workshop on inner city schools, sponsored by the Superintendent of Schools, Archdiocese of New York, November 11, 1965.[40] There were moments when that address was interrupted by

---

38. *New York Times*, May 26, 1985.

39. *Make Something Happen*. National Commission on Secondary Education for Hispanics, 1001 Connecticut Avenue, N.W., Washington, D.C. 20036, 1985.

40. This address was later published as "The Catholic School: Its Place in the

tumultuous cheering and applause, some of which took me by surprise. But it made clear to me that the Sisters and Brothers who were present were deeply concerned about finding the methods that would enable them to respond effectively to the problem, not only in the Catholic, but in the public schools as well.

ASPIRA

In 1961, Antonia Pantoja created Aspira, a remarkable organization designed to promote the education of Puerto Rican children. By organizing Aspira Clubs in the schools, by workshops and counselling, Aspira sought to motivate the students to excel and to prepare themselves for college and professional life (see p. 10). It became probably the most successful of all the Puerto Rican organizations.

Toni invited me to be a member of the Research Advisory Panel for Aspira, a distinguished group of scholars and community leaders, to evaluate the role of Aspira, and to recommend further projects. It was an interesting group to work with and any association with Toni was a lively event. I do not recall that the group contributed very much to Aspira. Its success was really through the student clubs in the elementary and high schools. But there is no doubt that Aspira developed an unusually large group of young people who became the leaders of the Puerto Rican community in the 'seventies and 'eighties. The existence of Aspira was further evidence of the maturity of the Puerto Rican community in the development of strong institutional structures.

THE PUERTO RICAN COMMUNITY DEVELOPMENT PROJECT

It was about this time that I became involved in an interesting conflict between two groups of my Puerto Rican friends. The Puerto Rican Forum had prepared a proposal asking for substantial funding to strengthen the Puerto Rican community. It was written by Dr. Frank Bonilla and was based on a very creative and important concept. He proposed a self-help project for the development of the community by strengthening family life, opening opportunities for youth, and making full use of education. The concept, which I had often emphasized, grew out of the awareness that "one integrates from a position of strength, not from a position of weakness." What enabled the earlier immigrants to move into the mainstream of American life was the existence of a strong,

Witness of the Church," *Catholic Mind*, March 1966: 28-35. See Part II.

immigrant community which gave them a sense of self-reliance and self-confidence. It was also a community in which they were at home, and which provided relief while they struggled to move into contact with the larger and sometimes hostile society.

The proposal was first challenged by American groups who claimed that it was divisive, and was likely to create a ghetto of Puerto Ricans. They were evidently not aware of the important role the immigrant community played among the earlier groups of which they were members. Far from isolating them from the larger American society, it was the one factor which enabled the immigrants to move with confidence into the mainstream of American society. As a member of the Research Advisory Panel, I strongly supported the concept and the proposal. I was convinced that the existence of a strong community of Puerto Ricans would give them the strength and self-confidence that would help them advance in American society.

However the real problem came from another direction. Paul Screvane, Deputy Mayor under Mayor Robert Wagner, claimed the proposal was too nebulous and intangible and should emphasize "nuts and bolts realities" such as jobs. Joseph Monserrat, then director of the Office of the Commonwealth of Puerto Rico, together with other Puerto Rican leaders, supported Screvane. The Forum split on the issue and it was never funded. I knew Screvane and had tried to influence him in favor of the proposal. As a member of the Advisory Panel, I also tried to mobilize some prominent New York citizens to act as advocates for the proposal, but to no avail. The article, "The Integration of Puerto Ricans," (see p. 115) which I had previously published in *Thought*, indicates why I supported the proposal. I was firmly convinced that a strong community, like the immigrant communities of previous years, was essential for the economic and social advancement of the Puerto Ricans. The Forum project, had it been implemented, would have been another strong institutional structure for the community.

THE ROLE OF THE PARISH IN THE SPIRITUAL CARE OF PUERTO RICANS IN THE ARCHDIOCESE OF NEW YORK

In all the discussions by New York priests of the Puerto Rican experience, the role of the parish was the center of attention. The parish is the front line of evangelization and spiritual care. It is also the religious institution which provides a basis of identity and strength. Thus, the response of the parish to the increasing presence of Puerto Ricans was a central point of discussion in the 1955 Conference in Puerto Rico on the Spiritual

Care of Puerto Rican Migrants. It was also central in the 1953 Sermon on World Sodality Day, and the subsequent meeting in Cardinal Spellman's office; in the *Thought* and *Integrity* articles of 1955; and in all the planning meetings of the priests thereafter.

In order to provide some perspective for these discussions, I had studied the role of the parish in the experience of earlier newcomers to New York City. It was evident to me that the strategy of establishing what were called "national" or language parishes for the different nationality groups had been a remarkably creative response (see p. 5). There had been constant criticism that the national parish would fragment the Church and destroy its unity at the very moment when its unity was most important. The German parish, the French parish, the Italian or Polish parish, etc., was one little segment of the Old World that was reestablished in the New. When the immigrants found themselves as strangers in a strange land, frequently struggling for their rights and against discrimination, the one oasis of solidarity, of security and self-reliance, was the parish, which became the heart of the immigrant community. As noted before, I had long asserted that "one integrates from a position of strength, not from a position of weakness." Without the stability and security of the parish and the immigrant community, the newcomers would be isolated and helpless in the presence of forces they could not control. They would have been in a position of weakness, subject to social disorganization. They found their strength in the immigrant community and the parish. From there, they moved with confidence into a relationship with the larger society.

One thing that made the national parish possible for Germans, Italians, and others was the large number of their own priests, sisters, and religious brothers who came with the immigrants. The priests particularly were a significant influence in demanding these parishes for their own people; and the priests were the community leaders who encouraged them to build the churches and schools and institutions of service. *Piety and Power*,[41] a book by Father Silvano Tomasi, a former student of mine, focuses on the role of the parish in the adjustment of Italian immigrants, and is an excellent study of the Italian experience.

I had conducted many workshops and given many conferences for bishops and priests about this issue. The fear, however, still persisted that separate parishes would be divisive. There was even the concern among some pastors that religious services in Spanish and in a Puerto Rican style would hinder the migrants' adjustment to the Mainland. I

---

41. *Piety and Power.* Staten Island, N.Y.: Center for Migration Studies, 1975.

sought to allay these fears and anxieties by reiterating that the national or language parish, far from hindering the adjustment of immigrants to American life, actually made it possible and hastened it.

It was clear to me that the Church and the parish should play the same role for Puerto Ricans as it had for earlier groups. However, there were some problems. In the first place, the Puerto Ricans had no priests to bring with them. Most of the clergy ministering to them on the Island were from Europe or North America. (The reason for this is historical – a consequence of Spanish Colonial policy that discouraged indigenous clergy in the colonies.) Furthermore, at the time when the Puerto Ricans were arriving, many of the national parishes had few if any immigrants still present among their congregation. Over two or three generations, the children and grandchildren moved to the suburbs, leaving many national parishes with few members. Given the almost empty German or Polish or Italian parish in the very areas where Puerto Ricans were settling, the Archdiocese could hardly be expected to build other churches for them. Furthermore, they would have to be staffed by priests who were not themselves Puerto Rican. As a result, Cardinal Spellman decided to follow a policy of what he called the "integrated" parish, namely, his priests would learn Spanish and become familiar with the background of Puerto Rican culture, and minister in Spanish to the Puerto Ricans. However, they would continue to minister in English to the remaining English-speaking parishioners. In any event, Illich and I and a number of our colleagues insisted that, if this policy were followed (and it seemed reasonable), a form of ministry would have to be developed which provided for Puerto Ricans the same opportunities for stability, security, and self-reliance that the national parish provided for the earlier immigrants. As one effort to provide some background for this, I published "The Role of the Parish in the Spiritual Care of Puerto Ricans in the New York Archdiocese."[42]

Certainly a major concern with ministry to Puerto Ricans was the parish. The Institute of Intercultural Communication (see p. 25) had prepared hundreds of priests, sisters, brothers and lay persons for apostolic work among them. These had revolutionized the response of the Church and, although it has never been adequate, the response has been impressive. I do not think that an effort similar to that of the New York Archdiocese had ever been made before to receive a foreign language and culture group into its own. The detailed history has not yet been

---

42. See Part II: "The Role of the Parish in the Spiritual Care of Puerto Ricans in the New York Archdiocese," *Studi Emigrazione*, III, No. 7 (Oct. 1966): pp. 1-27.

written but it must be written in the future. By the year 1993, there were 114 parish churches in the New York Archdiocese where Sunday Mass was offered in Spanish. Most of these parishes also offered a complete array of other services and devotions. In the course of the years, as "white flight" continued, many became quasi-national parishes; practically all the parishioners were Hispanic and they considered it their church. Many of these parishes are among the most vital and lively of the Archdiocese.

At the same time, more than half the services of Catholic Charities are provided for Spanish-speaking people, and a large percentage of patients in Catholic hospitals are Spanish-speaking. The Church has also been involved in housing developments. Father Louis Gigante, a priest of the Archdiocese and one of the early students of the Institute of Intercultural Communication, has rebuilt Hunts Point and created a vital Hispanic, largely Puerto Rican "barrio." The housing office of the Archdiocese, under the direction of Father Donald Sakano, has rehabilitated hundreds of units, many of which are occupied by Spanish-speaking persons. And, of course, the major investment has been in the Catholic school system. In Manhattan, more than 50% of the students are Spanish-speaking. Thus the Church has been deeply involved in the experience of Puerto Ricans and other Hispanics in New York. However, the decline in the number of priests and sisters has been a handicap. Some of those who returned to lay life were among the most active in the apostolate, and they are not being replaced.

The 1960s, and later the 1970s, brought new populations into the Archdiocese and the multicultural parish became a new challenge to the Church. The 1965 U.S. Immigration Law made visas equally available to all peoples of the world under established conditions, and increased the number of visas substantially. Asians of many nations, formerly excluded, began to come in large numbers. This, together with the refugee populations of the 1960s and 70s, made the situation more complicated. Parishes now had three, five, sometimes ten or more language and cultural groups among their congregations. The possibility of establishing national parishes for all newcomers was very remote. The parish staff faced the challenge of ministering to a diverse, multicultural group of parishioners. I have since been lecturing and directing workshops on this issue, to give the parish staff some insight into the problem and to assist them to respond effectively to this kind of pastoral challenge. This is very difficult when distinct language and cultural groups have no clergy of their own to minister to them. Some of the parishes have responded remarkably, but this will remain a major challenge to the pastors of the coming generation.

THE EVANGELICAL AND PENTECOSTAL SECTS

One of the great preoccupations of the Catholic Church has been the loss of Hispanics to the Evangelical and Pentecostal sects. I had long been aware of the many small, storefront churches in Puerto Rican areas. I had also noticed them in large numbers in Puerto Rico, and I shared the concern of Catholic leaders about the loss of Catholics to the Sects.

Toward the late 1950s, I began to direct my students in a series of studies of the Sects. We came to know them a little better. What impressed the students was the friendly reception they received when they visited the churches. The members would greet the students, inquire whether there was any way in which they could help them. It was clear to us why they were attracting the Puerto Ricans. These sects were small communities, mostly between sixty and one-hundred persons. The minister lived in the neighborhood among them, and frequently would have a regular occupation as a store-keeper, a factory worker, etc. The services were long but very lively, with vigorous participation by the congregation, which was small, familial, and of a style in which the poor Puerto Ricans felt at home. Furthermore, many of the congregations became active evangelists themselves, manifesting a zeal not found among Catholic populations. One of my students, Father Renato Poblete, S.J., a Jesuit priest from Chile, established some remarkable contacts with the Pentecostal ministers. Together with a Professor of Sociology on the Fordham Faculty, Dr. Thomas F. O'Dea, Father Poblete published an article, "Anomie and the Quest for Community: The Formation of Sects among the Puerto Ricans in New York."[43] This is still one of the best studies of the Evangelical and Pentecostal Sects.

I later came to know some of the ministers and to respect them. Many were very humble, sincere men and women, dedicated to the Gospel and the service of the Lord and their neighbor. I would often share with them the prayers at the beginning or end of a dinner or a conference: I giving the Invocation, they giving the Benediction. I often remarked how tame my prayer seemed in contrast to the fiery, emotional prayers of the ministers.

All the pastoral conferences I participated in had a major plan for protecting our Catholic people from the attraction of the Sects. We saw

---

43. *American Catholic Sociological Review*, V. 21 (Spring 1960), pp. 18-36.

the need to create small groups for study of the Bible and for prayer, and to cultivate a strong sense of community. There was also the need to reach out to people in the neighborhoods, enable them to become familiar with the Catholic Church and its services, and to become involved in the social and political action by which they sought to protect their rights and interests. There is still considerable controversy about the numbers who have been lost to the Sects. It is substantial. This is a problem that will continue and it will require a very zealous apostolate on the Church's part to enable Catholic people to find their satisfaction of community in the Catholic Church rather than in the Sects.

What was clear to me was that the greater problem was not the Sects; rather it was the large numbers of Hispanics who had no contact with any religious group at all. It remains a field ripe for the harvest.

A SUNDAY AFTERNOON WITH FATHER FITZPATRICK

On April 13, 1969, my Puerto Rican friends got together and gave me a celebration in thanks for many of the things I had done for them. It was inspired mainly by Mrs. Matilde de Silva and Joe Monserrat, who had been the Director of the Office of the Commonwealth of Puerto Rico. I had given numerous workshops and conferences for the Office of the Commonwealth both in New York and in Puerto Rico. As noted earlier (see p. 10), Mrs. de Silva had organized many summer trips to Puerto Rico for New York teachers and social workers to acquaint them with the background of the Puerto Ricans. Since I was generally in Puerto Rico during the summer anyway, I would always volunteer to meet the New Yorkers and provide a workshop for them on Puerto Rican culture and the problems of migration to the Mainland. They were very grateful for this. As a result they put together the wonderful party at the Tavern on the Green in Central Park and named it: "A Spring Sunday Afternoon with Father Joseph P. Fitzpatrick, S.J., in Recognition of His Outstanding Continuing Career."

It was a remarkable afternoon. So many of my friends – Jesuits, Fordham students, Puerto Ricans, and others – turned out to make it an unforgettable event.

Matilde had asked many people to write a testimonial letter and she collected these in an album which I still have. It is quite an experience to look back over those letters. Many were from friends like Father Michael Walsh, then President of Fordham. But others read like a "Who's Who" of the Puerto Rican community at that time. There were letters from Luis Ferre, then Governor of Puerto Rico; Felisa Rincón de

Gautier, Mayor of San Juan, and many others from Puerto Rico. There were letters from Mayor Lindsay of New York City; Herman Badillo, Borough President of the Bronx; Timothy Costello, Deputy Mayor, and a number of others. Many of them were at the luncheon together with members of my family. There are pictures of me with my four brothers, and with Ruth, wife of my brother Cy, and pictures of many of the Puerto Rican friends who had organized the luncheon. They recall wonderful memories of those earlier days. At the end of the luncheon the organizers gave me a round-trip ticket to Spain with a gift of one thousand dollars. Matilde de Silva said they wanted me to become acquainted with the land from which so much of Puerto Rican culture had developed. I went to Spain the following year, 1970, for one month; a remarkable visit. I travelled all over Spain and met many of my Jesuit friends in the various cities of that nation.

"A Spring Sunday Afternoon . . ." was a wonderful and joyful tribute. Although some of the people who were there are now dead, many are still alive and active. It was a remarkable gesture of thanks and affection from so many Puerto Ricans with whom I had worked in the previous twenty-five years.

PUERTO RICAN AMERICANS:
THE MEANING OF MIGRATION TO THE MAINLAND

In the late 'sixties, I devoted most of my attention to the preparation of my book, *Puerto Rican Americans: The Meaning of Migration to the Mainland* (see p. 4). This book incorporated the best of my insights into the experience of the Puerto Ricans. A second edition was published in 1987, with up-to-date figures and whatever new insights I had developed about the Puerto Rican migration. The focus of the book was the struggle of the Puerto Ricans to retain a strong sense of identity as they faced the problem of adjustment to the social situation in the Continental U.S. This is the persistent problem for any group of immigrants or migrants who move from one cultural and language environment to another. The book sought to provide some background on the problem of identity on the Island where Puerto Ricans have been struggling with three competing political situations: independence, statehood in the U.S.A., or the Free Associated State, a sort of commonwealth status, which had been created under the leadership of Luis Muñoz Marin, the first elected Governor of Puerto Rico. It includes demographic data about the migration, and has a long chapter about the organizations of the Puerto Rican community in New York City. However, what apparently made the book attractive were the chapters dealing with some of the main features of Puerto Rican culture, the family, the problem of color, and religion. It has a lengthy chapter about the experience of Puerto Ricans in the schools of New York City, another chapter on problems of welfare, drug addiction and mental illness. The concluding chapter is my own attempt to interpret the meaning of the migration both for the Puerto Ricans and for the U.S. Mainland.

The census data indicated that the pattern of increasing intermarriage which was characteristic of earlier immigrants was also appearing among the Puerto Ricans. In my study of Puerto Rican intermarriage, 1949 and 1959, the percentage of marriages of Puerto Ricans with non-Hispanics increased noticeably in the second generation over the first. There was also evidence of a decrease in the use of Spanish. However, it was clear to me that there were many unique characteristics of the Puerto Rican migration: the first large migration of the aviation age; American citizens by birth but from a different cultural and language area; the first large migration of people who had a tradition of the widespread intermingling of persons of different color; the first large migration of Catholics who came without their own clergy. I expressed the hope that these characteristics would enable the Puerto Ricans to retain their culture and their language as they entered mainstream American life.

NEIGHBORHOOD YOUTH AND FAMILY SERVICES

In 1969, my colleagues at Fordham and I began the effort to develop community-based programs for delinquency prevention and correction. This was the result of a Commission that President Lyndon B. Johnson had established to investigate the criminal and juvenile justice systems. The President's Commission on Law Enforcement and Administration of Justice, as it was called, issued its report, *The Challenge of Crime in a Free Society*,[44] in which, among many other things, it pointed out that juvenile correctional facilities were the best crime schools in the nation. The Commission recommended keeping the youths out of the juvenile justice system; keeping them at home in their families and neighborhoods with their peers, and providing youth advocates, big brothers and big sisters, to work with them, support them, encourage them and help move them on to a healthy and productive adulthood. One consequence

---

44. *The Challenge of Crime in a Free Society*, Washington, D.C.: U.S. Government Printing Office, 1967.

of this was the creation by the Congress of the Youth Development and Delinquency Prevention Administration, in the Department of Health, Education and Welfare. This agency was to fund community-based programs of delinquency prevention and youth development.

In 1969 we submitted a proposal for the development of a program in the East Tremont section of the Bronx, a very poor section of the City which had deteriorated badly after the building of the Cross Bronx Expressway, a depressed highway cut through the mid-Bronx. The proposal was funded and we established "The Neighborhood Youth Diversion Program" to divert young people from the juvenile justice system and work with them in their neighborhoods to enable them to achieve a creative life. Many of our clients were Puerto Ricans from the area as were many of our staff. The Director was a capable young Irish American lawyer, John Whalen, who had previous experience with neighborhood based programs. The program was very successful. With the help of youth advocates, the juveniles – both boys and girls – responded well. It has been a great benefit to the neighborhood, a refuge for children diverted from the courts, as well as hundreds of other children who simply show up to enjoy the program. It has expanded considerably under the able direction of Ms. Lizette Tait, who established a "Young Mothers Program" for pregnant teenagers who are experimenting with drugs. They get excellent counselling, the best of prenatal care; the Board of Education supplies teachers for their education; and they can stay for a while after the birth of their children. The staff conduct programs of parenting and independent living. After the program the young mothers go off on their own. Another program, "The Family Enrichment Program" has also been added for addicted mothers with children under six. Previously, when an addicted mother had very young children, the City would place them in foster care until the mother went through a rehabilitation program. The City discovered that the only concern of the mother was to get the children back. She would do anything and say anything until this occurred, then she lost interest in any rehabilitation. With the Neighborhood Youth Diversion Program, the children stay with the mother. They come to the program together for breakfast, the children are on the same floor in a day care center while the mother goes through her counselling. They have lunch together, recreation in the afternoon, and they return home together at night. Thus the mother has no preoccupation about her children. As a result, she cooperates much more enthusiastically with the rehabilitation.

The entire program has been renamed, Neighborhood Youth and Family Services, and after twenty-five years it continues to serve this deprived neighborhood well.

CENTRO SISTER ISOLINA FERRÉ

About the same time, 1969, Sister Isolina Ferré (see p. 38) had returned to Puerto Rico, to the poorest section of Ponce – the large city on the South Coast. My colleagues and I at Fordham had received a government grant to provide technical assistance for the development of community-based programs for youth development and delinquency prevention. The funding agency, Youth Development and Delinquency Prevention Administration, was guided very much by the theory of delinquency which John M. Martin and I had published in our book, *Delinquent Behavior: a Redefinition of the Problem.* Sister Isolina asked me if I would help her develop a community-based program for delinquency prevention in the Playa de Ponce, Puerto Rico. Sister Isolina and my colleagues at Fordham consulted the authorities in Puerto Rico and they encouraged us. But the proposal had to be approved by the Regional Office of the Youth Development and Delinquency Prevention Administration, and they had many misgivings about the ability of anyone in Puerto Rico to write a successful proposal. I invited three of the top criminologists in New York to join me for a weekend in Ponce. There, together with the financial office of the funding agency, and Sister Isolina, we put together a proposal that impressed the regional office. They had never seen one like it, and this was coming out of Puerto Rico!

Sister's Project was started in 1970 to divert youngsters from the juvenile court. It has prospered remarkably under her able direction. Her motto is "God's Glory is the Human Person Fully Alive in a Community that is Fully Alive." Sister has linked the project to a series of job training programs and community development efforts. She later started a Diagnostic Center in the Playa where not a single doctor, nurse or dentist had ever practiced before. This has blossomed into a community health center with five doctors, five nurses, dentists and a staff of para-professionals, to keep the Center in contact with the Community. Sister has since established numerous training programs, educational programs, programs for runaways, and more recently, a junior college. In the twenty-five years of its existence, the Centro Sister Isolina Ferré has transformed the Playa de Ponce. She has replicated the program in four other cities in Puerto Rico. I have remained a consultant to the Project since its beginning and, in 1990, Sister dedicated a new building to me, the Edificio Padre José Fitzpatrick, in recognition of my help in funding the project and keeping it going. As a result of her work, Sister has become one of the most prominent women in Puerto Rico and her Project is acknowledged by the federal and Island governments as one of the best that either has funded.

INTERMARRIAGE OF HISPANICS IN NEW YORK CITY, 1975

In 1975, together with a colleague, Douglas Gurak, I did a study of Hispanic Intermarriage.[45] The results caught us by surprise. We had expected a continuing increase in out-group marriage with non-Hispanics in the second generation. This was confirmed in the case of all other Hispanic groups except the Puerto Ricans. For Puerto Ricans, there was only a slight increase in the case of Puerto Rican brides, and an actual decrease in the case of Puerto Rican grooms. We had no convincing explanation for this. We hypothesized that it might be related to: 1) an increasing sense of nationalism among Puerto Ricans; 2) the development of a new sense of identity as "Nuyoricans"; 3) the greater density of the Puerto Rican population in New York City, and their segregation along class lines; and 4) a selective out-migration of Puerto Ricans of higher socioeconomic status. Possibly all these factors were involved. But a convincing explanation is not yet available, although analyses of the 1990 Census data may throw some light on this (see p. 89).

PUERTO RICAN INTELLECTUALS

By the 'seventies, a significant number of Puerto Rican social scientists was appearing, many of them challenging my own writings as reflecting "assimilationist" theories. Actually, I have always taken a position of cultural pluralism, the importance for Puerto Ricans to retain their own sense of Puerto Rican identity and their Puerto Rican language and values, while they become involved in the mainstream of American life. The Center for Puerto Rican Studies of the City University has been calling attention to the functions of the labor market in a capitalist economy; the need for an available, but disposable labor force. One consequence of this is continuous migration of poor, working men and

---

45. Hispanic Research Center, Fordham University, Bronx, N.Y. 10458, 1979. This was later published as an article, "Intermarriage Among Hispanic Ethnic Groups in New York City," *American Journal of Sociology*, 87:4 (1982).

women to areas where jobs are available, and their migration elsewhere when the need for them disappears.

Puerto Rican and other Hispanic scholars and their publications offer a promising future. The work of Lloyd Rogler, Frank Bonilla, Marta Tienda, Virginia Sanchez Korrol, Anthony Stevens Arroyo, and Clara Rodriguez, to mention only a few, is providing data and analyses that will help in the explanation of the Puerto Rican experience in the coming years. However, it is the continuing poverty of the Puerto Rican community that has raised important questions in recent years. Data are abundant, but explanations are scarce. Why Puerto Ricans, the only newcomers who are born American citizens and who do not have the immigration restrictions that other Hispanic newcomers have, should continue to be at the lowest poverty levels, has not been adequately explained. Puerto Rican poverty is concentrated in the female-headed families, which constituted about 34.5 percent in 1990.[46] Until this problem is solved, poverty will remain high. Moreover, large numbers of dark skinned Puerto Ricans are identified as black in the United States and face the same discrimination on the basis of color as African Americans. Finally all variables considered equally, educated Puerto Ricans do not yet enjoy the same level of income as non-Hispanic whites. In this perspective, I wrote an article about the problems this has created for the Church in its effort to receive the Puerto Ricans and other Hispanics as our own. I discuss this at length in the article, "The Hispanic Poor in the American Catholic Middle-Class Church."[47] I define the problem of the Church as that of a predominantly middle-class Church and clergy seeking to relate effectively to poor Hispanics. Bridging the gap between different social classes is much more difficult than bridging the gap between two different cultures. This is what I see as the basic problem: There are no Hispanic clergy who can relate to poor Hispanics as "their own" in the way Irish clergy related to Irish immigrants, or Italian clergy related to Italian immigrants, etc. Until this challenge is successfully met, the problem will continue.

---

46. *Puerto Rican New Yorkers in 1990.* City of New York, Department of City Planning, September 1994, Table 3-1.

47. See Part II: "The Hispanic Poor in the American Catholic Middle-Class Church," *Thought*, 63:249 June 1988.

THE 1970s

The character of the Puerto Rican community shifted considerably during the 1970s. Their organizational activity, especially around issues of
their civil rights, increased. Their involvement in higher education
issues was given more attention, and the number of Puerto Rican elected
and appointed officials also increased.

The Puerto Rican population had practically stabilized; there was
no noticeable increase. The 1980 population was 860,552 in contrast to
860,584 in 1970. This was due to the large numbers migrating out of the
City either back to Puerto Rico or to other parts of the United States. The
second generation increased by about 40,000. However, the 1970s saw
the influx of immigrants from Colombia, Ecuador and Peru, and refugees, mostly from Central and South America, from El Salvador especially, and from Nicaragua. Thus Puerto Ricans constituted only half the
Hispanic population of New York City. As a result of the 1965 immigration legislation and the defeat of South Vietnam, Asians came to the City
in large numbers (see p. 61). Thus the Puerto Ricans faced the problem
of adjustment not only to the Hispanics but also to large numbers of
Asians. One other demographic phenomenon occurred: the recognition
of large numbers of undocumented aliens, the so-called illegals. No one
knew how many there were, but numbers were probably well into the
millions across the United States. This was to create further complications for the Puerto Ricans. Many illegals tried to identify themselves as
Puerto Ricans, i.e., U.S. citizens who did not need papers. And Puerto
Ricans began to be challenged by employers and U.S. agents as being
among the illegals. The attempt to remedy this would not take place
until 1986.

There was evidence of substantial socio-economic progress among
the Puerto Ricans, especially the second generation. But the concern
focused on the continuing poverty of the Puerto Rican community, the
poorest community in New York City.

THE PUERTO RICAN LEGAL DEFENSE AND EDUCATION FUND

In March 1973, Cesar Perales called me. He and a number of other
distinguished Puerto Rican lawyers had recently founded the Puerto
Rican Legal Defense and Education Fund (PRLDEF), an organization to
provide legal advocacy and protection for the Puerto Rican community.
Cesar had been named its Executive Director. It was modeled on the
National Association for the Advancement of Colored People (NAACP)

and the Mexican American Legal Defense and Education Fund (MAL-DEF). The objective was to have an organization of lawyers who could represent the community in class action suits against public or private agencies where evidence of discrimination against Puerto Ricans existed. The educational division sought to prepare students for admission to law school and to assist them during their training. Cesar told me that most of the Board consisted of lawyers, but they needed some community people as well, and he was inviting me. Of course, I said, "Yes." The founding of the Fund was evidence of the continuing maturity of the Puerto Rican community. A number of excellent organizations already existed such as the Puerto Rican Forum, Aspira, and the Puerto Rican Family Institute, but the existence of an influential, high-powered organization such as PRLDEF was a sign that the community had really come of age. It would have highly competent representation before the Courts on issues that affected the welfare of the community.

Cesar had been born and raised in New York and was a graduate of the Fordham University School of Law. He had participated in the effort of Fordham professors to establish Community Action Legal Services to provide legal assistance to the poor in civil cases such as landlord problems, consumer fraud problems, etc. He also served as general counsel for the Model Cities Program where I had originally met him. He was selected by the Board to be the first Executive Director (President and General Counsel, as it was called) where he served until he was appointed to the position of Assistant Secretary of Health, Education and Welfare by President Jimmy Carter. When President Ronald Reagan was elected, Cesar returned to New York where he was again named to the position of President and General Counsel. He was later named New York State Commissioner of Welfare by Governor Mario Cuomo. In 1990, he was appointed Deputy Mayor for Health and Human Services in New York City by Mayor David Dinkins. He is now on the staff of Columbia Presbyterian Hospital.

When I walked into my first meeting of the Board, I had the impression of walking into a Who's Who of distinguished Puerto Rican lawyers. Victor Marrero, who later became a Professor at the Yale Law School, was the Chairman. There I met Jorge Batista, later to become a member of the New York State Board of Regents. Jorge and I became very good friends and he continues to be for me a source of abundant information about the Puerto Rican community. José Cabranes was there, who was teaching at Yale Law School and later became General Counsel for the University. He was the first Puerto Rican to be appointed to a federal judgeship. He also became Chairman of the Yale Board of

Trustees. José was very helpful to me and my colleagues when we were involved in delinquency research, and he has remained a very good friend ever since. Herman Badillo, whom I had known for many years when he was Borough President of the Bronx and then a Congressman in Washington from the Bronx, was an honorary member of the Board. There were many others. It was an unusually interesting Board to serve on. As we reviewed the cases in which the Fund was involved, it gave us a great deal of insight into the extent of discrimination against Puerto Ricans and other Hispanics, and how important the Fund was to the welfare of the Puerto Rican community, not only in New York, but in many neighboring states as well. The Fund challenged the use of discriminatory tests in the hiring of Civil service employees; it successfully won a number of cases against discrimination in housing and against private employers.

One of its most important cases was the Aspira Consent Decree it won from the New York Courts. The Supreme Court had upheld the complaint of a plaintiff in California (Lau *v.* Board of Education) who insisted that, when children did not know English well enough to be instructed in English, they had a civil right to be instructed in a language in which they could learn. This means bilingual instruction. Aspira brought suit against the Board of Education in New York City demanding bilingual education for Hispanic students who did not know English well enough to be instructed in it. The Fund represented Aspira in the Court and won a Consent Decree that the Board of Education would have bilingual programs in place by a certain deadline. Another well-known case was the redistricting of election districts which enabled more Hispanics to be elected to city, state or federal government positions. The Fund continues to distinguish itself in its service to the Hispanic community.

In 1984 a crisis broke out in the Fund that threatened its existence. The staff organized in a union and, for some reason or other, a great deal of hostility developed between the staff and the newly-elected President and General Counsel, Jack John Olivero. Cesar Perales, although he had agreed to serve a minimum of three years, asked the Board to release him so that he could accept the appointment as Commissioner of Welfare of New York State. Olivero had to deal with the early days of union organizing and negotiations. At one point, with the approval of the Board, he dismissed one of the attorneys for misconduct. The staff reacted militantly, occupied the offices, and the Board instructed Olivero to have the police remove them. All of this complicated relations between Olivero and the staff and created very serious problems for the

Board. Olivero had recommended the dismissal of the most militant of the demonstration leaders, but the Board refused and reappointed some of them. At this point, Olivero resigned. Board meetings were tense and troublesome events. At one point we met in Washington in the House office building to avoid disruption. I tried to be an influence for calm and patience. At one very tense meeting I read the prayer of Saint Francis ("...Make me an instrument of your peace.") and I think it had a quieting effect on the Board members. Jorge Batista agreed to be acting President until a new President, Ms. Linda Flores, was chosen. With the efforts of Batista and Flores, the situation calmed down and the Fund was able to get back to business. Flores resigned after four years and we chose Ruben Franco as President. He had been one of the early Board members, and was still on the Board when elected. Franco resigned in 1992 to go into politics and the Board chose Juan Figueroa who shows the promise of being the best President PRLDEF has ever had.

PUERTO RICAN STUDIES PROGRAM

During the college demonstrations of the late 'sixties, one of the proposals which continued to come from protesters, whether black or Hispanic, was the establishment in colleges or universities of programs in Black Studies or Puerto Rican Studies or the foundation of departments in Black Studies or Puerto Rican Studies. These proposals developed at Fordham as elsewhere. The Puerto Rican students at Fordham College founded a club called *El Grito de Lares* (*El Grito* for short). *El Grito de Lares* was the popular name of a revolutionary effort that broke out in Puerto Rico in 1888. The revolt failed but the effort is commemorated widely in Puerto Rican history and folklore.

The Puerto Rican students submitted their first proposal for a Puerto Rican Studies Department. It had three components: 1) to introduce a course of studies which would give adequate attention to Puerto Rican history and culture, 2) to create linkages with the Puerto Rican community and develop programs at the University which would redound to the benefit of the Puerto Rican community, and 3) to increase the number of Puerto Rican or other Hispanic professors on the staff of the University. I personally did not favor the creation of a Department. I was convinced that a degree in Puerto Rican Studies was far too limited in scope to enable the degree holders to compete for teaching positions throughout the nation. I felt it would be better for them to take their degree in a recognized discipline with a concentration in Puerto Rican Studies. Thus they could compete for jobs as specialists in American history, or sociology, or English literature, while they would have the background to offer courses in Puerto Rican Studies. This was acceptable to the students and we proceeded to set up a Puerto Rican Studies Program, later to be extended to a Puerto Rican/ Latin American Studies Program. We identified related courses in history, political science, Spanish language and literature, sociology, etc. Thus an abundance of courses was available to the students, both Hispanic and non-Hispanic, if they wished to take them. A Faculty/Student Committee was formed to supervise the Program and a fairly reasonable budget was provided.

From the very beginning, problems began to appear. It was evident that we needed a full-time professor to direct the program. The problem was to find one! The competition for recognized scholars of Hispanic background was so great that we found it almost impossible to recruit one. When we did locate one and offered him or her a position, other universities would make the person a better offer and we would be left without one.

Fordham students were under great pressure from outside. Students from other colleges and universities were contacting them and asking how their efforts were going to establish a Puerto Rican Studies Program. Meantime, a department had been established at the Manhattan Campus of the University at the College at Lincoln Center, but the Chairperson did not have his doctorate and, for this reason, was eventually terminated amid much controversy.

Later a disagreement broke out between the Director of the Puerto Rican/Latin American Studies and the Dean of Fordham College, mainly about budget problems. Shortly after, the Director received a very good offer from Rutgers University which he accepted. Meantime, I was retired in 1983. Although I remained on the Committee, I was no longer teaching, and my courses had been among the strongest in the Program. The Program slowly deteriorated and died. It interests me that the Afro-American Department still flourishes, but the Puerto Rican and other Hispanic students do not complain that their Program has ceased to exist. The Department of Puerto Rican Studies still exists at the Lincoln Center Campus.

THE HISPANIC RESEARCH CENTER

In 1974 Fordham had the good fortune to attract Professor Lloyd Rogler Canino as the Distinguished Schweitzer Professor. The Schweitzer Professorships in the Humanities and Social Sciences, and the Einstein Chairs in the Physical Sciences had been established and funded by the

State of New York in 1964.[48] These Distinguished Professorships were awarded competitively in response to proposals. I wrote a proposal for a Schweitzer Professorship in Sociology and Anthropology, and Fordham was awarded one. We were particularly interested in bringing an anthropologist to Fordham since our well-known expert in the field, Father Franklin Ewing, S.J., had become ill and incapacitated. We had practically signed up Professor Edward Hoebel, a prominent anthropologist from the University of Minnesota. But when the University President heard of it, he called Professor Hoebel and told him they would exceed any offer that Fordham would make. Hoebel stayed at Minnesota.

A short while after, a lawsuit was inaugurated challenging the award of the Professorship to Fordham because it was a religiously affiliated Institution. Everything was on hold until the legal issue was settled in favor of Fordham in 1975.

Shortly after we learned that the Schweitzer Professorship was available again, we discovered that Rogler Canino, whom I had previously tried to bring to Fordham, was interested in leaving Case Western Reserve University. I asked him to come to Fordham as soon as possible for interviews. With his help we wrote the proposal and it was accepted in Albany. Fordham finally had its Schweitzer Professor.

Rogler Canino's appointment was as full professor in the department of sociology and anthropology. Shortly after he arrived in the Fall of 1974, he was awarded a grant to do a study of second generation Puerto Rican men who married second generation Puerto Rican women. Both husbands and wives had to come from stable families of two Puerto Rican parents. The objective of the study was to determine the extent to which these second generation Puerto Ricans had preserved a sense of Puerto Rican identity. It was a carefully selected sample. But the study showed that they had prospered remarkably, were perfectly bilingual in English and Spanish, and were completely at home in both a Puerto Rican and American environment. The study, *Puerto Rican Families in New York: Intergenerational Processes* (see p. 54), is still one of the most significant studies of second generation Puerto Ricans in New York City.

Much more important was the establishment by Rogler of the Hispanic Research Center at Fordham University in 1977. The Federal Government had set up a program to establish a number of regional centers which would do research related to the needs of the minority

---

48. There was an interesting condition to these chairs. The professors could not be chosen from among those already teaching in New York State. The program was designed to attract out-of-state professors to New York.

communities in their respective regions. Some were for African Americans; others were for Hispanics; some for Native Americans. Rogler prepared a proposal to establish a Hispanic Research Center at Fordham and it was funded in 1977 with him as the Executive Director. The original plan was a program of sociological research which would serve as a valuable resource for the Hispanic communities in the New York area. My own study of "Hispanic Intermarriage in New York City, 1975," was funded and published by the Center, as was a study of health problems and a study of discrimination in the parole system of New York State. There were studies of the Cubans in West New York, of child care in New York City, and numerous others. In its first five years, the Center had distinguished itself by the quality and importance of its research and publications.

However, once President Ronald Reagan came to power, the situation changed. When Rogler submitted his application for renewal in 1982, his proposal received outstanding recommendations by the reviewers. But the Director of the National Institute of Mental Health turned it down: the Reagan Administration was not funding sociological research. If the Center wished to be renewed, it would have to redirect its activities to areas of clinical psychology. This was a blow to the Center, but Rogler and his team worked intensely to revise the proposal and it was funded for research mainly in the clinical area. Rogler focused the Center's research on the problems of clinical services in relation to culture. He recognized in the mental health field what Professor John Martin and I had recognized long before in the area of delinquency, namely, that the cultural element was given little if any attention in the diagnosis and treatment of mental illness. Under his leadership, the Center published a series of research projects which were to make a significant contribution to the areas of cross cultural diagnosis and treatment. These included: "Unitas, Hispanic and Black Children in a Healing Community"; "The Minority Foster Child," "Hispanics and Human Services: Help-Seeking in the Inner City;" and many others. But his great contribution was his own book, *Hispanics and Mental Health: a Framework for Research*,[49] which set out the method of introducing the element of culture and cultural difference in the diagnosis and treatment of mental illness. Thus, despite the change of policy of the Reagan Administration, the Center continued to produce research and publications which were of direct value to the Hispanic community. In fact, the

---

49. *Hispanics and Mental Health: A Framework for Research*, Malabar, FL: R. E. Krieger, 1989.

influence of his work can be seen in the introduction of culture into the *Diagnostic and Statistical Manual of Mental Disorders, IV,* the standard manual for diagnosis and treatment of mental illness. It now contains a section on the cross cultural element in diagnosis and treatment.

The Hispanic Research Center is now nationally known and respected as one of the most important of its kind. It has established the reputation of Fordham University as an important resource for the Hispanic communities, not only of the New York area but of the nation. Rogler has been the recipient of numerous awards. He is one of the most highly respected Puerto Rican sociologists in the U.S. and serves as a link in the network of Hispanic research centers throughout the nation. He resigned as Director of the Center but remains as the Schweitzer Professor of Fordham University. He was succeeded as Director of the Center by Dr. Orlando Rodriguez.

THE CITY UNIVERSITY OF NEW YORK

During the 1960s, as militant student activity spread throughout the Nation, it also broke out among Puerto Ricans in New York City. It was centered largely in the City University's colleges and took the form of demonstrations against tuition increases; against the take-over of the financing of the City University by the State; demand for open enrollment, and demands for the establishment of Puerto Rican Studies Programs. The first such Department was established at City College in 1970. It was followed shortly by the establishment of similar Departments at Lehman College and at Hunter College. Dr. Maria Teresa Babin was named Director of the Puerto Rican Studies program at Lehman College. And Dr. Eduardo Seda Bonilla was named Director of Puerto Rican Studies at Hunter College. There was a great deal of turbulence in the development of these Departments. The students at Hunter College became so disruptive that Dr. Seda Bonilla resigned.

At an early moment the idea began to surface of establishing a City-wide Puerto Rican Studies Center that would be affiliated with the City University. A Committee was formed to study this issue and I was asked to serve on it. There were numerous meetings of the Committee, some of them quite stormy, but the idea progressed. The Ford Foundation agreed to fund the Center but only on the condition that it be a Center of genuine scholarship and research for Puerto Rican students and for the Puerto Rican community. Thus they demanded that its Director be a Puerto Rican scholar of national reputation who would guarantee the academic respectability of the Center. The Ford Foundation was concerned that it not be a center of militant propaganda. The City University finally prevailed upon Dr. Frank Bonilla to accept the position and the Center of Puerto Rican Studies came into being. It is located at Hunter College, but has a great deal of autonomy to pursue its own objectives. Bonilla's appointment was a joint appointment as a Professor of Sociology and Director of the Center.

I had known Dr. Bonilla for many years. I had met him at numerous meetings, some of them scholarly, some meetings of the Puerto Rican community. I considered him the most outstanding Puerto Rican sociologist in the country, and often tried to lure him to Fordham without success. He had been born in Puerto Rico but had come to the Mainland at an early age. He did his doctorate studies at Massachusetts Institute of Technology and remained at the University in a research capacity, where he became internationally recognized for his studies not only in the United States, but in Latin America. As I mentioned earlier, he wrote the proposal for the Puerto Rican Community Development Project which was never funded (see p. 58). But it was a fine proposal which should have been revised and published as a book. He did an excellent job in getting the Center established, and he linked it with a series of other research centers throughout the country which deal with questions of interest for the Puerto Rican and other Hispanic communities. Many of the research studies deal with the Puerto Rican migration, with educational and occupational problems of the Puerto Rican community, and with the question of poverty.

Bonilla had a theory of the migration which gained much attention and enjoyed much respect. He conceived of capitalism as a system which could not prosper unless it had a pool of disposable cheap labor that it could call upon at moments of high productivity, and discard at moments of low productivity. He saw Puerto Rico as one source of that labor; and he interpreted the migration as a response of that pool to the demand for labor by the industries of the United States. The return migration and the continued unemployment of many Puerto Ricans was interpreted as the disposal of the labor force in times of low productivity.

I have kept in close contact with Frank over the years. We used to meet at the meetings of a small group of scholars called the Puerto Rican Exchange. The group was called together by Edward Gonzalez, then Director of the Cornell University School of Labor and Industrial Relations in New York City. We gathered periodically to discuss with each other the research we were doing, and to discuss areas where research was needed. It was a very interesting and helpful gathering, but when

Eddie Gonzalez relocated to California in the late 1980s, the Exchange lost its patron and has practically ceased to exist.

In 1991, the Chancellor of the City University decided to have an evaluation done of the Center and, probably at Frank's recommendation, asked me to do it. It proved to be an interesting and very informative experience. I came to know many of the personnel of the Center and became familiar with their activities. I submitted a favorable evaluation with a number of recommendations for improvement.

Frank announced his retirement in 1993. There was a search for a replacement and the search committee recommended unanimously that Dr. Maria Canino be appointed. The officials of the City University had been resisting this and, once again, the Center has become a center of controversy. Maria has had a long history of involvement with the Puerto Rican community in New York. She was a Professor at Rutgers University in New Jersey for some years; and for many years was a member of the Board of Trustees of the City University. There are no indications yet how this controversy will be resolved. Maria is no Frank Bonilla, but she knows the City University, the Center and the Puerto Rican community. Perhaps the same issue has surfaced again; some people may be demanding a scholar of Bonilla's stature. There are not many of them in the country and all are probably in very important positions already.

My own relation to the Puerto Rican community in these days reflected to some extent the situation of the community itself. I was no longer acting as their advocate. The Puerto Ricans had numerous advocates of their own. I was reacting mainly with scholars in academic matters and matters of research. The community was still poor and struggling for the most part, but the struggle was being played out now on many levels, one of them being the level of higher education and scholarship. I was associating with Frank Bonilla, Lloyd Rogler, Maria Canino, Anthony Stevens, Clara Rodriguez, and Isaura Santiago, President of Hostos Community College. More studies were appearing produced by Puerto Rican scholars, whom it was no longer possible to neglect. By producing its own scholars, the community was taking its place on the level of higher education and scholarship.

THE 1980s

The 1980s were strange years for the United States and for the world as well as for the Puerto Ricans. They were the Reagan and Bush years, a period during which poor people like many Puerto Ricans did not fare well economically. The early 1980s were marked by a deep concern about the threat of nuclear war. Much of my own time was involved in lobbying and demonstrations against the building of nuclear weapons. The later 1980s saw the collapse of Communism and the development of the so-called "New World Order."

The Puerto Rican population in New York City increased slightly from 860,552 in 1980 to 896,763 in 1990, a growth of about 4%. However, the growth was due to natural increase, since more Puerto Ricans left New York City in the ten years than had entered. Over half the Puerto Ricans were second generation, born here of parents born in Puerto Rico. The decade was to see the first decisive effort to have a determining vote about the status of Puerto Rico, and Puerto Ricans on the Mainland were demanding to be permitted to vote. The plebiscite, held in Puerto Rico, showed a slight preference for the Free Associated State, the present quasi-Commonwealth status. The vote did not require any further action of Congress.

For me it was a remarkable decade. I was retired from the Fordham University Faculty in 1983 and the University broke all traditions by granting me an Honorary Degree for my service to the University, but also for my service to the Hispanic community. John Jay College granted me an Honorary Degree that same year, largely because of my work with the Puerto Ricans. And in 1988 the Jesuit School of Theology at Berkeley awarded me an Honorary Degree for my influence on the development of the Apostolate to Hispanics. I published the second edition of my book, *Puerto Rican Americans* in 1987, as well as another book that became well known, *One Church, Many Cultures: The Challenge of Diversity*.[50] In 1988 I completed *Paul: Saint of the Inner City*.[51] The following year I did a nationwide study of Jesuits in Hispanic Ministry. This was privately circulated but it verified the extensive involvement of the Jesuits of the United States in ministry to Hispanics. I spent the Fall of 1989 as a Fulbright Lecturer in Montevideo. Shortly after my return, on November 16, 1989, we received the terrible news of the massacre of the six Jesuit priests and their two housekeepers by the army in El Salvador.

---

50. *One Church, Many Cultures: The Challenge of Diversity*. Kansas City, MO: Sheed and Ward, 1987.

51. *Paul: Saint of the Inner City*. Mahwah, NJ: Paulist Press, 1990.

HISPANICS IN NEW YORK: AN ARCHDIOCESAN SURVEY

Late in the 1970s, it was clear that the Catholic Church in New York was dealing with an entirely different situation than what had prevailed in the 'fifties. Not only had the new Hispanics arrived – the Cubans, the Dominicans, the many refugees from Central America and immigrants from South America – but the Puerto Rican community had become largely second generation and was beginning to move into the third generation. Cardinal Cooke was aware of this and he commissioned a study of Hispanics in the New York Archdiocese. It was to be conducted by his office of Pastoral Planning and Research under the directorship of Mrs. Ruth Doyle and Dr. Olga Scarpetta. A strong advisory group had been formed of which I was a member. The study was planned and carried out in 1978 and 1979 and the two volumes were published in 1980 as *Hispanics in New York: Religious, Cultural and Social Experience.*[52] This was the first extensive study done of the religious life of Hispanics in New York. A summary of the study is included in my readings. A selection of background readings was included in the second volume of the study to provide a context for it and its interpretation.

The diversity of the Hispanic population was clear in the results, although the Puerto Ricans still remained the great majority (65%) and the Dominicans second (25%). The generational change was also very clear: 51% of all Hispanics in the sample had been born in the continental United States. One striking finding was the strong adherence of Hispanics to the Church, although many seldom or never went to Mass. The use of folk practices was very strong although diminishing in the second generation. Despite their lack of involvement in parishes or Mass, the great majority expressed a favorable attitude toward the Church and Catholic Schools. Few were well informed about Church activities: 60% had never heard of Vatican II, and only 14% had ever heard of the two national Hispanic Congresses (*Encuentros*).

Following the publication of the Study, a Pastoral Plan was prepared and shared with all agencies of the Archdiocese. Every aspect of religious life was covered, with a special emphasis on family life and youth ministry. It has often been remarked that another study should be done at the present time (1994) to determine what success the Pastoral Plan had in its implementation.

---

52. See Part II: *Hispanics in New York.* . . . New York Archdiocese, 1011 First Avenue, New York, NY 10022, 1980.

HOSTOS COMMUNITY COLLEGE

In September 1970, after two years of planning and organizing under the direction of Candido de Leon, Hostos Community College opened in the South Bronx. I had known Candido for some years when he had been a Professor at Saint Peter's College in Jersey City. It was largely his initiative and vision that gave form to Hostos Community College and gave it its name. The College was designed to serve a largely Puerto Rican population in the South Bronx, with a special emphasis on the preparation of students in health services. It was strategically located close to the new Lincoln Hospital which could serve as a site for field training of students in health services. The College had a stormy history during its early years. After two years in office, its first President, Dr. Nasry Michelen resigned amidst student protests. In 1971 Dr. de Leon was named President. He resigned in 1979 after years of repeated outside attempts to close the College, but only one year after the State of New York had guaranteed its continued existence. He was replaced by Dr. Flora Mancuso Edwards. Dr. Mancuso Edwards saw the College through seven years of development, the construction and opening of new buildings, the addition of new programs, and the adoption of a Master Plan for the development of a permanent campus in the South Bronx. Dr. Mancuso Edwards resigned in 1986 and was replaced by Dr. Isaura Santiago Santiago.

I had known Dr. Santiago for some years. I had served on the committee for her dissertation at the Fordham University Graduate School of Education. I had also collaborated with her in a number of research projects she developed while she served as a Professor at Columbia's Teacher's College. Shortly after she became President, she created a Community Advisory Council to link the College to community resources, and to assist her in the development of programs related to the community. She asked me to serve on this Council, which I agreed to do. It has a wide representation of community people. But, apart from whatever contribution I have made, my service on the Council has given me an insight into the activities of the College which I had never had before. I think most citizens of New York, like myself, who knew little of the College, tended to look upon it as very minor league. But I was surprised by the extent of its activities, both educational and in collaboration with the community. It serves a full-time student body of 5,200 (in 1994), 75% of whom are women, many of them single parents, and almost all living in poverty. It is a remarkable example of the response of an educational institution to the needs of the surrounding community. It is developing a Culture and Arts Center which will bring artists from Central and South America and the Caribbean to the South Bronx, and provide an opportunity for the development of the arts among the people of this neighborhood. It has also created a mini high school which is located on the property and has received national recognition for its excellence. The College serves as an anchor of stability in the redevelopment of the South Bronx.

It has been an interesting and exciting experience to serve on the Advisory Council, although our contribution has been limited. The significant developments are the result of the creative efforts of President Santiago and her staff.

In 1992 a charge was made in the public press of discrimination in hiring on the part of Hostos Community College, especially by its President. The charge claimed favoritism toward Hispanic applicants and against African Americans. This seemed strange to me since the College has a specific mission of service to a largely Hispanic community. I was asked to serve on an ad hoc committee to study the hiring practices and determine if there was any evidence of discrimination. Already in place were Committees of New York State and of the City University to oversee hiring and to assure non-discrimination. Both had officially declared the practices of Hostos as non-discriminatory. We interviewed all the people involved in the process and found no evidence of discrimination. Our report to the Advisory Council was accepted. This settled the issue, at least for the time being.

The Advisory Council is now involved in the preparation of the celebration of the 25th Anniversary of the founding of the College. This will involve the opening of a new East Campus facility, and particularly the new Culture and Arts Center. I have been very grateful for the opportunity to serve on this Council. It has brought me into close contact with an important educational resource for the Puerto Ricans and other Hispanics. The new Campus has been called: "The Gateway to the Bronx," and represents a significant element in the rebuilding of the South Bronx. It is also another indication of the "coming of age" of this Puerto Rican community.

PUERTO RICO DISCOVERY DAY MASS

In 1986 the Bronx Arts Ensemble gave a concert in the Fordham University Church which I attended. One item on the program was the performance of the *"Misa En Do Mayor"* (Mass in D Major), composed by Manuel Gonzalez, a Puerto Rican. It was performed as a concert piece. I was very much impressed by it. The music and the singing were beautiful. Following the concert I had the opportunity to meet the composer who was present at the performance. We talked a bit and I said to him: "We have to find an occasion to do this Mass as a Liturgical celebration." He was fascinated by the idea. His music had never been performed within the context of an actual Mass. That afternoon I mentioned this idea to William Scribner, the Director of the Bronx Arts Ensemble. He encouraged me to find some suitable occasion to have the *Misa* performed as a Liturgy.

The chorus at the concert was from Boricua College, an institution of higher education originally founded for Puerto Ricans in New York City. I had heard the chorus some years before at a graduation of Boricua College. They were remarkable – really one of the best college choruses I had ever heard. Their performance of the *Misa* was likewise remarkable. I was determined at that moment to invite the Boricua College chorus to sing the *Misa* if we could arrange it. Director Abraham Lind-Oquendo was an accomplished professional singer. I got to know him well as things developed.

I knew that the Puerto Ricans in New York celebrated Puerto Rico Discovery week in November, at a date conveniently close to the November 24th date of the actual discovery. All the celebrations were civic events, either of Puerto Rican music or conferences on Puerto Rican culture. There was no religious celebration at all during the events. I decided that we would inaugurate a celebration of Puerto Rico Discovery Day at Fordham University with a Liturgical ceremony, featuring Manuel Gonzalez's composition, sung by the Boricua Chorus and accompanied by the Bronx Arts Ensemble. Abe Lind-Oquendo and Bill Scribner were enthusiastic about the idea and agreed to work with me on it. And Mannie Gonzalez was delighted that his *Misa* would be given prominence in a Liturgical celebration.

The New York Telephone Company, through the intervention of Mrs. Milagros Torres, contributed to the event; Consolidated Edison Company, through the intervention of Carlotta Maduro, also contributed; and Boricua College supported it as well as did the Puerto Rican students' club at Fordham, *El Grito de Lares*, which also sponsored the event. Many of my relatives and friends contributed the rest of the necessary funds.

The first performance took place on November 22, 1987, in the Fordham University Church. It was a very successful and impressive event. Both Father Joseph O'Hare, President of Fordham University, and Dr. Victor Alicea, President of Boricua College, greeted the audience. I offered the Mass in Spanish and gave the Homily. The chorus and orchestra were excellent. This Mass, the only religious event in the celebration of Discovery Day, was also significant since it featured this important example of Puerto Rico's musical tradition, and the creativity of one of its artists, Manuel Gonzalez. The response of the Puerto Rican community was very favorable. Many of them appreciated this aspect of Puerto Rico's religious, as well as musical, traditions.

The Mass has been celebrated each year since, with increasing success. A close tie has developed between Fordham University and Boricua College, an association which has been helpful to both. It represents another link of Fordham to the Hispanic community. With the help of Abe Lind-Oquendo and his associate director, George Dunbar, we also have had the Boricua College chorus do some spirituals during the regular Sunday Mass at Fordham. In 1993, the 500th year of Discovery, Abe Lind-Oquendo wanted to add *Puerto Rico: A Canticle* to the celebration at Fordham. This was a famous poem written during the last century which was put to music by Manuel Gonzalez. I did an English translation of it for the program, and the chorus sang it as a prelude to the Mass. It is a beautiful piece of music and received an enthusiastic ovation after its performance.

I have always appreciated the *Misa* since it has given me the opportunity to contribute something of a religious and artistic character to the Puerto Rican community in New York. One thing impresses me about Abe Lind-Oquendo: he trains his chorus in classical music. They can do the folk music and popular Puerto Rican music, but Abe has a full repertoire in place. Even at the Boricua College graduation, Abe has them perform the "Resurrection Chorus" from Handel's *Messiah*, together with a folk piece. Thus, while proud of their tradition of folk music, the chorus includes a wide range of the best classical music.

PUERTO RICANS IN NEW YORK CITY, 1990

In December 1993, New York City was in the midst of one of the worst winters in its history. The Puerto Ricans have always complained about "*El pais frio*" (the cold country), and they had good reason to complain more than ever that winter.

The Department of City Planning of New York had just issued its extensive study of all the data available about Puerto Ricans in New York on the basis of the 1990 Census. Deputy Mayor Cesar Perales had organized a public meeting to review the study and I was asked to be one of the discussants, focusing on the statistical description of the

Puerto Rican Community in New York City. Another panel was to discuss the policy implications of the report.

The report itself, much too long to be incorporated here, is a remarkable compilation of data. Similar analyses had been done before, on the basis of the 1970 Census by A. J. Jaffe et al.[53] Another analysis was done on the basis of the 1980 Census by Frank Bean and Marta Tienda, *The Hispanic Population of the United States*.[54] Both these books were rich sources of information, not only about Puerto Ricans but about all Hispanics in the United States. The 1993 City Planning report dealt only with Puerto Ricans in New York City.[55]

For the first time, the Census showed that the majority of the Puerto Ricans had been born on the Mainland. In other words, they are predominantly second generation. The report is significant since, for the first time, abundant data are available about the second generation in contrast to the first. The second generation are better educated and hold better jobs. In brief, they show considerable socio-economic improvement over the first.

However, the important finding was that there are two distinct Puerto Rican communities. The economic situation among Puerto Rican married couples was relatively good; income was high, almost 70% higher than the average for all Puerto Rican families, having increased about 40% during the 'eighties. This was significantly more than the 26% increase for all married couples in the City. During the decade the income of Puerto Rican married couples was three quarters that of all married couples in the City. In sharp contrast, the economic situation for the female-headed families had deteriorated; real income gains did not keep pace with gains for all female-headed families and some, especially those with grown children, actually experienced a decline in real income. The income ratio had declined since 1980 and was in the range of 50 to 60%.

In other words, of the two Puerto Rican communities, one consists of stable, relatively affluent, two parent families: (35% of Puerto Rican

---

53. *The Changing Demography of the Spanish-speaking of the United States.* New York: Academic Press, 1980.

54. *The Hispanic Population of the United States.* New York: Russell Sage Foundation, 1987.

55. The report was released in a more formal version in 1994. See *Puerto Rican New Yorkers in 1990*, Joseph Salvo, Ronald Ortiz and Peter Lobo, (New York: New York City Department of City Planning, Sept. 1994). The remainder of this section is a summary of the more important points contained in the report.

families); and the other of female-headed families, (34%) who are locked in poverty. Some of the female-headed families are the result of separation, abandonment or divorce; but many are the result of the high percentage of out-of-wedlock births to Puerto Rican teen-agers. Forty-five percent of Puerto Rican births in 1992 were out-of-wedlock. The problem of the continuing poverty of the Puerto Ricans is located here in the female-headed families: 57.4% in 1990. Although this was down from 67.8% in 1980, it is still extremely high.

There are two related issues: first, many mothers who are on welfare receive a stipend which brings them to only 67% of the poverty level; second, if they are working, the women may be in menial, low paying jobs. And it is clear that, in New York, a family must have two incomes in order to maintain a reasonable standard of living. This is the single most important challenge to the Puerto Rican community and the larger community of New York City.

The educational data in the Census are also significant. Once the second generation is considered apart from the first, the improvement in education becomes noticeable. In 1990, of those born in the United States, 66% had finished high school in contrast to 37% of those born on the Island. Nevertheless, Puerto Ricans still lag behind the total population in every category. They still have high drop-out rates from high school and the percentage of college graduates (6%) is still very low. However, the evidence of improvement is present and will probably continue.

Thus in assessing the Puerto Rican community in 1990, attention must be given to the 35% in successful families. Many of the Puerto Ricans have done well. At the same time, even more attention must be given to the 34% female-headed families, many of whom are still locked in poverty. Until this is corrected, it is not possible to be overly optimistic about the Puerto Rican experience.

A footnote is important here. Not all female-headed families are in difficulty. In the study of "Puerto Rican Addicts and Non-addicts" noted above (p. 46) there were as many addicts among two parent as among single parent families. Some of the single parents were remarkable mothers who knew where their children were, knew how much money they had and where they got it, exercised consistent discipline, and guided their children to a strong, positive adulthood. If these parenting skills could be communicated to others, improvement would be evident.

ANOTHER SUNDAY AFTERNOON WITH FATHER FITZPATRICK

In June 1993, I celebrated the Golden Jubilee of my Ordination to the priesthood. On October 17, my students and friends put on a celebration for me that will never be forgotten. After the Mass of Thanksgiving in the University Church, we gathered at McGinley Center for the reception. The celebration was organized by Dr. Madeline Engel Moran, and former students came from California, Puerto Rico, Illinois, Florida, Maine, and elsewhere; I was deeply impressed by the number of former students who appeared.

At the reception, representatives of the various organizations with which I had been active made presentations. Among them was Sister Isolina Ferre, whose great Center in Ponce, Puerto Rico, I had helped start. She gave me a beautiful silk-screen reproduction of the Ponce Cathedral. Mrs. Maria Elena Girone, Executive Director of the Puerto Rican Family Institute, gave me a Medal of the Institute. I had been a member of their Board since its beginning in 1963. Jorge Batista represented the Puerto Rican Legal Defense and Education Fund, whose Board I had served on since 1973. Sister Barbara Lenniger, Executive Director of Thorpe Family Residence, a transitional residence for homeless unmarried mothers in the Bronx, spoke about my service getting that project started. I was on their Board until 1994. A staff member represented Lizette Tait, the Director of Neighborhood Youth and Family Services, a community-based program in the South Bronx that I had helped found in 1970. I am still Chairman of their Board. All of these organizations were serving the Puerto Rican community and reflected my extensive involvement in it. Then there were my former students and representatives of other organizations. The students used the occasion to reactivate the Fitzpatrick Scholarship at Fordham. It will provide partial tuition for an academically qualified minority student in need of financial assistance.

It was an unforgettable day, one which made me aware of how many people greatly appreciated what I had tried to do, and how much gratitude I owed to all of them.

CONCLUSION: ASSIMILATION OR INTEGRATION?

Finally, what is the relationship of Puerto Ricans to the larger society of the United States? As I have mentioned before, assimilation is not a politically correct term among Puerto Rican scholars. Nevertheless, the process that was evident among earlier immigrants is appearing equally now among Puerto Ricans. The important evidence is in the area of intermarriage. Intermarriage of Hispanics, or Puerto Ricans with non-Hispanics, is the major indicator of the weakening of ties to the ethnic origin group and their involvement in the larger society of the United States.

I have just finished the third study I have done about the intermarriage of Puerto Ricans with non-Hispanics. The decrease in intermarriage noted in the 1975 study (see p. 68) has reversed and the pattern of intermarriage of Puerto Ricans is similar to that of all other Hispanic groups. There is a substantial increase in intermarriage with non-Hispanics in the second generation over the first. Below are the figures for Puerto Rican intermarriage from my first study in 1949 to the last one of 1991.

Table 1
Comparison of 1991 Puerto Rican Intermarriage Rates with those of 1975, 1959 and 1949, and with All Foreign-Stock Marriages during 1908-1912, by Generation

	First Generation %	First Generation No.	Second Generation %	Second Generation No.	Increase in Second Generation %
Brides					
Puerto Rican 1991	17.3	1,621	34.0	3,437	16.7
Puerto Rican 1975	12.9	3,606	20.7	1,943	7.8
Puerto Rican 1959	6.0	7,257	33.1	717	27.1
Puerto Rican 1949	8.5	3,077	30.0	523	21.5
1908 to 1912	10.1	61,823	30.1	14,611	20.0
Grooms					
Puerto Rican 1991	16.0	1,802	28.3	2,938	12.3
Puerto Rican 1975	9.4	4,003	21.3	2,344	11.9
Puerto Rican 1959	3.6	7,078	27.4	638	23.8
Puerto Rican 1949	5.2	3,079	28.3	378	23.1
1908 to 1912	10.4	64,577	32.4	12,184	22.0

Source: 1975-1991: New York City Marriage Records; 1949 and 1959: Fitzpatrick (1966); 1908-1912: Drachsler (1921)

[a]Intermarriage to non-Puerto Rican Hispanics omitted for this table in order to render the 1991 and 1975 data comparable to that for 1949 and 1959.

[b]Increase is presented as the difference between the percent in the third and first columns.

In 1991, 34% of Puerto Rican brides, second generation, married non-Hispanics, an increase of 16.7% over the first. Among the grooms, it was 28.3%, an increase of 12.3% over the first generation.

The evidence across the years is a reliable indicator that Puerto Ricans are following the same pattern of assimilation into the larger community as the immigrants of the past century and early part of this century. Thus within another generation or two the Puerto Rican population may be indistinguishable from the larger society of the United States.

Two things will affect this, the proximity of the Island and the constant flow of Puerto Ricans back and forth. This link to the Island will continue to be strong and will give, even to intermarried Puerto Ricans, a sense of identity that has been lost to European immigrants. Secondly, the emphasis on culture, multiculturalism, and cultural pluralism have become strong currents in American thinking. Sensitivity to cultural origins is much more important among newcomers than it was among earlier immigrants. And anthropologists have noted that the Hispanic culture is a strong and deeply rooted one. Thus, although Puerto Ricans become more and more similar in cultural style to the mainstream of American life, their sense of origin will continue to be strong. What remains to be seen will be the influence on the United States of the presence of so many millions of persons of Spanish-speaking background. This will not become very evident until another generation or two.

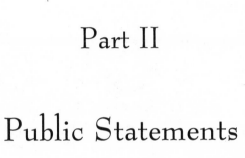

Part II

Public Statements

1

The Newcomer
Becomes Our Own[1]

I WOULD LIKE TO SAY A FEW WORDS TO YOU ABOUT THE "DILEMMA OF THE newcomer," the strong desire of immigrants to become part of our American way of life or our New York way of life, and the equally strong desire to retain their identity with the way of life from which they came. This is not a problem that is unique to the Spanish-speaking. It has been the classic problem of all newcomers to our American way of life. Two great dangers in the dilemma are obvious in the experience of earlier immigrants; they will be obvious in your experience also. They are: first, the danger of those who are so anxious to become American as quickly as possible that they cut themselves off from all identity with their own background and their own people; second, the danger of those who try so hard to retain their identity that they isolate themselves from participation in American life. It is clear that virtue lies somewhere in the middle, in a vigorous participation in New York life or American life, but a participation in which you are identified as Puerto Rican or Spanish-speaking members of the community.

In the first place, it is important to try to preserve the best things from the way of life from which you come. Eventually, in your grand-children, this will have become part of the great stream of American life – this seems to be the law of immigrant experience. But, if you are going to contribute to the greatness of New York and the greatness of our Nation here, you will do this obviously, not by ceasing to be yourselves, but by bringing with you the best of yourselves from the world from which you come.

---

1. Address on the Occasion of Installation of New Officers, Consejo de Organizaciones Puertorriqueñas e Hispano-Americanas de Nueva York, January 21, 1961.

It is always sad to see the loss of the great values of the people who come to us. There is a strong temptation to give up the ways of the past. This has generally been the problem mainly of those who are second generation, those born here of parents who came from a different culture. There is an old, old saying about the earlier immigrant groups: "The son tries to forget; and the grandson tries to remember." The son wants to be identified as an American and he frequently tries to dissociate himself from anything that might make him appear different. The grandson, fully confident that he is American, tries to recover some things from his past that will make him distinct as an American.

But for yourselves, it is so important to try to bring with you to the life of New York or the Nation those wonderful qualities which were part of the life from which you came. Let me give you one instance of how impressive that life is. Recently a wonderful new book was published about Puerto Rico. It was the life history of a poor, uneducated sugar cane worker on the south coast of the Island.[2] We might be inclined to say: what can there be that is great or impressive about the life of a cane worker? Yet, the Yale Professor who was making the study was profoundly impressed by the greatness that he found in the life of this ordinary man. Let me read the summary of his impression.

> But what I regard as bigger things I learned are hard for me to describe. In my growing friendship with Don Taso, and probably for the first time in my life, I learned to look down the corridor of time through which a man had walked. I found myself deeply stirred by what I could dimly understand. Taso, though only a few years older than I, had lived so differently, so hard, had suffered so much more, even in terms of the fundamentals of life, that knowing him and feeling his liking for me made me humble.

Any ordinary New Yorker, seeing the little wooden houses near the cane fields of Santa Isabel might ask: "Could anything good come out of there?" Yet a University Professor who came to know that way of life felt himself humbled, brought low before the greatness that he found, before the loyalty, the human qualities of devotion, the ability to suffer, to sacrifice, that shone out of the life of the cane worker. Those qualities shine out in the lives of thousands more in Puerto Rico, in Mexico, in Latin America. If you can bring those qualities with you: loyalty, devotion to God and fellow men and women; the ability to bear trial and suffering, the courage to endure; if you can give these to the way of life

---

2. Sidney Mintz, *Worker in the Cane.* (New Haven, CT: Yale University Press, 1960).

of New York or of the Nation, you need never be ashamed of that from which you have come. You can boast proudly of the greatness of the way of life which you have left, and contribute this greatness to the way of life to which you have come.

But, remaining the best of what you are, you must still try to become part of the way of life that is New York or the mainland United States. How do you do this?

With reference to this difficult question of integration, let me say first that, in the long run, the school is the great instrument of integration. But this is something that will touch your children rather than your-selves.

Compulsory education in a common American school system, whether public or private, has been for earlier immigrants, and will be for the Spanish-speaking, the great channel of integration. This is the institution that formally communicates to the child the American way of life. The child cannot avoid it. Therefore, any doubt about eventual integration of newcomers is groundless in view of the system of educa-tion which is necessarily the common experience of the children of all newcomers. This raises a serious difficulty of another kind in your experience, a difficulty which would require a whole speech to describe, the difficulty of the change in generations: the fact that a child is taught one way of life in the school while he lives in another way of life in the home; the fact that you will never completely understand the way of life of your children, and they will never completely understand yours.

A second important channel of integration, the one that touches you more directly, has always been organized activity, generally some form of political activity, a participation in the political life of the City or the Nation. It is here that your own organization is important. Note what it is and what it does. It is an organization that represents the interests of the Puerto Ricans and the Spanish-speaking, but it represents them within the framework of American political institutions and American community activities. It is just such an organization that enables you to participate vigorously in the life of New York or of the Nation, while you retain your identity as Spanish-speaking citizens.

I see no fear that such organizations interfere with your integration in American life. Occasionally older citizens, many of them very sincere, become anxious about your organizations and urge you to give them up and become part of the organizations which already exist. But if your organization is effective, the one thing it prevents you from doing is staying by yourselves. It brings you, as a group, into vigorous contact with American life. It has always been in the best of American traditions for various groups to have organizations to represent their interests. There have been German organizations, Irish organizations, Italian organizations, Jewish organizations, and so on. Indeed, America is one great and complicated system of interest groups, making their voices heard, striving to advance the interests of their members, striving to contribute to the common welfare through organizations which represent them. There seems no reason why you should not do the same. It is just such activity which enables you to resolve the dilemma of the newcomer. You participate actively and vigorously in American life, but you participate as Puerto Ricans or as Spanish-speaking citizens. Your organization is formed, not to participate in the political and community activity of Puerto Rico, but in the political and community activity of New York; not to participate in the political and community activity of Mexico or Colombia, but in the political and community activity of the United States. Thus, while you participate for the common welfare of the city or the nation, you promote also you own interests as respected citizens of Puerto Rican or Latin American background.

Therefore, I congratulate your new and old officers, and all the members of your organizations. I pray always that God will give you the guidance and the vision to be proud of the great qualities of the way of life from which you come, and to preserve them so that you may share them with the people of New York and the Nation; I pray that He will guide you also in your efforts to be yourselves while you participate in that organized activity through which you hope to give the best of yourselves to the new world and the new way of life of which you wish to be a part.

2

Puerto Ricans in New York

The Great Challenge to the Charity of Catholics[1]

ONE EVENING BACK IN THE YEAR 1902, WILLIAM FOLEY WAS GLAD TO SEE the work day at an end. He closed the wooden bins on his stocks of tea and coffee, turned the gas jet down to a dim flicker, and locked the door of his shop with a song in his heart. Great things were afoot for that night. He started home beneath the roar of the Second Avenue El where steam trains puffed and spouted as they pulled along. He may have stopped in at Murphy's Saloon where many respectable Irishmen of the East Side settled the little troubles inside of them and the big troubles outside of them with a short whiskey or a glass of ale. He turned into 23rd Street, and with a great chuckle, looked at the hall he had rented from the Masons for the use of his stalwart Catholic men. There, in that hall, William Foley's idea was to be born that night.

Little did he know that, fifty years later, in the Grand Ballroom of a fine hotel, the achievement of his great idea would be honored after fifty golden years by his faithful followers. He had founded his Council of Knights of Columbus to meet the challenge of charity and brotherhood. Had he been able to look ahead, he would have seen that the great challenge to charity and brotherhood was to parallel this vital development that was taking place in this City of New York.

For William was in the center of things now. Just up 23rd Street, Madison Square was the hub of the great world, and country cousins would take a Sunday outing to journey there to see the tallest building of the world, The Flatiron, rising to the dizzy heights of twenty stories. But in a sense, this was not the real New York. Rather, William Foley saw the real New York when he passed Lexington Avenue, and there in the pits beneath the street, were hundreds of strange men, digging the

---

1. Address: Golden Jubilee Breakfast, Vera Cruz Council, Knights of Columbus, May 18, 1952.

97

new subway. They spoke a strange language, these new men from Italy; they acted in ways the Irish did not understand; they lived in horrible dwellings on the Lower East Side. But soon they were to move northward, soon they were to invade this Irish stronghold of Murray Hill. This was the real New York, the New York of the poverty-stricken immigrant struggling for a better life. This was the New York his own Irish people had known during a century before when they dug the Erie Canal and hacked out the road bed for the New York Central. Here in the struggle of the immigrant was the real drama of the City. This was the challenge to charity and brotherhood for which he was founding his Council. And here we see its fulfillment in the unity of Irish and Italian in the Vera Cruz Council today.

William Foley might have thought to himself that night, what a foolish thing it would be to discredit these new immigrants. For here we are founding an organization, dedicated to a great Italian, Christopher Columbus; here we will forever bring charity to the world in the name of one who spoke their language, who followed their customs – a man who had never heard of Dublin and would have found the Irish even more puzzling than the Irish find themselves. Here in devotion to a genius of the Italian people, was the basis for a bond in charity and brotherhood that has flourished into this wonderful organization to which I speak today.

This was the challenge of the past fifty years, and you have met it well. For this you deserve the greatest praise and honor.

But there is another challenge arising for the next fifty years, one that will be just as great and just as pressing. If today, you rode the Lexington Avenue subway where William Foley heard the strange harmony of Italian dialects, you would be jostled in the crowd of other strange people speaking another strange language, acting in other strange ways that neither Irish nor Italians find easy to understand. These are the new immigrants, the new development in that dynamic life that has always been New York, the latest challenge to the charity and brotherhood of fellow Catholics. These are the Puerto Ricans. Already they are dislodging the Italians from the Lower East Side, taking over the worst of impossible housing; soon they will begin to invade what is left of the Italian-Irish stronghold on Murray Hill. Soon they will be knocking on the doors of the Vera Cruz Council.

I have called this the greatest challenge to the charity and brotherhood of the Catholics of New York; and I say this with careful deliberation. It is part of the challenge that includes all groups – Negroes and

Jews and Central Europeans. What I say could apply to all of them. But as the newest group – as a predominantly Catholic group, I wish to center my attention directly on the Puerto Ricans. The success or failure of the next fifty years will depend on the way in which not only you, but all Catholics in this City, meet the critical problem of our brothers and sisters from Puerto Rico. I would like to dwell on this for a few moments because I am sure that, when you see this thing in its real meaning, you will respond to this challenge as generously as you have met the problems of the past.

Just as there was a basis in Columbus to unify the Irish and Italian, so also is there an equal basis in Columbus to unify the Irish, the Italian and the Puerto Rican. For although Columbus was an Italian, he sailed under the King and Queen of Spain, supported by that very tradition from which the Puerto Ricans have been born. In fact, the very symbols of your order are expressed in the language that the Puerto Ricans speak. The very title of your Council, Vera Cruz, the name of the First Council in New Haven, San Salvador, these are words ever on your lips in the language of the Puerto Ricans.

The Puerto Ricans are the newest immigrants to New York City. As immigrants, they are no different than the many waves of immigrants who have gone before them. They are misunderstood, frequently criticized in exactly the same way that all our people were criticized before them. They are called dirty, unkempt, half-civilized; they are considered irresponsible, shiftless; and the crime and delinquency statistics are used to show that they are a people prone to crime. How frequently the remark is made that they come to New York to be put on relief and to vote for Marcantonio. And so, the litany continues.

What I wish to show you is that this type of criticism is not new. In almost identical terms, it was leveled at the Irish, at the Jews, at the Italians, at the Negroes. And as the children of immigrants ourselves, if we reflect on the experience of our own people, we should be best prepared not to make the mistake of judging the Puerto Ricans in the unjust way in which our people were judged themselves.

Let me just run through some of the documents and official statements made about the Irish one hundred years ago. I think it will show you exactly what I mean. Suppose we begin with the criminal records of New York City for the year 1859. On the list of criminal convictions we find the following:

80 Canadians were convicted of crimes
118 Scotchmen
666 Englishmen

1,403 Germans
And the Irish......11,305

Now when you get down to the reasons for those convictions among the Irish, a few were convicted of running disorderly houses; a few for theft or manslaughter; then 7,000 for drunkenness and disorderly conduct.

You laugh when you hear this, and rightly so. Because we know that you cannot use a chart of criminal statistics to tell you much about the real life of an immigrant group. We know that, despite this failing of drunkenness and disorder for which our people were severely criticized, in the neighborhoods where those men were, there was tremendous personal loyalty, deep reverence for women, love of children and family life, and the heroic struggle of the Irish mother to keep the family strong and secure. We know that this was the real picture of the Irish neighborhood, and we know how bitterly we resented it when native New Yorkers used the criminal records to brand us as an irresponsible people.

Similarly, in the case of the Puerto Ricans, despite the records of delinquency and crime, despite the almost unbearable burdens of poor immigrants, there is similarly many an example of heroism, of deep devotion to family, of love and loyalty, and faithfulness to God. And we, who have suffered from misrepresentation, should make sure that we never visit misrepresentation on others.

A report of the Commissioner of Almshouses for 1837 as the great Irish migration began stated: "Europe is casting upon us the refuse of her Almshouses and her prisons. . . ."

The Irish were accused of worming their way into the City and casting themselves on public charity. In 1847, the Report of the Board of Assistant Aldermen had this to say: "There are so many paupers at the Almshouse in Bellevue Hospital that they have to be lodged in cells and garrets, in the chapel and even in the morgue."

When we are tempted to speak glibly about the Puerto Ricans on relief, it may be wise to recall the reports about our own people a century ago. Finally, just a word of criticism that came from the Irish themselves. It appeared in the *Irish American*, November 29, 1856. It was a comment on Irish women. We all know the respect we have for Irish women, those heroic and devoted souls who made the Irish home a place of love and security. The paper has this to say:

> The Irish girl often mistook forwardness, if not impertinence, for independence. They dress too expensively and showily for their calling and assume unbecoming airs. Some forget them-

selves to the extent that they hire the employer instead of the employer hiring them.

Finally, let me quote a passage from the Report of the City Inspector to the Mayor of New York, 1864. He was talking about a predominantly Irish section.

> The tenants seemed wholly to disregard personal cleanliness and the very first principles of decency, their general appearance and actions corresponding to their wretched abodes. This indifference to personal and domiciliary cleanliness is doubtless acquired from a long familiarity with the loathsome surroundings, wholly at variance with all moral and social improvements.

This does not refer to Puerto Ricans in East Harlem – it refers to our own Irish people. Note the kind sympathy of the Commissioner who places very little blame on the people, but remarks that no one could live decently in that environment.

This was the experience of our fathers; this was what we went through. Surely the memories of that experience should never die. We should be the first to be able to say to the Puerto Ricans: We appreciate what you face; we have gone through this before you. Depend on us for understanding.

This should be even easier for us when we understand something of the background from which they come. In the first place, they come as United States citizens. They have as much right to come to New York unhampered, as you or I have to move to New Jersey or Connecticut. Their sons fight in our American armies, and many a boy from San Juan, Mayagüez and Ponce, has stood on the hills of Korea beside the boys from Brooklyn and the Bronx. Secondly, they come here because they are forced by desperate economic necessity. They come from a little island, 100 miles long, 35 miles wide, with one of the densest populations in the world. They come here for the same reason the Irish and Italians came here, in search of the opportunity to escape hunger and to find a better life. They have the same problem of language which the Italians found such a terrible handicap. They range in color from very light to very black; thus many of them, God help them, must face the terrible, unchristian prejudice against color.

Many of them, it is true, are poorly instructed in their Faith. But that is not their fault. They come from a tradition where they never had to fight for the Faith as the Irish did for centuries against the English; they come from a culture where the State always supported the Church and Church activities; they come from an area where priests have been too few to reach them. But they are not to blame for this. They come now into our land, where we point with pride to the achievements we have made, the Churches we have built, the schools we run. And as they seek to share for the first time in this vigorous Catholicism we boast of, should we not make sure that they will be greeted with charity, the root of all practice of religion? Rather, we should approach them with understanding, appreciation, and a willingness to receive them as our own and teach them in patience. In saying this, I am not asking for pity for the Puerto Ricans. They do not want pity any more than our people wanted it. They want respect, understanding, and the opportunity to be accepted by us as our brothers in Christ.

This, then is the challenge of the next fifty years. Your greatness will consist in your ability to meet it. In a sense, should we not often recall the story you have heard of Damien the Leper? You recall that, when he first went among the lepers, he was not received, no one listened to him, his teaching was rejected. But eventually, he contracted the disease himself. Then when he came to the lepers, he showed them the marks of the leprosy on his flesh and addressed them as "We lepers." At that moment, everything changed. They respected him as one who knew what they were going through, as one who shared their suffering, who knew what leprosy meant. At that point, they all turned to him, listened to his instructions and they became a flourishing Christian community. Similarly, of all people, we can turn to the Puerto Ricans and say, "We immigrants." We know how it feels, we understand. And with that they should be able to turn to us for the greatest of appreciation, the greatest of understanding and help.

This then is the future. And I trust that your example in meeting the challenge of charity in the past is assurance that you will meet this challenge of charity in the future. Were William Foley alive today, were he riding on the Lexington Avenue Subway with the Puerto Ricans instead of watching it being built by the Italians, he could have looked forward to one hundred years instead of fifty – and he might have said: What a strange plan of God's Providence that I should have founded a Council so strikingly designed to be a bond of unity for all these people. The Vera Cruz Council of the Knights of Columbus, a living tribute to the heroic Irishman who founded it; a living tribute to the genius of an Italian to whose name it is dedicated; a living tribute to the traditions of Spain, and marked by the symbol of the Cross in the language of the Puerto Ricans.

3

A Plea for Christian Unity[1]

THIS IS "WORLD SODALITY DAY." I WONDER IF YOU REALLY KNOW HOW important this is. I wonder if you really know that this act of devotion is not just a pageant which you enjoy. I wonder if you really know that this is one of the most important things that is happening in the world this afternoon! For while the world is trying desperately, through tears and bloodshed, to find some power that will bring men into one, you are gathered here to proclaim to the world that you have found that power in the life of Our Lord, and in the love of Our Lady.

For in every war of recent years, whether men and women have been aware of it or not, they have been fighting in the vague hope that they would find the power that could unite them, that could reach the children who play in the snows of Alaska, and make them one with the children who run in play along the banks of the sacred rivers of India; some power that could reach to the black children in the forest of Africa and make them one with the children who pray for bread in Italy; who hope for freedom in China. That is the issue of the world today. That is why your presence here is one of the most important things that is happening this afternoon.

For as we stand here before the shrine of Our Lady, are you not joined throughout the world by her other children? Some of them stand to honor her beneath the beautiful mountains of Japan; others chant their hymns to her this afternoon in the bamboo groves of the Philippine Islands; brown children of Our Lady gather for their devotions in Bombay or Calcutta; black children in the Congo say the same Hail Mary to her as the children of Paris, of Buenos Aires, of Berlin. In English, Spanish and German; in the many languages of Asia and the Islands, Our Lady hears herself called Mother this afternoon. This is the miracle of unity, of love. This is what makes your devotion here so terribly important. To a world that is praying and crying for unity, you must proclaim

1. Sermon, *World Sodality Day*, Fordham University, May 10, 1953.

the unity which you have already worked out in the love of the sodalist for Our Lord, and the devotion of the sodalist to Our Lady.

This should show you all the more what the theme of today's celebration means: Your apostolate must be Catholic. We use that word Catholic so often! I wonder how many of you really know what the word "Catholic" means? It is one of the four marks of the Church; one of the four great signs by which all men and women were to know that this was the true Church of Christ. Unless men and women see that the Church is Catholic, they will not accept it as the Church of Christ. The word Catholic means that the life of Christ in His Church is perfectly suited to any way of life in the world that is not sinful. It means that a person does not have to stop being a Negro in order to be another Christ; that a person does not have to stop being an Indian or a Japanese in order to be another Christ. It means that the life of Christ can express itself in a Chinese way of life as well as an American way of life without making them all the same. The power of Christ is great enough to make all people one no matter how different they are in everything else. As long as there is no injustice, it means that the life of the Church can express itself just as richly among the poor in their huts in a Philippine village as it can in the inspiring atmosphere of a Western monastery; that the beating of tom-toms in an African tribe can be turned into a hymn of praise as pleasing to God as a Cathedral choir. Our Lord made it clear from the earliest days that His Church was never to be identified with any particular way of life, with what we could call today, any particular culture. God even gave a special revelation to Peter to drive it home to him. As you can read in the tenth chapter of the *Acts of the Apostles*, when Cornelius the first Gentile asked to become a Christian and Peter went to visit him in his home, Peter spoke the words that should burn in your hearts and minds always: "You know well enough," he said, "that a Jew is contaminated if he mingles with one of another race, or visits him: but God has been showing me that we ought not to speak of anyone as profane or unclean. . . . I see clearly enough," he said, "that God makes no distinction between man and man; he welcomes anybody, whatever his race, who fears Him and does what piety demands." (*Acts* 10: 28; 34-35.)[2]

---

2. In the Old Law, in order to preserve the purity and truth of the religion of the One True God, God had explicitly forbidden the Jews to mingle with foreign peoples who worshipped false gods. If a Jew mingled with them, he was considered ritually unclean, i.e., he was not permitted to rejoin his Jewish brethren in their religious rites until he had gone through a ceremony of purification.

Now the great danger to your apostolate today is that it may not be Catholic. You may begin to think that, unless people do the ordinary things of life your way, they cannot live the faith in Christ's way either. At a time when the greatest numbers of people in the world are fighting to be recognized as equal to ourselves, when they look for the faith that will show them the meaning of existence, we may give them the impression that they cannot be Christian unless they become like Americans; that they cannot be like Christ, unless they first become like us.

This is why the theme of your devotion today is the Catholic apostolate. In your effort to bring this great unity of the faith to all men and women, you must never force that faith into the narrow limits of your own social class, your own likes or dislikes, into the narrow limits of our American way of doing things.

But why should we talk only about the great world? Why speak about a Catholic apostolate to the nations of the East if you are not busy about a Catholic apostolate on your own block? Why talk about the Negroes in Africa if you have not busied yourself in a thoroughly Catholic way about justice for the Negroes in New York? Why talk about missions to India if you have not shown concern for the greatest challenge that God has given us in the coming of the Puerto Ricans to New York?

If we are thrilled at the thought that here at our Devotion, the children of Our Lady, white and colored, are assembled in a unity of love, that the black children of Our Lady in the Congo are united with us in prayer and praise today, we should be tireless until every colored child of God is certain that his color will not prevent him from mingling with us on our own block, in our own club, in our own business. If we fail in this, we may fail because we have not been Catholic; because we have locked our faith within the limits of a neighborhood or a race – we will not allow the life of Christ to break across the boundaries of color in order to make us all one.

Likewise with the Puerto Ricans: This is a question not of bringing them to the faith of Christ; because almost all of them are Catholics. With them it is a question of showing them love and respect and understanding which they deserve from us as their brothers and sisters in Christ.

Many of them are among the finest Catholics in New York; many others through no fault of their own, nor through any fault of the priests who have labored so generously among them, have never received the training in the faith which you enjoy. Last year in Puerto Rico, for about 2,200,000 Catholics there were 290 priests. At the same time in the New

York diocese with 1,300,000 Catholics, there were 2,400 priests. Is it any wonder they do not have instruction! It seems to me that, in the face of the difficulty of sending priests to Puerto Rico, God in His Providence has decided to bring the people here to enjoy the more abundant care we can provide. God brings them to us now, by thousands every month, and our love and respect and understanding will have much to do in deciding whether they will learn to enjoy the richness of a full Catholic life, or whether they will lose the faith they now have.

And if we fail here, it may also be due to the same fault which our Devotion here this afternoon is aimed at correcting. We may fail because we are not Catholic enough, because we do not think the Puerto Ricans can be Catholic unless they become just like us. We want them to do things our way the minute they step off the plane. We may forget that they come from an entirely different culture: they come from a tradition of Spanish Catholicism, into a city which is entirely different. What is more, they suffer all the trials that every group of immigrants before them has suffered; uprooted from the Island they love, they are thrown into the bewildering city of New York. Strangers in a strange land, unfamiliar with the language, anxious and afraid, they come here looking for a better life. The one thing that they should find here which is the same in Puerto Rico is their Catholic faith. This should be their refuge, this should be the bridge to make the passage easy. We should be the ones whose understanding and love should make their welcome a Christian one. This is the challenge that God gives to your apostolate. This is not easy. It has never been easy for people to understand the stranger. But of what value is our faith unless it gives us the grace and strength to receive the stranger as our own?

This is your apostolate then. To be caught by the great vision of the meaning of your faith. To rise above the petty limits of your own life, your own likes, your own social class; to see the meaning of the unity which our faith and our faith alone can bring to men and women. And above all to be "Catholic," determined that all men and women must be embraced in a faith that makes them one with us in Christ, but leaves them their own identity as children of God.

4

Catholic Responsibilities and New York's Puerto Ricans[1]

ALMOST A HUNDRED YEARS BEFORE HENDRICK HUDSON TOOK POSSESSION of New York in the name of the Dutch, a Spanish mariner, Esteban Gomes, sailing for the King of Spain, found his way into New York harbor, looked around at it, decided it wasn't promising enough, and sailed away. It is interesting to speculate what might have happened if Esteban had stayed and if the Spanish had begun to colonize what is now Manhattan Island.

Strangely enough, the spot that did not become a Spanish settlement then shows many more signs of being a kind of Spanish settlement now. The language is heard in every corner of the city; many a bus might be travelling a main route in San Juan, so many of its passengers are Puerto Rican; and riders on the East Side or the Broadway subways will find the language quite as common as Italian or Yiddish must have been fifty years ago.

For the newest of the New Yorkers have been arriving in fairly large numbers in recent years, and New York is conscious that the latest of the great migrations to the city has been under way. At the beginning of 1955, it was estimated that more than half a million Puerto Ricans were living in the city, that is, either people born in Puerto Rico or children born here to Puerto Rican parents. During 1954 the number coming from the island dropped off sharply, but latest reports indicate that the trend has reversed again and that 1955 may see almost as many coming from the island as came during the record year of 1953.

Of course, this has raised a cry of distress from the older citizens of the city. Those who are more favorably disposed toward the Puerto Ricans think it is unfortunate that they should be allowed to come to an overcrowded city and live in poor conditions. Something should be done

---

1. *Integrity*, July 1955, pp. 12-21.

to keep them on their beautiful island, or at least to get them out to other sections of the country. Those less favorably disposed repeat the familiar accusations that they are the cause of our delinquency, that they ruin every neighborhood they move into, that they will not learn English and mingle with "Americans"; in brief, that with the coming of the Puerto Ricans, the great experience that was New York is coming to an end.

This is familiar criticism to one who knows something of previous migrations to the city. The same accusations have been levelled at every new people as they arrived. Yet each new group has brought new energy, new ideas, a new challenge that would not let the city rest. New York is much more New York in 1955 than it was in 1855, and it is what it is because the stranger came from the cities of England and Germany, from the hills of Ireland and the farms of southern Italy. There is every reason to hope that New York will continue to be great as the Puerto Ricans lend a touch of Latin America to the mingling of the nations that has made the city what it is.

To Catholics in particular this new migration offers a great challenge, but an even greater promise. The day is not far past when all our people were strangers themselves in this strange land. As the children of immigrant peoples, there should be no one more alert or anxious than the Catholics of the city to understand what a migration means, and to receive the newcomers who seek to share the blessings that God has so abundantly given to us. But furthermore, the Puerto Ricans are Catholics themselves. If they are accepted into the community of Catholics in the city, they will become an important and dynamic part of the life of the Church in the next generation. If they are not accepted, and many of them lost to the faith, the responsibility will rest heavily on our consciences in the years ahead.

In examining the nature of this migration, it is important to keep it in perspective. Actually, in numbers, it cannot begin to compare with the great migrations of the past. Thus far only about half a million Puerto Rican-born have come to all parts of the United States. But during the great migrations, more than six million German-born came here; almost five million Italian-born and more than four and a half million Irish-born. The Puerto Ricans have a long way to go before they begin to match the movement of peoples from Europe in the past. Nor is there any need to fear an avalanche of people from the island. They come from a tiny island, no larger than Long Island. There are 2,400,000 people in the island population. If they all came, it would still not amount to a migration comparable to those of earlier years.

Puerto Ricans on Relief

Secondly, in estimating their impact on the city's life, it is important to keep in mind the experience of earlier people. The earlier migrations were a much heavier burden on the life and resources of the people of New York. Nevertheless, despite the difficulties and conflicts, New York residents received the earlier immigrants with surprising charity and generosity. New York has been a great, great city. In the early days of the city's history, many of the eastern states had laws forbidding ship captains from unloading poor immigrants at their shores. On their way to those states, the ship captains would stop at New York to leave the immigrants at this port which would never turn them away. New York received them, sheltered them, poured out money to care for them. As early as 1790, the largest single item on the city's budget was the relief of the poor. In 1796, the Commissioners of the Almshouse reported that this expense was the result of ". . . the prodigious influx of immigrants into the City. . ." and cited as an example the Irish immigrants ". . . many of whom having paid their last shilling to the captain, are landed destitute and emaciated."[2] If it was this way in 1796, one can imagine what it must have been when the flood of immigration began to sweep in fifty years later. There were 40 Irishmen on relief in 1785, 148 in 1796, and 2000 in 1855.[3] Relief, it seems, is no new phenomenon in the city's history. This must be kept in mind by anyone who wishes to estimate the significance of Puerto Ricans on relief. Considering the difficulties which the Puerto Ricans face, the number on relief is surprisingly small.[4] Granted that the nature of relief has changed considerably in the last century, nevertheless it seems that children of former immigrants should only rightly look upon this generosity as a means to repay the debt that we owe for the great generosity shown to our own people when they came. There is little doubt that social historians, reviewing the behavior

---

2. S. L. Pomeranz, *New York, An American City* (N.Y., 1938), pp. 333-34.

3. Robert Ernst, *Immigrant Life in New York City* (N.Y., 1949), p. 40.

4. Estimates in 1954 indicated that about 8% of the people on relief were Puerto Rican, most of them dependent children. At that time about 5% of the City's population was Puerto Rican. Cf. A. J. Jaffe (ed.) *Puerto Rican Population of New York City* (N.Y. Bureau of Applied Social Research, Columbia Univ., 1954), p. 47. *The New York Times* (6/9/55) reported Commissioner McCarthy as saying that the number of Puerto Ricans on relief has increased during the past year. Most of them were seeking "supplementary relief." They were working but not earning enough to support their families.

of New York toward the immigrants of the 19th century, will look upon the past hundred and fifty years of New York City as a social miracle.

As a matter of fact, the city was probably never as well organized or equipped to handle an influx of people as it is today. A century ago there was no public housing, no Department of Welfare, no employment services, no organized Catholic Charities, no extensive hospital and health facilities. It is a marvel that the older immigrants survived as well as they did. Now all of these highly organized services are at hand to assist the poor and the newcomer.

Why do the Puerto Ricans come? They come for the same reason that all the earlier people came before them. They come from a very crowded island, fleeing from poverty, looking for a world that offers a better opportunity for work and advancement. The island government has been engaging in some remarkable programs for social reform, but in a few years, has not been able to correct the difficulties which accumulated over the course of a few centuries. What is more, the Puerto Ricans are American citizens and have every right to come to the mainland unimpeded. When they arrive, they face the main problems that every immigrant group has faced before them.

Housing

As with every other immigrant group, as with the Negroes and many other people today, the problem of housing for the Puerto Ricans is a terrible nightmare. These are days, certainly, when the Spirit of the Lord should be urging every conscientious soul most strongly to face the problem of housing. It is interesting to note how concerned Our Lord was about "giving homes to the homeless." When He spoke about the last judgment, He did not emphasize as the *first* law that His followers would get to Heaven because they were sober, or industrious or chaste. Rather He emphasized: "Come, ye blessed of my Father. . . . When I was homeless, you took me in." Far from being zealous to keep the Puerto Ricans out, the spirit of Christ should prompt us to help them find a decent home and to protect them from becoming victims of conditions that will turn their neighborhoods into slums.

The conditions that create a slum are fairly well recognized today. One cannot simply say that Puerto Ricans or any other group create them. They move into them because they are too poor to move into better houses. Or, when they have the money, the "respectable" citizens do not want them around. They are forced to take whatever they can get. Unscrupulous landlords exploit their terrible need by putting twenty families in a house that was built for ten; never fixing the place properly because the Puerto Rican people cannot complain. They have no other place to go. Thus a speculating landlord can turn an apartment into a slum by overcrowding it for his own profit.[5] I could run down the list of my Puerto Rican friends and it is a sorry litany: one had to slip a $350 bonus to a landlady to get a meager three room place for five people; another paid $1200 to buy the furniture of the apartment from the previous tenant. He then sold it all as junk for fifteen dollars. A third paid a $600 bonus to a supervisor and was trapped into an eviction a few months later. The neighbors then make it worse by running away because: "The Spanish are coming." Puerto Ricans themselves often extend this overcrowding, many times out of a desperate effort to help their relatives or friends. As long as the poor have been coming to New York, the pattern has been the same. The marvel of it is that so many Puerto Rican families can put up with these incredible surroundings, and maintain a wholesome family life in a home that they keep remarkably neat and clean despite the environment.[6]

Once again, in estimating the housing situation of the Puerto Ricans, perspective is important. Irishmen will recall with sadness the old sixth ward and the "Five Points." Here where the earliest of the Irish gathered was a neighborhood notorious for bad housing, crime and disease. The better citizens shunned the spot, but thousands of good Irish families lived there, law abiding and respectable in the midst of its attics, cellars, etc., anywhere where they could find room within their tiny income. Others, Germans and Irish alike moved out to the edge of the city where they put up little shacks for themselves, the Germans in the area around Murray Hill, the Irish on the West side between 40th and 18th Streets. There was no place else to go. Cellar dwellers became a problem. Out of a population of about 500,000 in 1850, 29,000 lived in cellars. These were not the neat, trim basements of today. They were damp, unsanitary and unventilated, water was not plentiful for washing, and sewage was inadequate if it existed at all.[7]

Italians should still be alive who remember "Mulberry Bend." The city had to level it in 1890 and turn it into a park. But, by 1890 many a poor family had spent years there. Jacob Riis gave a description of the area in 1890:

---

5. For a vivid description of the experience as it happens, cf. A. Yezierska, "The Lower Depths of Upper Broadway," *The Reporter*, Jan. 19, 1954.

6. Cf. John McKeon's beautiful story of a fine Puerto Rican family, "The Ortiz Family," *Jubilee*, June 1953.

7. Ernst, *op. cit.* p. 49.

> Something like forty families are packed into five, old, two story and attic houses that were built to hold five, and out in the yards, additional crowds are, or were until recently accommodated in shacks, built on all sorts of old boards and used as drying racks by the Italian stock.

This was not East Harlem, 1955. It was the Lower East Side, 1890. It appears that history repeats itself.

The real danger involved in all judgments about living conditions is the danger that the poor condition of a neighborhood may be turned into a moral judgment against the people themselves. Their homes appear dilapidated and worthless; therefore the people in them must be worthless too. The dirtiness of the neighborhood is attributed to something dirty or irresponsible in the people themselves, and, in a very large number of cases, this is not true. In the light of this, it is helpful to recall a Report of the Select Committee appointed to examine the conditions of tenant houses in New York and Brooklyn, 1857:

> But we must pass over without description hundreds of dilapidated, dirty and densely populated old structures which the committee inspected in different wards and which come under the head of *re-adapted, reconstructed or altered* buildings. In most of them the Irish are predominant as occupants; though in some streets Negroes are found swarming from cellar to garret of tottering tenant houses. In this connection it may be well to remark that in some of the better classes of houses built for tenantry, Negroes have been preferred as occupants to Irish or German poor; the incentive of possessing comparatively decent quarters appearing to inspire the colored residents with more desire for personal cleanliness and regard for property than is impressed upon the whites of their own condition. . . . [8]

I have italicized three significant words: re-adapted, reconstructed and altered buildings. That means putting ten families in a house that was built for two; throwing up partitions in a warehouse and renting them as apartments, etc. History does not change, and the exploitation of the poor continues by the same elementary methods. The Germans and the Irish involved in this a century ago need no defense. Most of them were stable, devoted, good family people, caught in the grind of poverty in a strange world. Knowledge of their experience may help us get a new perspective with regard to the difficulties of Puerto Ricans with housing today.

---

8. Quoted in Edith Abbott, *Historical Aspects of the Immigration Problem* (Chicago, 1926), p. 635.

Delinquency

When delinquency strikes the Puerto Ricans, it is part of the problem of their "uprooting" from their native land, of being lost as strangers in a strange world. They come from a beautiful island where they are never cold, where life moves at a much more quiet pace, where they are close to the love and devotion of family, friends and neighbors. They live for the most part in little single houses of two or three rooms, away from traffic where children can run and play without care. They have never ridden on a train or seen a subway in their lives. Then they are uprooted, swept quickly into the bewildering confusion and speed and noise of New York. Not knowing the language, not familiar with our ways, they begin to know the suffering that all other immigrants have felt so acutely before them. Their lives can become disorganized, their children are taught a way of life which they, as parents, do not understand, and if there is any weakness in the family, the slip toward delinquency can be an easy one. Unfortunately, there is a weakness in a large number of these families which leaves them exposed to these difficulties. There is a background of consensual marriages in the tradition of the island (a type of common law marriage) which, among other things, has not made for stability in some of the Puerto Rican families.

However, in any discussion of delinquency, a number of points must be kept in mind. In the first place, delinquency is not something that Puerto Ricans bring with them. It is something that happens to them when they get here. As we are realizing to a greater degree every day, delinquency is a characteristic of the large American city, and it is increasing alarmingly all over, in many cities where there are no Puerto Ricans as well as in cities where there are many. When the control of the family over the child weakens, the child is exposed to the types of delinquency that are prevalent here, and the sad story starts. It would be well to read the summary of the Senate Subcommittee Hearings on Juvenile Delinquency if anyone needs assurance that delinquency is not the difficulty of any particular race or class or ethnic group.[9] It is striking all segments of American society to a very disturbing degree.

Secondly, although the types of delinquency have become more serious, it is important to keep in mind that delinquency was a problem of earlier immigrants also. . . . If the Germans and the Irish with their remarkably strong faith, their good family life, were unable to protect some of their children from delinquency, it would be unreasonable to

9. Richard Clendennen and H. W. Beaser, "The Shame of America," *Saturday Evening Post*, Jan. 8 through February 5, 1955.

expect the Puerto Ricans to do better, especially since they are living in a much more troubled world. The important thing for Catholics to do in this situation is to center their attention, not on the troublesome families among the Puerto Ricans, but on the large majority of sincere and honest people who are trying to bring up their families in the midst of trying circumstances. The most effective way of helping the Puerto Ricans avoid delinquency or diminish the delinquency that exists does not consist of casting criticism at the Puerto Ricans, but of trying to make the "uprooting" a little easier through understanding, respect and charity, and of accepting them as brothers and sisters in Christ. . . .

Will We Give them Opportunity?

This, then, is the challenge: to receive the Puerto Rican with respect as our brother or sister in Christ; to give them the opportunity to develop their Catholic life beside us, as our equals in the same school, the same parish, the same neighborhood.

The one thing that is the same in Puerto Rico and in New York is their Catholic faith. This should be the bridge to make their passage easy; this should be the link to bind us together into one. This is not easy. It has never been easy for people to welcome the stranger. But it has never been easy either to be strangers in our land. Nevertheless beneath all custom and culture is the common life of Christ that makes us one. If this is strong enough in the hearts of New York Catholics to express itself in their social relations as well as in their personal devotion, the challenge will be met, and with God's grace, hundreds of thousands of Puerto Ricans will give the Church new vigor in the generations to come.

5

The Integration of Puerto Ricans[1]

THE PRESENT STATE OF THEORY CONCERNING THE ADJUSTMENT OF PEOPLE to a new culture would seem to suggest the following: No strong effort should be made to disorganize the community which immigrants or migrants may form as they move into the area of a new culture; they should be permitted to form into communities of their own where they will have security, stability, and order as they gradually learn American ways; efforts should be made to help the immigrant preserve a genuine respect for his own culture as well as acquire a knowledge of the new one; similar efforts should be made to cultivate in the older residents a respect for the culture of the newcomers; opportunities for association with older residents must not be blocked for the newcomers, the job and the school being the two which will be first in order of time, the neighborhood second as the immigrant community begins to weaken and its members disperse. In this situation, the immigrant community will not shut its members off from a gradual integration with their new culture; neither will it be blocked off in a ghetto-like segregation by the resistance of the older residents.

This, of course, is an ideal pattern which will never be wholly carried out in practice. But it is the policy which seems to be suggested by current theories.

In view of this, it is important to examine some of the experiences of the latest group to move into the Eastern part of the United States in large numbers. These are the Puerto Ricans. They are citizens of the United States, and in that sense, do not come from a foreign country. But they do come from a culture quite different from that which prevails on the mainland, and their adjustment to life on the mainland involves difficulties very similar to those of the immigrants of previous years.

---

1. Reprinted by permission of the publisher from *Thought*, 30, No. 118 (Autumn 1955), Copyright© 1955 by Fordham University Press, pp. 402-20.

It is unfortunate that so little empirical data is available on the experience of the Puerto Ricans.[2] Nevertheless a brief review of their experience will be helpful in enabling an evaluation of their adjustment against the background of theory which has just been reviewed.

Dispersal in New York

One of the most striking things about the coming of the Puerto Ricans is their dispersal into almost every corner of New York. There are noticeably large concentrations of them in East Harlem, in the South Bronx, on the Lower East Side and in downtown Brooklyn. But in considerable numbers they are scattering into almost every section of the City. This is reflected in the large number of public schools that have Puerto Ricans in attendance in large numbers, and in the parishes, so many of which require the assistance of a Spanish-speaking priest.[3]

This scattering is due to a number of factors. In the first place, the city is terribly crowded and built up, and Puerto Ricans must seek any kind of housing anywhere they can find it. They find it in the areas where the old tenements, built for an earlier generation of immigrants, are beginning to decay. These were privately built tenements, rented to large groups of Jews or Italians or Irish who wished to stay together in a neighborhood where they knew others and were known themselves.

Now, as the second and third generation of the older immigrant groups move to the suburbs, the Puerto Ricans move in any place in the city where they can find space. Therefore the possibility of concentration is diminished.

When the city attempts to provide new housing, the situation becomes more complicated. The only new housing which is within the reach of poor people today is low-rent public housing. When this is provided, two interesting phenomena appear which had never affected

---

2. The latest survey published on the migration (and it is a survey rather than an intensive inquiry into specific questions) was the one prepared by C. W. Mills and Clarence Senior, *Puerto Rican Journey*. The data for this were gathered in 1947 and are already quite out of date. Much more limited surveys have been done by Oberlin College on *Puerto Ricans in Lorain, Ohio*, and of the Puerto Ricans in Philadelphia by the Mayor's Committee on Human Relations. These surveys are excellent as far as they go. But they do not go into detail on the problem of the "community life" of the Puerto Rican people.

3. In the area of Manhattan and the Bronx alone, there are at least seventy-five Catholic churches with special provisions for Spanish-speaking parishioners. Whatever else this may mean, it certainly indicates an extraordinary spread of Puerto Ricans.

the older immigrants. When slums are cleared and many square blocks of houses demolished to make way for new public housing, thousands of families are forcibly dispersed into any section of the city where they can find rooms, or where the city can find rooms for them. Therefore, if any concentration of Puerto Ricans had begun to form in this area, it is forcibly dispersed and the members of this growing community of migrants are scattered in many directions.

What is more, when the low-cost public housing is ready, families are not admitted on the basis that they are Irish or Jewish or Negro or Puerto Rican, and they would like to be with a group of families of their own kind. A very strict renting list is followed, giving priority to those who applied first, or who are veterans, or who are most in need, etc. Consequently, the low-cost public housing is, by policy and practice, integrated housing with no discrimination permitted on the basis of race, creed, color, or ethnic background.

The reasons for this firm policy of non-segregated housing are many and convincing, and they are rooted in some unfortunate historical situations. In general, segregated housing in the United States has not been segregated because the occupants wanted to be by themselves and away from others. Rather it was generally the result of racial discrimination which forbade Negro groups particularly, and occasionally other ethnic or religious groups simply because they were Negro or Jewish, etc., from moving out of their area into a new one when they tried to do so. In order to correct the injustices involved in this kind of discrimination, a strict policy of nondiscrimination is followed in public housing.

This obviously means that the concentrations of immigrants in neighborhoods which often reproduced the flavor of the old country will no longer be possible for the migrants from Puerto Rico who move into the housing projects.

The case histories of some of these families is a vivid indication of the way they are literally "pushed around" by slum clearance, housing development, new city projects or redevelopments. The insecurity, the rapid mobility to which these people are subjected can just about be imagined. This is further complicated by the fact that public officials, in a desperate effort to locate unused land where they can build without first demolishing existing structures, have located some of the low-rent public houses in the midst of old, established middle class neighborhoods where bitter resentment is frequently visited on the families in the projects, who are accused of ruining the neighborhood. A consideration of the merits of this policy is beyond the scope of the present paper. Nor is any criticism of this policy implied here. It may prove in the next twenty years to have been the wisest of policies. It is simply mentioned here as part of the situation which the new migrant to New York must face.

In this situation, it is doubtful whether the Puerto Ricans will be able to form the type of community which earlier immigrants formed. If they do, they will have done it in circumstances much more difficult than those faced by earlier immigrant groups. If this more rapid intermingling with other Americans prevents the formation of strong Puerto Rican communities, will that hasten their integration into American culture; or will the loss of that stability which the immigrant derived from his immigrant community show itself in a noticeable disintegration of their social life, psychological unrest, even forms of antisocial behavior? No one knows the answer to this yet. But the experience in process should be able to provide the answer within the next generation.

The Integrated Parish

Another important aspect of the Puerto Rican experience has been the apparent policy to integrate them as parishioners in existing territorial parishes rather than form national parishes for them as a particular group.[4] A number of rather convincing reasons have prompted this policy. It is a reflection to some extent of the scattered location of the Puerto Ricans in this city. If national parishes were created, at least one third of the parishioners in a great number of existing territorial parishes would be lost to these parishes, and this would involve a multiplication of churches and services which would apparently be unwise. Secondly, almost all of the dioceses in the country which have had the tradition of national parishes for the immigrant groups are now faced with the difficulty of what to do with these parishes as young people of the third generation move away, or no longer speak the language if they stay. Finally, there is a widespread conviction that a much more positive effort toward integration within the territorial parish will hasten the adjustment of the Puerto Rican to the customs of the mainland parish.

Where this practice of the integrated parish is adopted, it is clearly acknowledged that an intermediate process must take place, that special services must be provided in Spanish, and opportunity given for the practice of traditional customs and devotions by the new parishioners. Otherwise, the adjustment to an entirely American parish would be too great a shock for most of them to take.

---

4. I refer here primarily to the practice in the New York Archdiocese where the largest number of migrants have settled.

Nevertheless the process may inhibit formation of those closely knit communities, centered around the practice of the faith, which were characteristic of earlier immigrant groups, and it is one more factor impeding the development of a community of migrants.

Social Services

One final factor preventing the formation of a strong community of Puerto Ricans in the sense of the immigrant communities of earlier days is the fact that, within the past thirty years, the development of public social services has taken over so many of the functions of mutual assistance which the immigrant communities often provided for themselves.

This does not imply that there is not an extraordinary amount of loyalty to friend and family, of great charity and assistance for one another in their neighborhoods. Their informal adoption of children, their willingness always to take someone else in a home that is already overcrowded, their willingness to share their meager possessions – these are all impressive indications of the kind of mutual assistance which often fades out as people become more American.

Nevertheless, there are public benefits available today which relieve the new community of much of the burden which once was the basis for much of its solidarity. Public welfare exists for those who are in financial need; employment services, both of the State, of the Office of the Commonwealth of Puerto Rico, of the Archdiocese of New York and Brooklyn, are all available to help men and women to find work; social security, minimum wage laws and maximum hour laws, low-cost public housing for those who need homes. On the side of private agencies, Catholic Charities is a highly developed organization applying a great many of its resources to the assistance of Puerto Ricans; and labor unions can exert their power to protect the newly arrived worker.

All of the services just mentioned can be quite inadequate, can suffer from improper administration and inefficiency, can harass the needy person with red tape. Nevertheless, at the critical moment, they are often on hand to assist. And the immigrant community which years ago had to bear the burden of its own poor and needy now no longer plays as important a role as the generous supporter of the immigrants or migrants.

The accumulation of these services again weakens the bonds that used to hold together the members of a migrant community. Quite apart from the Puerto Ricans, it has been noted by some of the political writers that the old form of "boss politics" has declined since the time when the machine took care of the needs of its people.[5] One of the important factors in the decline of the "political machine" has been the shift to public welfare of many of the services once fulfilled by the political boss, often the patron of the immigrant community. And the solidarity of the machine was often only one aspect of the solidarity of the immigrant neighborhood.

In summary, therefore, all these factors seem to be working against the formation of a strong migrant community among the Puerto Ricans. With no such strong community to act as a society in transition for them, will they suffer from great disorganization which might otherwise have been avoided, or will their adjustment to American life be more rapid than that of the others? There are two favorable factors in the situation which must be mentioned – the familiarity of the Puerto Rican with American culture before he comes here, and the more favorable attitude toward people of other cultures that has been cultivated by increasing emphasis on the possibility of cultural pluralism.

American Influence

To some extent, the Puerto Ricans have a head start toward adjustment before they come to the mainland. The Island has been a United States possession for more than half a century, and Puerto Ricans have enjoyed citizenship for almost forty years. American methods of education were introduced into the Island shortly after it became an American possession. This was carried to a point where English became the standard language of instruction until after many years this was changed to Spanish in the mid-thirties. Since that time, English is a compulsory study at all levels of instruction.

It is doubtful whether classroom instruction alone can communicate an understanding of a different culture to children who all day long are immersed in their own culture. Nevertheless, the Puerto Rican has been given at least this much formal introduction to life on the mainland which earlier immigrants had not enjoyed.

Within more recent years, a much more noticeable impact has been made upon the Puerto Ricans by advertising, radio, magazines, movies, business houses from the mainland, American tourists, and the return of large numbers of students who have come to mainland schools. Missionaries, both Protestant and Catholic, have all made the culture of the mainland a very real thing to the people on the Island. Most significant of all, however, in more recent years, has been the return to Puerto Rico

---

5. Cf. Penniman, *Sait's American Parties and Elections*, chap. xvi-xvii.

of the migrant himself. Actually, the movement of Puerto Ricans to the mainland could be better described as a form of commuting rather than a migration, so many move back and forth every year.[6] There is no one better able to communicate an understanding of "the way it is done" on the mainland than the brother or cousin or father who has been here and is now returning. This is not the first time that this has happened. Italian immigrants moved back to Italy in large numbers. But it is doubtful whether the movement was ever proportionately as extensive as it is among the Puerto Ricans.[7] All those things taken together represent an impact of the mainland culture on the Puerto Rican much greater than had been made on earlier immigrant groups before they came.

It is possible that such an introduction into the culture of the mainland may make the transition easier; that the Puerto Rican may not find it necessary to rely so much upon the support of his fellow migrants.

Emphasis on Cultural Pluralism

It is a strange irony that, at a time when much more respect is being shown for the role of the immigrant community, a set of circumstances exists which may hinder its development.

Nevertheless, whether the immigrant community develops or not, there is much more widespread understanding of the nature of cultural transition today than there was half a century ago. This is accompanied by a greater respect for the culture of the migrant group and an effort to spare them the distress of the uprooting as far as that is possible. This has resulted in New York in admirable efforts to make the transition for the Puerto Ricans as smooth as possible.

This is certainly true on the level of official policy. On the level of community leaders, people of some influence and education, strong public statements against the Puerto Ricans would not be tolerated, or at least would be severely criticized.

---

6. Within the past few years, generally about half a million passengers per year travelled between San Juan and the mainland. Balancing the outgoing passengers against the incoming, the net out-migration of people in 1954 was only 21,000; in 1953 it was 73,000. Many of the other passengers are obviously tourists, students, business and government officials. But large numbers of them also are migrants going back to the Island after they have been here.

7. During the years of heaviest Italian immigration, from 1905 to 1914, often half as many Italians would go back to Italy as came here. Cf. Foerster, *Italian Emigration in our Time* (Cambridge, Mass., 1922).

Nevertheless, there is still a great deal of resentment against them among people of influence and education as well as among older city residents in the neighborhoods, the taverns, the workshops, the supermarkets, even in the church.

Which of these two influences will predominate is difficult to say. In widespread programs of education, the effort is being made, probably greater than ever before, to dispose the older New Yorker to accept the Puerto Rican. If this can neutralize the hostility or resentment that manifests itself also very widely, the influence of the emphasis on cultural pluralism may be able to smooth the transition in the areas where Puerto Rican is intermingled with Negro or Irish or Jew or Italian or any other of the many ethnic groups in New York City.

These are factors in the situation which make the migration of the Puerto Ricans somewhat different than that of the immigrants before them. The experience of the next generation will answer a number of questions and throw a great deal of light on the importance of the community that immigrants or migrants tend to form as soon as they move into a new culture.

It is possible that the Puerto Ricans will succeed in establishing a strong community in spite of the obstacles. If they do not, it may appear that their experience was a smoother one than that of the immigrant groups before them. In this case, it will be necessary to determine whether this was due to the fact that they were forced to intermingle with the older residents much more rapidly; or because they were somewhat familiar with American culture before they came; or because the emphasis on cultural pluralism created an atmosphere of acceptance which earlier immigrants did not enjoy.

Out of the experience, it should be possible for scholars to learn whether the immigrant community is so important that people will develop it against great obstacles, whether its absence retards the process of integration, or whether the understanding of culture and the emphasis on cultural pluralism can compensate for its absence.

6

Mexicans and Puerto Ricans
Build a Bridge[1]

IT IS BECOMING CLEAR THAT THE CATHOLIC CHURCH IN THE WESTERN Hemisphere may experience a period of triumph or tragedy during the century ahead. This issue may be settled largely in Latin America. It follows that the role of the Spanish-speaking Church will be a crucial one.

The Church in the United States will be called upon to take a serious part in meeting this challenge. Thus, Spanish-speaking Catholics in the United States may become a factor of increasing importance to the welfare of the Church. They may become the link which binds the Catholics of North and South America together in a new and greater era.

If this is so, then it throws a new and serious light on the apostolate to the Spanish-speaking in the United States. The teaching of catechism to Puerto Rican children in East Harlem or the organizing of Catholic Action among Mexican teenagers are no longer tasks that are "local" to New York or San Antonio. They are part of the larger challenge that the Church must face during the next few generations.

The problem of Latin America is a question of simple arithmetic. It has the most rapidly growing population in the world. It has also a very slow-growing clergy. Numbers are madly outracing available spiritual resources. In 1950, Latin America had a population of 162 million (Mexico and the Caribbean Islands included). This population is expected to double before 1980; by the year 2000, Latin America, with more than half a billion people, may have twice the population of the United States and Canada combined.

---

1. *America*, December 31, 1955. Reprinted with the permission of America Press, Inc., 106 West 56th Street, New York, NY 10019. ©1955 All Rights Reserved.

Population projections are risky, but there is no doubt that population-wise Latin America will demand a lot of attention in years to come. At the same time, the number of newly ordained priests in Latin America last year equaled only 671 or one new priest for every 7,000 new people. Moreover, almost one third of these priests were in Mexico. This population increase in an area nominally Catholic, where shortage of priests is alarming and lack of religious training appalling, highlights what people mean when they say that a major victory or defeat for the Church may be settled in Latin America in the next half century.

All this brings into new focus the importance of the apostolate to the Spanish-speaking in the United States, an apostolate which is assuming considerable proportions. There are now more than half a million Puerto Ricans in New York City, and 30,000 more will have arrived by the end of this year. Almost one-third of the Archdiocese of New York is now Spanish-speaking. The Puerto Ricans' birth rate is twice as high as that of the white population as a whole, and 40 percent of their population is under 15 years of age. Numbers, plus youth, plus a high birth rate, mean that the city and the Archdiocese will become noticeably Spanish.

Of course, New York is only one small part of the picture. A tradition of Spanish Catholicism had existed in the Southwest long before European immigrants brought the faith to our east coast. But now the increasing influx of Mexicans is coming into sharper contact with American cities, bringing the problems of the Spanish-speaking more vividly to the attention of Mexican and American alike. Estimates say there are at least three million people of Mexican origin in the Southwest. In 1953, 17,500 Mexicans came legally into the States; in 1954 the number exceeded 36,000; no one knows how many hundreds of thousands have come illegally as "wetbacks" and stayed here.

Apart from the Mexicans, 33,000 Cubans have come to the States in the past eight years; 14,000 more are expected to come this year. It appears that the population pattern of the Puerto Ricans holds true for these people also; high birth rates, large youthful population. This means that the Spanish-speaking population may soon begin to approach the proportions of some of the great migrations of the past century. If this is true, the success of our apostolate to the Spanish-speaking will be a critical matter for the welfare of the Church in the United States.

In view of all this, it is quite significant that only a month ago His Eminence, Cardinal Spellman, circulated among his priests the *Report of the Conference on the Spiritual Care of Puerto Rican Migrants*. This is a report of a conference, sponsored by their Excellencies, Bishop James P. Davis of San Juan, P.R. and Bishop James E. McManus, C.SS.R., of Ponce, P.R.

The conference was held last spring during Easter week. It brought together 35 priests from 16 mainland dioceses, and 77 priests from the two dioceses in Puerto Rico. They came to discuss methods of providing spiritual care for the Puerto Ricans before they come to the mainland, after they settle in mainland cities, or when they come as seasonal workers on mainland farms.

Many of the priests at the conference had had long experience climbing the steep mountains of Puerto Rico or the shaky steps of tenements in Harlem or the lower East side. They knew the satisfaction and frustration, the hope and discouragement of this great apostolate.

The Conference

One New York priest, for instance, had taken a census in April 1954. He had 3,000 Puerto Ricans in his parish, and he was overwhelmed by the work. He took another census in November; the number had risen to 5,000. In April, on one single block, he had found 26 Puerto Rican families. In November he found 26 families, but 21 of them were different – about an 80 percent turnover in eight months. The priest has his heart set on opening a school or a community center. Now the city officials tell him they are planning to demolish a large section of his parish for the erection of a middle-income housing project. Thus will the flock be scattered in the checker game of life that priest and Puerto Ricans lead in the shift and uncertainty of New York's neighborhoods.

One priest from an outstanding parish in Puerto Rico itself described the conditions under which he labors. There are 92,000 people in his parish; there are seven priests; the parish covers an area of one hundred square miles, much of it difficult mountain territory reached only on horseback. He has 500 children in his wonderful parochial schools; but 16,000 of his children are in the public schools.

These are typical accounts of a difficult apostolate, carried on in the face of great odds, frequent indifference and discouragingly increasing numbers. Sometimes, even to the zealous but overworked priests, it seems as though nothing were being accomplished.

Yet there was no pessimism at the conference. There was nothing but enthusiasm, generous devotion to the care of a people who, it was generally admitted, will reward that care abundantly in years to come. Signs were visible everywhere of the increasing vigor of Catholic life in the Island itself. Reports from the various mainland dioceses gave an inspiring account of heroic efforts being made. Testimony was universal that, if approached with understanding and respect, the Puerto Rican is most responsive and well disposed.

What makes the Puerto Rican migration unique in the experience of the United States is the fact that these are the first of our Catholics to come from a mission territory. They are the first Catholics who have come to the east coast from a land with a Spanish colonial tradition. They are the first Catholics who, in many instances, will face the situation of being integrated into existing territorial parishes, instead of into national parishes established for themselves.

All these factors add up to a new kind of apostolate. It is an extraordinary challenge, with unusual promise, but freighted also with unusual dangers. Success will bring to the American Church the added vigor, heroism and loyalty of the Spanish influence. Failure will leave unfulfilled the rich promise implicit in the migration of the Spanish-American to the United States.

The Missionary Parish

The fact that Puerto Ricans come from a mission territory means that spiritual care in a mainland parish becomes a missionary problem. The mission has simply been transferred from one place to another. It is true that many Puerto Ricans are well instructed and devout. But the level of their religious instruction in general is extremely low. It was clear to the priests who visited Puerto Rico why this is so. There is roughly one priest for every 7,000 Catholics. (New York City has one for 750.)

When the Puerto Rican comes to a mainland parish, he cannot be expected to fit into its established routine. He must be sought out; his confidence must be won; he must be patiently and sympathetically instructed and taught not only how to practice his faith, but how to practice it in a complicated, highly organized city parish.

Personal contact is essential. The Puerto Rican may not always be ready to follow a doctrine that is explained to him, but he will always follow a priest whom he has come to love. If this approach can be made – and this was the testimony of every priest who worked with them – the Puerto Rican will become a sincere and devoted Catholic.

The city parish, however, is not geared to a missionary apostolate. Nor has every priest the time or talent or disposition to engage in it effectively. But unless the city parish can adjust itself to the needs of its new flock, instead of insisting that the flock adjust itself to the parish, grave doubt was expressed whether the Puerto Rican apostolate could ever be successful.

Spanish Traditions

Secondly, the Puerto Rican comes from a land with a Spanish colonial tradition. His attachment to the Church was not founded so much on the basis of instruction and conviction as on that of social and religious customs – his medals, holy pictures, fiestas.

One of the great legacies of Spain was this immersion of its people in a culture which brought the faith into every corner of their lives and gave them a feeling of strong identification with what they called Catholic. They lived through the penetrating silence and reverence of Holy Thursday and Good Friday; wept with the Virgin in the great procession of the Sorrowful Mother; acted out in joyful drama the meeting of Mary and the Risen Jesus on Easter morning; brought the Infant into their homes before Christmas to assure Him of a shelter in their *posada*; took the place of the Three Kings bringing gifts to their children on Epiphany; recited the rosary for nine days after the death of a loved one; interspersed their speech with familiar reference to Our Lady and the saints; asked the blessing of parents on leaving or returning to their homes.

Respect for these customs, and an effort to preserve whatever can be salvaged of them, is not simply catering to trivialities. It is part of the effort needed to save what has been the faith for these many thousands of people. A pastor needs imagination and ingenuity in order to know what to try to preserve among his new parishioners' customs. But more important than that, he needs genuine reverence and appreciation for them and for the support they give to the faith until the day when instruction and conviction makes his new parishioners able to get along without them.

Added to this is the pain of the "uprooting" – inevitable in the transition to a new culture – the shift from a familiar world where they were at home to a new world where they are strangers. This strikes most sharply in the family, where Latin cultural patterns leave them exposed to serious difficulty. Twenty-five percent of the marriages in Puerto Rico itself are entered upon without civil or religious ceremony. It seems that half the Puerto Rican families on the mainland are not joined in Catholic marriage.

Integration in Existing Parishes

This change of culture and of religious customs would not be so great if Puerto Ricans were coming into parishes that were established just for them. When older immigrant groups came, whether German or Italian or Polish, they commonly established parishes where their own language was spoken, where many of their customs were preserved and where they were served by a clergy of their own culture and background. Some dioceses try to arrange this with the Puerto Ricans but often it is not possible or advisable.

They move into scattered sections of overcrowded cities, where they find themselves in the center of an existing parish, organized by Germans or Italians or Irish, with a clergy of different language and background, unfamiliar with Catholic life as the Puerto Ricans have known it. In such situations the practical policy adopted by some dioceses has been that of integrating them into the existing parish. There was no question that special services must be conducted in Spanish, and that the presence of a Spanish-speaking priest was essential.

Most important, the influx of new parishioners places on the older residents of the parish a special obligation to accept the Puerto Rican as a first-class member of the parish. Integration, as was frequently remarked at the conference, is a two-way street. If the Puerto Ricans are to be integrated with the older residents, this implies that the older residents must also be integrated with the Puerto Ricans.

As a consequence, "human relations" becomes not just a form of "do-goodism" but an essential part of this vital apostolate. It consists of the effort on the part of older residents to understand the background of the Puerto Ricans, to respect them, to share with them the opportunity of participating in the common life of the parish.

These were but a few of the important items discussed at the conference. There were high hopes that they would be the starting point of a more systematic and effective apostolate which would insure that the Spanish-speaking become a vigorous part of the Church in the United States.

To Build a Bridge

Here in the midst of a Caribbean Island, where the cultures of Latin America and North America meet, there was also a great confidence that the emigration of the Latin Americans may, in God's providence, be preparing for the future greatness of the Church in Latin America. If the Spanish-speaking in the United States become a vigorous and well-instructed Catholic people, they will be the very ones who can serve as the cultural and religious link between the two parts of our hemisphere.

Coming from the Latin tradition themselves, they will have an understanding of the Spanish-American which the North American has found it difficult to cultivate. They will share the background of the ideals and character that have made the Spanish great. What is more, they will have received the best that a vigorous and well-organized Church in the United States has been able to give them. They will, in their own lives, be the bridge between two worlds, a symbol of the Church itself – one in faith but manifold in culture. But they can do this only if we older Americans have the grace and the wisdom to accept generously the challenge that God has given us.

7

Commentary in *Fox-Sight:*
Telling the Vision of Robert J. Fox[1]

IT WAS IN THE PONCE BASKETBALL STADIUM ON A MILD SUMMER NIGHT in 1958. There he was, out on the court with Lou Gigante and some other New Yorkers, playing the Ponce Lions, the championship team of the Puerto Rico League. Well poised, competitive, yet quiet and smooth, Bob Fox, from New York. He was in Ponce to spend the summer with us at the Institute of Intercultural Communication, under the direction of Ivan Illich (then the youngest Monsignor of the New York Archdiocese). That was the summer when Illich had advised all of us: "It never rains in Ponce." It poured for days. Illich had built some temporary barracks for the priest students. They had to swim in and out of their residence after the rains came. Bob was one of them – one who could joke about it when many others had nothing but complaints. He listened to my lectures on intercultural understanding and communication. But, looking back, the situation should have been reversed. I was to learn much more about intercultural communication from Bob than he was ever to learn from me.

It was later when he became Director of the Office of the Spanish Apostolate that I came to know him better. It was clear, very early, that he had a different concept of the office than the previous directors had had. He saw so clearly that the Church was facing an entirely new kind of challenge with the coming of Puerto Ricans. He had not only grasped the vision of Illich that newcomers to New York from whatever culture – Puerto Rican or otherwise – had to be ministered to in their own language and in the style of religious practice that was familiar to them,

---

1. Bea McMahon (ed.), *Fox-Sight: Telling the Vision of Robert J. Fox.* Huntington, IN: *Our Sunday Visitor* Publishing Division, 1989, pp. 160-163. ©Fox House, 111 East 117th Street, New York, NY, 10035. Reprinted by permission of the Director.

130

in which they felt at home, which made sense to them. Bob saw many other things, a complicated city that was hopelessly bewildering to people like the Puerto Ricans; a situation in which pastoral ministry had to break through all the impeding blocks of a secular culture, and a solidly established style of Catholic life that made little sense to the Puerto Ricans who were arriving in large numbers. Leadership would have to come from the men and women going through the experience of the Puerto Ricans, and seeking to be faithful to the Lord and the Church in a world where, religiously, they were lost. This led to his innovative efforts to form lay leaders, never mind how much schooling they had. There, among the humble and unsophisticated poor, were qualities of faith, of devotion, of concern, one for the other that provided the promise of the Church of the future.

He had a gift for recognizing leadership, and the men and women with whom he came into contact will surely never forget him. "What do I care what they look like to people of our world? As with the apostles I want them to find Christ in the love I have for them and the respect I show them." Bob had an amazing combination of tremendous strength and determination together with a gentleness and a tenderness that was extraordinary. As we all knew, he was a "person-to-person individual," anything but an organization man. It was the person, no matter how unpromising, how deviant from ordinary social behavior, how difficult to understand. Bob's insight would find something of value, something that responded to the respect he had or the attention he showed to the person. It was just such a characteristic that impressed him about Jesus.

This was particularly true in the case of women. Listening to Bob talk about the women of the Gospels and Christ's relationship to them opened up a whole new vision into the character of Jesus and the women whose lives Jesus touched. Bob wanted to be the same way with women in his own life. He had little use for the restrictions and reservations about the relationship of priests with women. He would say things like: "If Jesus allowed a woman of the streets to fondle his feet and wash his feet with her tears, why shouldn't I show the same kind of love and regard for women who are cast aside in our society!" He felt that the emotional life of men and women should be nourished and given expression, rather than repressed in an over-intellectual theology and pastoral style. Certainly, what came through to the poor persons he worked with was the love he expressed for them. In so many of his remarks, or the phrases that used to dot his cards and publications, it was this spirit that burst forth in his imaginative expressions.

One of my closest associations with Bob was our mutual effort to bring Paulo Freire to New York. Bob knew of Paulo's work and was familiar with his method. He may have met him in Cuernavaca at the Center that Illich conducted there and where so many of us came into contact with Paulo. Bob and I were able to put a package together, partly Fordham University, partly Bob Fox, and Paulo came to spend a week or so in New York. It was Paulo's first visit to the United States. Paulo gave a few seminars at Fordham, but most of his time was spent with Bob, in meetings with the lay people who were going through Bob's leadership training courses. Bob always followed a Freire method in these programs. But to have the Master here himself was a great experience. Paulo developed a terrible cold the first day he got here, and the poor man suffered terribly during the whole week. But it did not dampen his spirit or impede his work. It was marvelous to watch Paulo in these meetings, and Bob's joy at having him here.

Bob's midnight celebrations of the San Juan fiesta were not the great celebrations he had hoped for. He was very critical of the way the fiesta had become a day of family picnics and parties, gambling and drinking in abundance; with smaller numbers in the stadium for the Mass, he decided to have the Mass at midnight. "Anyone really interested in the religious celebrations will be there." Yes, it was a really religious event, with Bob's posters and phrases. It was imaginative, real, related to the inner-city experience, but many of the Puerto Ricans steeped in tradition did not find the meaning in it that Bob had intended. Yet, never discouraged, he kept going, trying to find the word that would have meaning for the Puerto Ricans in New York. He was replaced in the office and, what he had always feared, it became highly institutionalized, American style.

I saw him occasionally in these later years. Whenever Illich came to town, he would often gather a group around Bob, and it would be a stimulating evening. I often wondered which of the two was the one really having the influence with the New York clergy: was it Illich or Bob? Aware as I was of Illich's tremendous influence on that whole generation of young priests, there was something about Bob that was more authentically New York; more rooted in the turmoil of the city and the pain of the Puerto Ricans; if I may use a bolder expression, more like Jesus walking the streets of East Harlem. Bob was one of the blessings of my priestly life. He taught me many things about Jesus as only Bob could.

8

The Changing Neighborhood and the Parochial School[1]

IF YOU READ THROUGH THE FOURTH CHAPTER OF GENESIS, YOU WILL NOTICE that the first city mentioned in recorded history was built by the first murderer, Cain. I do not know whether this is symbolic, whether this association of the city with the criminal, was anything other than accidental. There are quite a few writers at the present time who would indicate that the modern city is quite an inhuman thing and can readily be understood as the plan of a criminal mind.

On the other hand, we know that the city has been the center of man's greatest developments. It was in the city that schools arose, that art flourished; it was to the cities that Peter and Paul went, to the great cities like Antioch and Ephesus and Corinth and Rome, cities where the peoples of many races and nations and cultures met, where Greek came to know Jew, Syrian met African, and Macedonian met Roman. Out of this turmoil, sometimes vigorous, sometimes violent, came the mingling of energies, the clash of ideas, the stimulus of strange cultures that later blended into the great developments of the Catholic Church.

Therefore, if you are upset at times by the challenge of new and strange peoples who have different ideas and customs, it is well to remember that it was out of such experiences that many of the great advances of the Church have been born.

I have been asked to speak to you about the relationship of the shifting neighborhood to the parochial school, or the relationship of the parochial school to the shifting neighborhood. This is all part of the important role that the parochial school will be expected to play in the difficult task of assisting our Spanish-speaking newcomers to find themselves at home in the complicated culture of a mainland city.

---

1. Address, Committee for the Spanish-Speaking of Chicago, November 1, 1956.

I wish to center my attention on three things:

1) the problems that beset any person from a different culture as he tries to adjust himself to a new way of life. The less violent this uprooting is, the more harmonious and gradual it is, the less likely will be the disorganization of the immigrant's life, disintegration, and the evils that attend these.

2) this transition for migrants into our large cities today is complicated terribly by the problem of shifting neighborhoods, haphazard mingling of peoples for which little provision has been made.

3) in the midst of this situation, the parochial school is a crucial factor which can make the transition to a new culture considerably easier if it approaches its task with understanding and skill.

We can thank God that most of our people are well disposed to accept strangers, the migrants from Spanish lands. They are anxious to help them become Americans, Chicagoans, New Yorkers as quickly as possible. In this wonderful good will, certain cautions must be exercised.

The worst way to try to integrate the Spanish-speaking into the life of Chicago is to try to force them to stop being Mexican or Puerto Rican or Latin. People from a different culture will always be more responsive to our way of life when they recognize that we respect their way of life. Therefore, any over anxious effort on our part to get the Spanish-speaking to give up their Latin ways may be the surest method of persuading them to hold on to them. If the history of earlier immigrants tells us anything, it certainly tells us this.

It is not clear yet whether the integration of the Spanish-speaking will be easier or more difficult than it was for the immigrants of a century ago. In some ways it should be much easier because our large cities are probably in a better position today than they have ever been to handle a large migration, and the Puerto Ricans at least are much better prepared to come than the immigrants who came years ago. On the other hand, the shifting neighborhoods of our large cities presents them and us with a problem of instability which earlier immigrants never had to face.

In the remarks that I shall make, I do not want to give the impression of pleading for Spanish-speaking ghettos. The more intermingling of the Spanish-speaking with older residents, the better, provided this is accompanied by understanding and respect. Increased intermingling where there is no understanding and respect leads only to increased hostility and conflict. Therefore, the Spanish-speaking must be given the confidence and assurance that our way of life is completely open to them. Then they will accept it gradually, instead of resisting it if it appears to be forced upon them. What I am cautioning against is any resurgence of that old and pitiful mistake of the "Americanization" period when so much harm was done by trying to force the immigrants to accept American ways too quickly.

It is always well to remember, when we speak of integrating the newcomer that, in order to integrate him into our way of life, we must inevitably disintegrate the orderly pattern that his life knew before he came here. Disintegration is always dangerous and always painful.

Life is integrated when it has a meaning that gives a person satisfaction and security. When the big and little things of a person's day – the feeding of a baby, the gesture of politeness to a lady, a way of cooking food and eating it; the type of work persons do for which they are respected; prestige or prowess in work or play; the way people honor their fellows and are honored by them; the way they worship God and pray; the way a man loves a woman or a woman, man; the way they show reverence to the aged – when these and the other million things of a person's life are interwoven with a set of meanings that give a person respect, a sense that they are somebody, and they belong to something, then life is integrated. But when a person is shifted to another culture, when they do the things that brought them honor among their own people and they now receive ridicule; when they live according to a code of rightness they had known in their own land and now find themselves betrayed; when loyalties to friend and family which once brought a person respect now bring criticism, the meanings of life are gone; a person no longer knows exactly what to do to be honored, to be respected. They no longer know who they are, where they fit, where they are going. Life has disintegrated, fallen apart.

The crucial point in dealing with a migration is this: we must be extremely careful that the lives of the newcomers do not disintegrate before they have gradually learned the new meanings, the new ways of doing things that bring them security and respect in their new world. Therefore the clinging of the Spanish-speaking to their own groups, their perpetuation of old customs, their love of the old ways that gave meaning to their lives will not hinder them from becoming integrated into the life of Chicago. Rather this will give them the security, the support, the satisfaction they require as they learn gradually, but inevitably how to become Chicagoans. Integration is a matter of time. The inevitable process goes on and, consistently it seems the third generation child becomes definitely American. Therefore the real questions of integration are not: "How long will it take?" But rather, "How easy or difficult will it be?" and "How much may be lost in the process?"

There are many factors which indicate that this process will be easier for us and for the Spanish-speaking people who are coming to us. There are other factors which indicate that it may be more difficult.

The Spanish-speaking are beset, as most Chicagoans and New Yorkers are beset, by the problems of unsettled and shifting neighborhoods. Frequent changes of residence, or the scrambling and unscrambling of people in neighborhoods and housing projects, is not an automatic way to integration. This is simply a social situation which makes integration a much more pressing spiritual and psychological challenge. The process of integration, thrust on people as it is today, requires a greatness of mind and heart, a charity and vision which it has not required previously. This is not because Chicagoans or Latins are any better or worse. It is because all of us are caught in the intensive mingling of peoples, a mobility of residence which makes us acutely conscious of the differences of people while giving us less time to adjust ourselves to them. Therefore "understanding," and "good human relations," are not just a form of do-goodism; they are the essentials of a peaceful and satisfying life in the neighborhoods of our large cities. If respect and understanding are not present, hostility will breed disintegration, and disorder will beset our social life. . . .

I do not know what kind of a burden [extensive] turnover creates for a school. But it does represent the shifting kind of neighborhood which is so characteristic of our cities today. This could be documented at length. Housing projects bringing 1500 to 3000 families suddenly into an established parish; these are all aspects of the problem of unsettled and shifting neighborhoods which are the experience of large numbers of our people today.

These figures I have just given you reflect one of the important characteristics of these recent migrations to our cities. The newcomers, the Spanish-speaking, are not concentrating in a few, well defined areas of the cities. They are filtering into the interstices of declining neighborhoods in almost every section of the city.

It may seem very fortunate on the face of it that the Spanish-speaking are moving into areas all over the city. But this means that they do not enjoy that old type of immigrant neighborhood where everyone was Irish, or German, or Jew, neighborhoods that seemed to be almost a foreign land transplanted to the United States, where the customs of the old country were preserved, the old ways were followed, where the old loyalties and solidarities and social control kept a community strong and secure as it gradually learned to adjust itself to American life. In these neighborhoods, the immigrant groups had their own Church where familiar practices took place in a language that made the immigrant feel "at home" and "among his own kind" in the practice of the faith that was such a deep bond among them.

In the shifting neighborhoods of today, these conditions are much more difficult to achieve. Not only are they caught in the great mingling of peoples, in their own shifting from one poor section to another, but the integrated parish means that they face the problem of being strangers in the worship of God; they are not "at home" and "among their own" in the practice of their faith.

This creates considerable difficulty for the newcomer and the older resident. They cannot leave the newcomers "by themselves," because the social situation makes them present to us all the time. Nor can the newcomers stay comfortably "among their own," because the social situation throws them repeatedly into close and constant contact with people whom they do not know and seldom understand. If this close contact is not accompanied by understanding and is associated with hostility, misunderstanding, conflict, it may lead to rapid disintegration of parish and neighborhood, and sad consequences will follow for all.

It is in this context that the parochial school can be an extraordinary influence.

The school, we all realize, has been the great instrument of integration. Without it, nationalities and ethnic groups might have continued their old ways for generations. With it, the child is schooled into American ways; mingles with American children; makes friends with American playmates; learns the English language as a native tongue. The result: by the third generation, there are no longer immigrants, but Americans all.

However, it is also clear that the school does not represent an unmixed blessing for many children from a strange culture. It is the place where the second generation child learns the new culture that is so different from that of his parents. He lives at home in a Mexican or Puerto Rican world; he lives in school in an American and Chicago world. The things he learns at home may not be understood or respected at school; the things he learns at school may be strange and poorly understood at home. Caught between two cultures, the child can become bewildered, resentful, even rebellious. The setting for delinquent behavior is being formed.

Against this background, therefore, it is important for all of us in the schools to realize that we are not simply teaching a child; we are teaching a child who is trying to put together some unified meaning of life out of the conflicting cultures that he experiences in home and at school. If he is in a shifting neighborhood, the whole pattern of life around him may be disorganized. It is possible that he knows no consistent pattern of right and wrong; no consistent training in respect for himself and others; no form of behavior that he knows will bring him respect and recognition. To this may be added poor performance in school because of handicaps of language, and lack of strong motivation for learning.

And yet, despite these difficulties, the school can be the one bridge to ease the child's entrance to his new world. It seems to me that the school could explain, in simple manner, similar to the methods of elementary training, what it means to pass from one culture to another; could point out to him the wonderful qualities of the culture of his parents, but the reasons why he must inevitably move away from them; could explain to him why he must do things differently in America, and why his parents will not understand some of the things he learns.

In doing this, there are two things we must try to achieve: to try to cultivate in the newcomer a deep respect for the culture of his own people, even though he must be taught to move away from it. He can be taught to love the heroism of the Spanish tradition which he shares; the respect for those of other race and color that marks the poor of Mexico and Puerto Rico; the wonderful generosity of women who accept as their own the children left alone by economic distress, death or abandonment; a sense of personal pride and personal loyalty, these and numerous other traits he could be taught to love and respect. This would strengthen them against the disorganization that can easily follow if migrants lose respect for the culture of their older folks.

Secondly, this same respect for the newcomer can be cultivated in the children of the older residents of the area. If you are dealing with the coming of the Spanish-speaking, there are so many wonderful things that can be emphasized: the Spanish resistance to the Reformation; the respect of the Spanish for native peoples in Latin America; their deep sense of loyalty and personal dignity; the great traditions of sanctity and devotion to the service of God. These could all be emphasized in an effort to cultivate a sense of respect and reverence for the culture from which the Spanish-speaking come. If the school could dispose the children to this kind of a spirit of respect, it would go far to easing the integration of the Spanish-speaking in the shifting parishes.

Finally, beyond the children are the families. There is no more direct way to parents than through the children. Parents of newcomers, caught in the distress of unstable neighborhoods, lost in a bewildering environment, are not likely to understand the pattern of life that their child is being taught, and are not likely to understand the problem of the uprooting which they are going through. If the school could reach them, through parent-teacher meetings, through special conferences called for parents like this; if they could have explained to them the reasons why they do not understand what their children are learning; if they could have the nature of cultural transition described for them, perhaps they would be in a better situation to lead a more contented life at home and in the neighborhood.

However, even more important than the parents of the Spanish-speaking are the parents who are older residents of the City. These are the ones whose resentment and hostility against the Spanish may lead to bitterness among the Spanish, a sense of not being respected. If these parents can be reached through the children, through the activities of the school, would it be possible to explain to them the meaning of these migrations; explain to them the way all our people were despised when they first came here; explain the importance of respect and reverence for strangers in our land; cultivate in them a sense of obligation and zeal toward these new members of the parish who should be received as first class members of the parish and the neighborhood.

Is all this naive? I do not think so. If the members of the parish can be properly disposed to respect the Spanish-speaking, to realize that they cannot expect the Mexicans and Puerto Ricans to become like the Irish Catholics or the German Catholics or Italian Catholics overnight, the way will be smoothed for effective integration. It is so important that the Spanish-speaking be helped to preserve some of those wonderful customs that Father Illich must have spoken about yesterday, the religious practices that make the faith a living thing in their Latin lands and which may be abruptly cut off when they come here. If this can be done, the life of the Spanish-speaking may be able to avoid disintegration, and may enjoy a more peaceful, less violent transition to a new integration with American ways.

The school will be a crucial factor in the integration, whether this integration is peaceful or violent. I am sure that your interest and participation indicates that you will guide the education of children in the school so that the school will become an instrument to cultivate great respect for the newcomers in the hearts of the older residents; greater respect for their own culture among the Spanish-speaking themselves, and a spirit of Christian love and generosity among both. In this way, their faith will become the bond to resist the disintegrating pressures of our city neighborhoods.

9

Background Paper on Puerto Rican Culture and Organized Social Services[1]

Introduction

"Social Services" are the community's helping hand to a neighbor in need. It is the application of system, of organization, of trained skill to the age-old difficulties of the human family: hunger, cold, unemployment, homelessness, illness, isolation, abandonment and family disorganization. It is one of the great tributes to the generous and human spirit of Americans that its abilities at organization have gone not only into production and commerce; they have gone also into providing food for a hungry family, sharing a cloak with a neighbor who is cold, and giving shelter to the man without a home.

"Social Services" however, are a decidedly American institution. They "make sense" within the framework of American life. To people who do not share that way of life, they can be quite puzzling, bewildering. Sometimes they can be offensive. Therefore, in order to make social services effective – "better" as your title calls them – it is helpful to have some understanding of the background of the life from which Puerto Ricans come. This may throw some light on the way they react to the social services that are offered to them. Knowing their background, the American may be in a better position to offer social services in such a way that the Puerto Rican will accept them with gratitude for the gift, and with respect for the giver. The following sketchy notes are provided

---

1. Address: AFL-CIO Community Services National Advisory Conference, Labor and the Puerto Rican Community – Working Together for Better Social Services, January 15, 1960.

as a modest contribution to your understanding of the way of life from which the Puerto Rican comes.

Troubles

The common troubles of the human family are as much the lot of the Puerto Rican on the Island as they are of anyone. He is familiar with them on his Island; he knows how they strike in the death of his infant son, in the illness of his wife, in his own weeks without work, in the drunkenness of the man next door, in the flight from home of the girl across the way, in the family of his cousin that has just appeared at his doorstep. He has learned from folklore, from family and neighborhood gossip, from the tales of the older men how people cope with troubles. He has for the most part learned to bear with troubles with resignation and dignity. If faith lives in his heart, as it does in so many, he has learned to face trouble with a wonderful sense of God's Providence. *Si Dios Quiere*, "If God wills it," is as common a phrase on Puerto Rican lips as is the phrase on American lips, "Somebody ought to do something about it."

In the presence of troubles, the Puerto Rican is keenly conscious of one all-pervading resource: his family. The brother, the cousin, the *compadre*, the good neighbor, the parish priest, the store-keeper, are the traditional human institutions that make the difference between sorrow or joy, between pain or pleasure, between death or life. In the recurrent crises of human life, "troubles" have led the Puerto Rican to weave around himself the protecting net of human loyalties, of people he can count on, of people who will always "be there." Likewise, in the facing of troubles, in knowing what to do and on whom to count, a man enjoys prestige and respect. He is one on whom other people can depend.

To an increasing degree, the Puerto Rican is becoming conscious of another resource: the government. The district hospital, the health center, the unemployment and social security check, the milk station, the school children's lunch room, the public housing project, these are becoming more familiar to people of the Island. But for the most part, they are administered by people who come from the same Puerto Rican culture, who know the background of human feelings and family life, who as often as not, know how to relate themselves to the traditions and customs of Puerto Rican people

Poverty

Poverty is old and familiar to many of the Puerto Rican's as it is familiar to most people in the world. But poverty is a diminishing trouble on the Island. Average family income of wage earners in 1941 came to $360 a year; in 1953 it had jumped to $1,188 a year. The advance is remarkable. But Puerto Rico still remains poorer than the poorest of the Mainland states. Industrialization has made Puerto Rico the greatest example in the world of "the development of an underdeveloped area." But industrialization, while creating many news jobs of higher skill, has been eliminating many jobs of the unskilled. Staple foods are all imported and are costly. Therefore, the bananas in the yard, the mango and the bread-fruit tree, the chicken and the pig, are cherished possessions. They often mean the difference between food and hunger. And the credit of the store-keeper, the loaf of bread from the friend next door, the bag of vegetables from the cousin in the country are still familiar weapons in the struggle with poverty that is part of the life of many a Puerto Rican family.

The Family

Family life has developed in Puerto Rico under three influences: that of the native Borinquen Indians; that of the Spanish Colonists; that of slavery; a fourth influence from the U.S., is increasingly felt. The predominant influence was the Spanish one. Family life on all social levels in Puerto Rico is marked decidedly by Spanish characteristics. Parents play an important part in the selection of the marriage partner of the son or daughter; the husband has a dominant role in the family; the wife's role is subordinate, oriented to home and children. Children are loved – sometimes give the impression to Americans of being pampered – elders are respected, and the old folks have a position of influence and respect that is common in traditional rather than modern families. The husband expects to be the provider, to make the important decisions, often without consulting the wife; commonly he has controlled the money and has often done the shopping; he disciplines the children, and sometimes disciplines the wife.

This is the framework of a strong, traditional family in which stability does not depend on "togetherness" in the American sense, but on a clear understanding of roles, of expectations. By doing that which is expected of a man, a woman, a son or daughter, the Puerto Rican enjoys the satisfaction of being a good man, a good wife, a good child. He has a sense of personal dignity and pride, and enjoys the respect and esteem of his family and friends.

Tied in with these close family relations is an expanding network of *compadres*; Godparents at Baptism; sponsors at Confirmation, best-man and bridesmaid at marriage. This network of close personal loyalties and responsibilities acts like an extended family group to befriend, to support, to help, to correct, to criticize, to sanction.

The key to the stability of the system is the virtue that Puerto Ricans call *respeto*. The English word "respect" does not catch the meaning at all. *Respeto* consists of an understanding of my place, of what is expected of me as husband, wife, child; the carrying out of my obligations to others in a complicated network of personal loyalties. Husband provides support and authority because he has *respeto;* wife is faithful and properly submissive; child is obedient and dutiful because they have *respeto*. When this fails, family conflict and possibly disorganization is on the way.

Typical of the Latin tradition, a double standard of sexual morality has been common in Puerto Rico. The girl is carefully protected, regularly chaperoned. The family feels deep responsibility to bring her safely to marriage as a virgin. As a wife she is expected to be close to the home, protected by husband and relatives, faithful to her husband. On her chastity, marital fidelity and devotion, the strength and security of the Latin family is firmly built. More liberty is accorded to the boy. Sexual liberties outside of marriage are not considered a "problem" in the American sense of the word. Pre-marital relations with prostitutes or "bad" women are more openly accepted than on the Mainland, and outside interests during marriage are tolerated, often openly admitted. Illegitimate children have generally been openly and honorably acknowledged. It is a matter of law now that, if the father is known, he must "recognize" his illegitimate child, and the law vests the recognized child with certain rights of status, support and inheritance. These outside interests of the man are never considered "morally good;" they are tolerated as "humanly expected." They do not represent the "problem" that they would be in the culture of the Mainland, but they can be the occasion in Puerto Rico of frequent jealousy, conflict and personal violence.

Consensual Unions

According to the 1950 Census, 25 percent of the unions of men and women in Puerto Rico were classified as "consensual," that is what American law would define as a common law marriage, a union without civil or religious ceremony. Many of these are stable unions. They have been a common feature of Puerto Rican culture for centuries. The background of consensual marriage is quite complicated; it is partly related to the experience of slaves; partly to the practice of a colonial ruling class having outside interests among poor women; partly to lack of good religious training; partly to the attitude of poor people who were much more concerned about having a companion who treated them well than they were about an official ceremony.

Consensual unions have been a socially acceptable form of life in Puerto Rico despite the constant effort of the Church to correct them. People without embarrassment frankly admit that they are not married. Their moral judgment on the union is in terms of the behavior of the man or woman: "He supports me and my children"; "She keeps my home, prepares my meals, takes care of my clothes and is good to my children." Children of a consensual union are legally illegitimate, but are universally "recognized," and they enjoy the rights of recognized children.

The Unstable Unions

Finally there are the unstable unions. Divorce is relatively easy on the Island and the rate of divorce is high. Separation and abandonment may occur and frequently in cases of distress the women may seek support by living with another man, either consensually, or in a civil or religious marriage if the union can be regularized.

The abandoned family, the fatherless or motherless child, are as sad a human phenomenon in Puerto Rico as they are on the Mainland. But again the network of family relationships softens the shock of human distress. The relative, the friend, the *compadre*, becomes once again the reliable human resources. They regularly take in as their own, mothers and particularly children who are in need. It is not uncommon to find in Puerto Rican families a child or children, informally adopted, and being raised by parents who are not their own.

Youth, Recreation and Leisure Time

The world of a child in Puerto Rico fills the mind with images and associations quite foreign to the child of a complicated city like New York. The life of a boy is taken up with many of the small tasks of childhood; bringing water from the common fountain in converted five gallon oil cans; bringing meals in little containers to father or brother at noontime; hunting for crabs; shining shoes, selling papers, feeling quite useful in the manifold services he carries out for his family. Apart from that, leisure moments are filled with the simple play of childhood, along the beach if he lives near the sea; around the mountain home if he lives in the hills; seeking amusement with other children around the Plaza, along the streets, across the fields.

Even if he were very poor, possibly living in a slum, his life is likely to be filled with memories of waves breaking quietly against the shore, of trade winds whistling through the trees, the sudden downpour of tropical rain followed by brilliant sunshine, the sight of cane blossoms bending in the breeze, hibiscus growing wild beside the fields, flamboyants covering the highways.

As the child pushes into the teen ages, school finishes often when he is sixteen, sometimes before he is sixteen, and the desire for a job becomes a preoccupation for the boy. The girl generally helps around the house. Interest now begins to center in more organized sports, baseball, basketball, soccer; in the small fiestas in someone's home or the dance in a nearby hall or in social gatherings where he hopes to meet a girl who will someday be his wife.

Play and recreation are thus geared into the ordinary routines of a simple life. There are the special moments when hundreds gather in the Plaza for a patronal feast, a procession, a parade. The old, the young, the middle-aged participate in the common celebrations of a community, each one conscious that he belongs to a "pueblo," that he has an identity, that one's life is tied in with that of family, friends and neighbors. One feels always "at home."

Housing

A house in Puerto Rico is a different thing than it is on the Mainland; it serves a different function. It is a private house, to begin with, a little wooden structure built up on stilts and consisting of two or three little rooms. The Puerto Rican lives there with his family, often with parents and grandparents; sometimes sharing it with cousin or friend. It is a kind of symbol of his individuality and independence, for, whether rented or owned, it is his and it is separated by a little or a big space from the house of the man next door. The Puerto Ricans have put these up for themselves, climbing up the hills on the outskirts of the towns, along the river banks or the seashore, gazing out on the beautiful water, lining the steep mountain paths, and clinging to precipitous slopes over the green valleys. They are his house and his home. If we could allow the Puerto Ricans to put up their little houses in Central Park or along the Harlem River, they would settle their housing problem quickly. The houses all have electric light, most have an electric refrigerator and a radio, and the TV aerial is appearing more frequently above the little wooden dwellings. Children fetch water from public pumps; women wash in nearby streams; and life goes on in a vigorous lively, human way in the area around the house. The Puerto Rican generally sleeps in his house; but he lives around the house. It is a shelter only from the rain, not from the cold. Life in Puerto Rico is very much under the open sky. Public housing is now quite common; large, long multiple dwellings, two and three stories high, echoing with the sounds of activity and life. Middle class homes are becoming so numerous that the outskirts of most cities are beginning to resemble Levittown. Practically all the houses are detached, concrete private dwellings, open to the wind and the air, as is so much of Puerto Rican living.

Medical and Hospital Care

The one aspect of life that brings government and family close together is the matter of health. The control of illness and disease, the cutting down of the death rate is one of the great achievements of Puerto Rico. The death rate on the Island was cut from 31 per thousand per year in 1899 to 7 per thousand per year in 1957; and life expectancy at birth was raised from 38 years in 1910 to 68 years in 1957. In this victory over illness and disease, the Puerto Rican was particularly aware of the local health center, the small hospital in his town, the large district hospital, of public health services brought into the most crowded neighborhoods of coastal cities and the most distant hamlets of the mountains.

Folk practices are still widespread, the use of herbs and potions; recourse to the woman who has special powers to cure; reliance on superstitions. But the systematic efforts of the Government have reached the lives of the people in every section of the Island with results in health improvement that have been remarkable.

Race and Social Class

The Puerto Rican has been aware all around him of people of every variety of color from completely white to completely Negro. In his ordinary social relations, he never averred to the fact of a person's color. If a man was upper class, the Puerto Rican knew that man would be "white," although interestingly enough some of the "white" people in the upper class were darker than people who were not called "white." If a man were lower class, the Puerto Rican knew he might be any color. In the plaza, at social gatherings, at civil meetings, around the neighborhood, people of all different shades mingled together, took each other for granted, often intermarried and had children in their family of noticeably different color. Discrimination on the basis of color, as it prevails on the Mainland, was something an ordinary Puerto Rican would not understand.

However, as classes began to shift, as a middle class began to form and to be prominent (and it has been forming for a long time), as education, industrial development and government services began to break open many channels to higher status, the question of color became a troublesome source of anxiety to many Puerto Ricans. The influence of the Mainland has only contributed to the difficulty. When color no longer means that a man is lower class, what is it going to mean in Puerto Rico? And with this question, the Puerto Rican, especially the one who is moving up, is struggling in his mind and heart; whether he will slip into the injustice and inhumanity of an American pattern of discrimination, or whether he will make explicit the human values implicit in his tradition, of accepting a man on the basis of his personal worth and not on the basis of his color.

Religion

Puerto Rico as a Spanish colony was "Catholic" in its culture. As a man was born into the white or colored race, as he was born into an upper or lower class family, he likewise was born into the Catholic faith. This was the way a Spanish person thought about religion and its relation to society. It was part of the cultural environment. The Church dominated the plaza at the center of his town, for God had to be present in every community. Periodically in great festivals or processions, the community worshipped God, and the Puerto Rican ordinarily is deeply conscious that he belongs to a community where God is present in the Catholic Church, and in which God is worshipped in great public demonstrations. The Blessed Virgin, the Saints are almost like *compadres*, part of that network of personal relations on which the Puerto Rican depends for help, protection, support. He will tell you, therefore, when you ask him, that he is *muy católico*, "very Catholic" and there is a great deal of meaning to what he says.

In many cases, he will be as devout and faithful a practicing Catholic as one can find. In many other cases, he will have no formal knowledge of his faith at all. Despite its constant effort to provide sufficient priests, the Catholic Church has never come near the point where it would effectively reach with religious instruction and spiritual care the large numbers of Puerto Ricans who need these. In dealing with Puerto Rican people, therefore one cannot presume that they will understand their faith or base their behavior on a conscious knowledge of Catholic principles.

Protestantism has been active on the Island since the time of its accession to the United States, and in more recent decades, the Evangelical and Pentecostal sects have been very much in evidence. Estimates of the percentage of Puerto Ricans who are Protestant or belong to the Sects range from 10 percent to 20 percent. Almost every town has a Protestant church, and the Evangelical and Pentecostal churches or meeting places are scattered far and wide. The Puerto Rican, therefore, has generally become familiar with Protestantism before he leaves the Island.

Spiritualism is widely practiced, by wealthy and poor, by Protestant and Catholic, despite the efforts of the Church to correct it.

- - - - - - - - - -

This sketchy outline gives some idea of the way of life from which the Puerto Ricans come. It is presented as a "point of reference" against which Americans may try to judge how they should interest Puerto Ricans in social services that are available. With an appreciation of this background, it is hoped that the American may be given a bit more guidance in his noble and generous effort to make available to the Puerto Rican the benefits and services which the American wants so sincerely to give to any person who is in need.

Suggested Readings

Facts and Figures, 1959. Published by the Office of the Commonwealth of Puerto Rico, 322 West 45th St., New York, NY. Published every year, this little booklet keeps one up to date on the present state of the migrants, the extent of migration, population trends on the Island, education and economic development. Available on request.

Steward, Julian H., and others. *People of Puerto Rico.* Champaign, Ill.: Univ. of Illinois Press, 1957. This is the only extensive anthropological study of the Puerto Rican people available. Actually, it studies only five different segments of Puerto Rican life. But it does provide some excellent insights into the ordinary life of people in a number of sections of the Island.

Roberts, Lydia and Rose Stefani. *Patterns of Living in Puerto Rican Families.* Rio Piedras, Univ. of Puerto Rico Press, 1949. An indispensable book for an intimate knowledge of the practices of Puerto Rican families. Provides wonderful insights into home conditions, food, budgets, health care, etc. Somewhat out of date by this time, but still a very valuable book.

Padilla, Elena. *Up From Puerto Rico.* New York: Columbia Univ. Press, 1958. An anthropological study of Puerto Ricans in a very poor neighborhood in New York City. Helpful for insights into the reaction of Puerto Ricans on this level to New York life. The chapter on the family has some rather good detail about types of families. The section on the problem of "color" is excellent.

Wakefield, Dan. *Island in the City.* Cambridge, Mass.: Houghton-Mifflin, 1959. Few books give, as this one does, the "feel" of bewilderment of the Puerto Rican trying to cope with the complicated organization of a large city. It makes one very much aware of the very human Puerto Rican person trying to make sense out of the way New Yorkers do things.

Berle, Beatrice. *80 Puerto Rican Families*. New York: Columbia Univ. Press, 1958. Case studies of 80 Puerto Rican families and their response to medical care. Invaluable for the insights it provides for anyone who intends to provide services for Puerto Rican people.

Handlin, Oscar. *The Newcomers*. Cambridge, Mass.: Harvard Univ. Press, 1959. The latest word on the present state of the migration together with an evaluation of the impact of the migration on New York life. Written by one of the great authorities on the history of migrations to the United States.

10

New York City and Its Puerto Rican "Problem"[1]

NEWSPAPERS TELL US THAT DELINQUENCY IS A SERIOUS DANGER IN NEW York City. Indeed it is. But a far more serious danger would be a sense of panic in the minds of New Yorkers; a fear that our fair city has begun to decay; a sense of pity that older and peaceful and prosperous times are being snowed under in a new phenomenon of teenage crime, of slum living, and of poverty.

This would be a strange state of mind for New Yorkers to fall into. There must be something in the heavy air of the Hudson or the East River that causes it. New Yorkers have been assigning their fair city to the dust heap for the past hundred and fifty years, but it always seems to come out fairer than ever. They have another old tradition – something like a tribal practice, I suppose – of always blaming her recurrent ills on the latest strangers who arrive to populate her slums. It takes a bit of maneuvering to substitute Idlewild Airport for Castle Garden, but the New Yorkers look as if they are going to succeed in doing it.

There are signs of life in the old lady yet. The Irish and the Germans, the Italians and the Jews have now become respectable. It seems, however, as if the Puerto Ricans will enable the old tradition to survive. For they are joining the company of all the great peoples who went before them. They are getting their initiation into the noble heritage of the immigrant by having all the crime and the ills of the city attributed to their coming.

---

1. An address at the Fordham University School of Business, New York, New York, October 8, 1959. Published in *The Catholic Mind*, January-February, 1960, pp. 39-50. Reprinted with the permission of America Press, Inc., 106 West 56th Street, New York, NY 10019. ©1960. All Rights Reserved.

The New Yorker's Delusion

The interesting thing about this strange attitude that affects New Yorkers is this: the older, more peaceful and more prosperous times never really existed. New York has always been a rough city, often a violent one. Turbulence and upheaval, conflict and adjustment, change and struggle have always been her way of life. That is what made her great. One contemporary judge wants us to slow things down to give the city time to catch up. New York has never had time to catch up. Wave after wave of newcomers kept driving the city onward. Struggle and change have kept her on her toes. The city is great precisely because destiny never allowed her to take a rest. Effort and energy, challenge and striving have drawn from her mind and soul a constant burst of creativeness, imagination, and drive that has made her what she is. I give you the quotation, for what it is worth, of an old friend of mine, a hard-bitten Irishman who spent his life in the excitement of the Stock Exchange – where New York was so very much New York. "Father," he said, "you are privileged to be living in New York these days. You are witnessing the greatest moments of the city's life."

The one simple prescription to cure the New Yorker's recurring delusion is a sense of perspective, a realization that these are not the worst times of the city's history. They may be the best. Let's forget about Mayor Wagner for a few moments and listen for a while to the man who was mayor of New York in 1825. Philip Hone never thought the city would last long enough to have a mayor in 1859, much less 1959. He wrote in his diary on Monday, December 2, 1839 as follows:

> One of the evidences of the degeneracy of our morals and of the inefficiency of our police is to be seen in the frequent instances of murder by stabbing. The city is infested by gangs of hardened wretches, born in the haunts of infamy, brought up in taverns, educated at the polls of elections, and following the fire engines as a profession. These fellows (generally youths between the ages of twelve and twenty-four) patrol the streets making the night hideous and insulting all who are not strong enough to defend themselves; their haunts all the night long are the grog shops in the Bowery, Corlear's Hook, Canal Street and some even in Broadway, where drunken frolics are succeeded by brawls, and on the slightest provocation knives are brought out, dreadful wounds inflicted, and sometimes horrid murder committed. The watchmen and police officers are intimidated by the frequency of these riots, the strength of the offenders and the disposition which exists on the part of those who ought to

know better to screen the culprits from punishment. (*Diary of Philip Hone, 1828-51.* N.Y.: 1936, p. 434.)

This is a description of those more peaceful and prosperous days that modern New Yorkers long to have back again. One doesn't have to look very far to see whom Philip Hone blames for this distress. The doom of the city was already assured by the worthless element that was there in abundance:

> [These Irishmen] . . . are the most ignorant and consequently the most obstinate white men in the world, and I have seen enough to satisfy me that, with few exceptions, ignorance and vice go together. . . . These Irishmen, strangers among us, without a feeling of patriotism or affection in common with American citizens, decide the elections of the City of New York. . . . The time may not be very distant when the same brogue which they have instructed to shout 'Hurrah for Jackson!' shall be used to impart additional horror to the cry of 'Down with the natives.' (id. p. 190.)

Can you imagine what chance Mr. Hone would have of becoming Mayor today!

Philip Hone was not by any means alone in his prejudices. John Pintard was another outstanding man of those days, a very spiritual and generous soul who spent much of his time raising funds for the building of St. Patrick's Cathedral and for the support of Irish orphans. Pintard had doubts on many things but he was a true New Yorker. He knew the city was going to the dogs and he knew the reason why:

> But the beastly vice of drunkenness among the lower laboring classes is growing to a frightful excess, owing to the cheapness of spirits and the multitudes of low Irish Catholics, who, restrained by poverty in their own country from indulgence, run riot in this . . . .We have 3,500 licensed dram shops in this city, two or three on every corner; but if we stop one half . . . the consumers will all go to the other corner . . . As long as we are overwhelmed with Irish immigrants, so long will the evil abound . . . .Thefts, incendiaries, murders which prevail, all rise from this source. (*Diary of John Pintard*, Vol. III, New York, 1941, p. 51.)

It is too bad that Philip Hone and John Pintard did not tell us more of the really peaceful, and orderly and prosperous days that came twenty years later. Another generation had come; more immigrants had arrived; the city was worse than ever. And who gets the blame? You guessed it. By this time, the United States Congress had become interested. And we owe to them the following sketch of New York in the 1850s:

> It has been stated in the public journals that of the 16,000 commitments for crimes in New York City, during 1852, at least one-fourth were minors, and that no less than 10,000 children are daily suffering all the evils of vagrancy in that city. In 1849, the chief of the police department of that city called attention to the increasing number of vagrant, idle and vicious children of both sexes growing up in ignorance and profligacy, and destined to a life of misery, shame and crime . . . He stated that there were then 2,955 children of the class described, known to the police in eleven patrol districts, of whom two-thirds were females between eight and sixteen years of age. Most of the children, as was stated at the time, were of German or Irish parentage, the proportion of the American born being not more than one in five. (Foreign Criminals and Paupers. Report from the Committee on Foreign Affairs, August 16, 1856 [U.S. 34th Congress, 1st session, House Report No. 359] pp. 16-17. Quoted in Edith Abbott, *Historical Aspects of the Immigration Problem*, Chicago: University of Chicago Press, 1926, p. 621.)

The good members of the House Committee did not confine themselves to New York. They thought on a national scale. It was not only New York City that was going to the dogs. It was the entire nation. However, they had spent enough time in New York City to catch the spirit of that strange tribal practice of finding the roots of all evil in the strangers to our land:

> . . . The source of this great moral evil may be almost wholly traced to the many vices of the foreign population, who afford no other examples to their children than habits of disorder, idleness and uncleanliness, and degrading vices of all kinds, and who exercise no parental authority whatever on them. (*Id.* quoted in Abbott, p. 621).

19th-Century Gangdom

Really, if a New Yorker wants to get the spice of life, a real image, in vivid pictures, of what was going on; if he wants to know the names of some of these vicious children and the methods of their trade, he can turn to that extraordinary bit of historical reporting that so many New Yorkers so quickly forgot – Herbert Asbury's *Gangs of New York* (N.Y.: Knopf, 1929). Asbury puts flesh on the bones of statistics. And it amazes me that no publishing house, in these days of mild panic, has thought it fit to bring out a cheap paperback for the edification of all New Yorkers.

It is a heartening reassurance that things are not so bad. If New York survived the 1850s, it should be able to survive anything.

> Conditions such as these soon prevailed throughout the Fourth Ward, and by 1845, the whole area had become a hotbed of crime; streets over whose cobblestones had rolled the carriages of the aristocrats were filled with dives which sheltered the members of such celebrated river gangs as the Daybreak Boys, Buckoos, Hookers, Swamp Angels, Slaughter Housers, Short Tails, Patsy Conroys, and the Border Gang. No human life was safe, and a well-dressed man venturing into the district was commonly set upon and murdered or robbed, or both, before he had gone a block. . . . The police would not march against the denizens of the Fourth Ward except in parties of half a dozen or more . . . .(pp. 48-49)

> Nicholas Saul and William Howlett, who were hanged in the Tombs when the former was but twenty years old and Howlett a year his junior, were the most celebrated leaders of the Daybreak Boys, although membership in the gang included many noted criminals, among them Slobbery Jim, Sow Madden, Cowlegged Sam McCarthy and Patsy the Barber. . . . (pp. 66-67)

About this time, new rays of light began to appear in public statements. Crime, indeed, preoccupied everyone's mind. Its association with the immigrant poor was taken for granted. But as public officials began to look into the housing conditions of the time, they began to see the situation in new perspective:

> That crime, in general, is on the increase in our community, is a melancholy fact, in spite of the prevalent taste for reading, the multiplication of means of education. . . . Where shall we look for the rankest development of this terrible combination, but in the hideous anomalies of civilization which are to be found in the tenant-house system? . . . (*Report of the Select Committee Appointed to Examine into the Condition of Tenant-houses in New York and Brooklyn*. N.Y. State Assembly Document No. 205, 1857. Quoted in Abbott, p. 635.)

The Committee had pointed out earlier who was living in these horrible slums. If I may quote a bit more:

> But we must pass over without description hundreds of dilapidated, dirty and densely populated old structures which the committee inspected in different wards and which come under the head of re-adapted, reconstructed or altered buildings. In most of them the Irish are predominant, as occupants, though in some streets Negroes are found swarming from cellar to

garret of tottering tenant houses. In this connection it may be well to remark, that in some of the better class of houses built for tenantry, Negroes have been preferred as occupants to Irish or German poor; the incentive to possessing comparatively decent quarters appearing to inspire the colored residents with more desire for cleanliness and regard for property than is impressed on the whites of their own condition . . . . (*Id.* quoted in Abbott, p. 635.)

Make no mistake. This Committee had no particular respect for the foreign poor. They did not think good housing would enable good foreigners to remain good; rather good housing would enable Americans to reform the evil ways of foreign people. The tribal practice had been given a new tone; but they were the same words.

As a surety we must, as a people, act upon this foreign element, or it will act on us. Like the vast Atlantic, we must decompose and cleanse the impurities which rush into our midst, or like the inland lake, we will receive the poison into our whole national system (Ibid).

All this time, of course while the Daybreak Boys were breaking the skulls of rival gangs or decent citizens, and while committee after committee spoke philosophically about the evil immigrant poor, hundreds of thousands of these supposedly evil immigrants were pushing their way courageously through poverty and exploitation, were working hard to bring up decent families against hopeless odds; were laying the solid bricks, with human courage and human hope, of what was to be the greatest city of the world.

But the 1850s passed. Came the Civil War, the draft riots, and after the Civil War, amidst the flowering of industry and commerce, the flowering again of those persistent elements of New York life – crime, slums and poverty. John Francis Maguire, the well-known Irish writer, came to observe how his fellow Irishmen were doing in America. Interestingly enough, he caught the fever of New York's writers very quickly. He found the city in a hopeless condition, with little indication that it would ever overcome the difficulties that faced it:

The evil of overcrowding is magnified to a prodigious extent in New York . . . . There is scarcely any city in the world possessing greater resources than New York, but these resources have long since been strained to the uttermost to meet the yearly increasing demands created by this continuous accession to its inhabitants: and if there be not some check put to this undue increase of the population, for which even the available space is altogether inadequate, it is difficult to think what the consequences must be. Every succeeding year tends to aggravate the existing evils which, while rendering the necessity for a remedy more urgent, also render its nature and its application more difficult. (John F. Maguire. *The Irish in America*. New York: 1868, pp. 218-19.)

There were less than 800,000 people in New York when Maguire wrote. If the available space was altogether inadequate then, I wonder what he would say about the nearly eight million who live in the city today . . . .

It is a rather disturbing and upsetting picture, isn't it? And if one saw nothing else, or failed to see these dismal situations against the background of all the other aspects of the city's life, he could easily conclude, as so many did, that the city was facing its last days.

There was one other group that was concerned about the situation, and we must not overlook the things they had to say. They were the Catholic Archbishops and Bishops of the United States, who met in the Second Plenary Council in Baltimore in 1866. Urging the establishment of Catholic reform schools or industrial schools, they wrote in their Pastoral Letter:

It is a melancholy fact and a very humiliating avowal for us to make, that a very large proportion of the idle and vicious youth of our principal cities are the children of Catholic parents. Whether from poverty or neglect, the ignorance in which so many parents are involved as to the true nature of education, and of their duties as Christian parents, or from the associations which our youth so easily form with those who encourage them to disregard parental admonition, certain it is that a large number of Catholic parents either appear to have no idea of the sanctity of the Christian family, and of the responsibility imposed on them of providing for the moral training of their offspring, or fulfill this duty in a very imperfect manner. Day by day, these unhappy children are caught in the commission of petty crimes which render them amenable to the public authorities; and, day by day, they are transferred by hundreds from the sectarian reformatories into which they have been placed by the courts to distant localities where they are brought up in ignorance of, and most commonly, in hostility to the religion in which they were baptized. (Martin J. Spalding, Ed. *Concilii Plenarii Baltimorensis II, 1866*, Baltimore, 1868, p. cxviii.)

New York's Triumph

This, then, is part of the record of that old and peaceful and orderly life which so many New Yorkers long for when they read of the Royal Crowns and the Egyptian Kings. It was a life, like so much of New York's life, of crime and violence, of struggle and effort. But with it all, the strong, human, creative elements won out. New York has not become what it is without struggle. If the struggle of the past gave us the greatness of the present, can we not expect that the struggle of the present will give us the even more impressive greatness of the future?

As we reach the time when my quotations end, about the year 1870, certainly we could say the city needed a rest. If only they could have stopped migrations to allow the city to catch up, to clear the slums, to eliminate the crime. And what happened? New ships appeared with new faces, bringing an even stranger babble of new tongues. The Italians and the Jews began to crowd in just about the time when the Irish and the Germans were finding themselves. Whereas the Irish may have brought 100,000 a year at some times, the new migration was to bring a million a year. New York had not seen the beginning of strangers. There developed a new challenge, new distress, new slums, new poverty, new crime – and hundreds of thousands of new immigrants to be blamed for it.

The record need not delay us. Jacob Riis was around to write some of the record for us. *How the Other Half Lives* (America Century Series, N.Y.: Sagamore Press, 1957) is fortunately out in paperback. Read it for yourselves. Were things bad in 1870? They were worse in 1890. Riis tells us there were gangs on every corner.

Where did they come from? Here we have not only a new tune, but a new script. Riis saw what many an intelligent person had seen before him. The gang was not the product of evil foreigners. It was the product of life in New York; the by-product of generations lost in the confusion and bewilderment of the uprooting. The weak ones fell by the wayside when they faced the shock of molding a new way of life for themselves in a new world. It was the price we pay for a system that urges people of talent to advance socially and economically. Some people are ground down in the process. This is the unfortunate result of a system in which parents of one culture will never fully understand the way of life of their children, and children will never fully understand the way of life of the parent.

These are some of the things we began to see more clearly toward the close of the last century. But the record of that century's history is eloquent. The crime that distressed the city, the slums and poverty that created such a constant burden on its life did not destroy the city's greatness. They were a part of the goad, the stimulus, the challenge that evoked the effort that made the city great.

Now again we have crime. We have slums. We have poverty. Again we face the traditional malady of the New Yorker. We hear the lament that the city is going to the dogs, and see the revival of the old tribal practice of blaming our crime and poverty on the Puerto Ricans who now find themselves socially in the slot where the Germans and the Irish were a century ago.

In the perspective of the past, therefore, we can now take a brief look at the present. There is nothing in the record of the past or the experience of the present that gives us reason for composure. Crime and the poverty of city slums are terrible evils. But there is much in the record of the past that gives hope for the old New Yorkers, for the Puerto Ricans and for the Negroes. The record does not tell us that crime and poverty were ever easy. It simply tells us that they have always been here and that the citizens of New York have always had to exert enormous energy and courage to deal with them. That they have done surprisingly well.

Where the Problem Lies

Indeed, when one looks back over the experience of the immigrants, and when one looks closely at the experience of the Puerto Ricans, the marvel is not that there has been so much delinquency, but that there has been so little. As with every group of newcomers in the past, so with the Puerto Ricans: they are not nearly as great a problem for New York, as New York is a problem for them.

In the first place, delinquency is not something the Puerto Ricans bring with them. It is something that happens to them when they get here. They come from a way of life which they cherish. They have traditions of respect. They know what to expect of others and what others expect of them. They know the things for which they will be honored and the things for which they will be punished or despised. Then they come to New York and all the expectations change. Uprooted from a way of life they once took for granted, they find themselves as strangers in a way of life they do not understand. Things that were right in Puerto Rico, they find are wrong here. Things that were wrong in Puerto Rico, they find are right here. Things that brought them honor in Puerto Rico invite ridicule in New York. The values are different; norms are no longer consistent. Life becomes confused. They are the "uprooted," and the suffering that has marked the coming of every group of immigrants now begins to shake the framework on which their life was built.

One young Puerto Rican man whom I know stopped me the other day and remarked: "Father, things are not going too well with my little girl. She is fourteen now and in the ninth grade. But her mother goes to school with her and calls for her when school is over. The girl is beginning to rebel against this. The other girls make fun of her and of her mother. I don't know what to do." How many sincere and interested teachers both in the Catholic and public schools have remarked to me in regard to the Puerto Rican mothers who wait outside the school for their children at the end of class: "Father, why don't you tell them to let up on the children? They're making babies out of them."

Here we have the case of conscientious Puerto Rican parents try-ing, in the best way they know how, to protect their children, especially their young girls. Protection of the young girl is a serious responsibility for a good family in Puerto Rico. They do not escort them to school and back because they know what to expect in Puerto Rico. They understand the situation and have no fears. But in New York fear prompts them to exercise their responsibility in the best way they know how. As they do so, the child may be ridiculed; the parents may be criticized or laughed at. Family authority is weakened. Old norms of control are shaken, and conflict between the generations is in the making.

Another young Puerto Rican I know has a young boy about six years old. The boy has been in school now for two years. I asked the father recently: "How is the young boy making out?" The father replied with a shrug of the shoulders, half in amusement, half in bewilderment: "Father, he is a true American; he is already telling me how much I do not know."

Many children in Puerto Rico have the beautiful custom of asking their parents or their elders for a blessing when they go out or come home or when they go to bed. It is part of that wonderful pattern of "respect" that is often taught to Puerto Rican children. Explaining how these customs are undermined in New York, a wonderful young woman, a Puerto Rican school teacher, deeply devoted to her people, told me the following story: "I was visiting an aunt of mine one day, and two of my small cousins, recently arrived from Puerto Rico, came in to see her. They bounced in gleefully and, when they saw my aunt, they called out 'Bendición, Tia' ('Your blessing, please, Auntie.'), Father," she said, "I feel humiliated to tell you what happened. But, I laughed. The children turned to me, puzzled and confused. A practice of reverence, for which they were praised in Puerto Rico, had become an object of laughter in New York."

In how many other aspects of life does this not occur: behavior of a wife which we would define as part of "togetherness," the self-reliance, the alertness of the American woman might strike a Puerto Rican wife and husband as a sign of sinful disrespect. The devotion of a woman to her husband, schooled in them by centuries of tradition, they find criticized as excessive subordination, the lack of proper female independence.

When you talk with so many good Puerto Rican parents, one refrain is constant: "It is impossible to bring a child up in New York." The qualities of independence, of self-reliance, of assertiveness which we admire, which we try to teach children as necessary virtues in our competitive American system strike the Puerto Rican parent as a lack of proper childhood respect. The child lives in one way of life in the home. He is taught another way of life in the school. Parent will never fully understand child, and child will never fully understand parent. The seeds of the conflict between the generations are being sown.

These are the difficulties which come from the uprooting. Millions of immigrants have faced them before. The Puerto Ricans are facing them now. Fortunately, most people manage to become adjusted to them without serious distress and the Puerto Ricans will do the same. But in the process, if there is weakness in the family or weakness in the personality, disorganization sets in, mental illness and delinquency appear, and the price for the great values of migration and urban living are paid in the distress of old and new resident in the turmoil of social and cultural change.

This was so vividly illustrated in the case of Julio Rosario, the young Puerto Rican who died in the gang warfare of the Lower East Side last August. Julio apparently came from a good family. His father, with the strength and spiritual qualities of a patriarch, bore the trial of his death with a dignity, a composure, an acceptance of God's will that brought tears to the eyes of many who watched him. At the end of the Requiem Mass, he embraced each of the priests and the altar boys in gratitude for this service to his son. How much he had wanted to give to his son that wonderful dignity of the man from the hills of Puerto Rico, that quality which would bring so much richness to New York if we could save it. How much he wanted to give his son that which he was himself. And how much the son would have been blessed in receiving it. But life in New York got in the way. Things that gave a boy dignity and honor in the countryside of Puerto Rico were not the things that gave a boy dignity and honor on Forsyth Street. Things that were rewarded in a Puerto Rican village were not the things that were rewarded in the churning life of the Lower East Side. What a new and strange world of values, of struggle, of loyalty, dignity and pride was reflected in Julio's words. After he had received the last rites, he slipped into semi-consciousness, mumbling: "Tell the guys they can count on me, tell them I'll be there."

How easy it is to blame delinquency on the parents. In many cases they must certainly share the blame. But how unfair we can sometimes be in giving the impression that any decent family should be able to avoid the tragedies that strike frequently in the troubled neighborhoods of a city like New York.

Toward a Remedy

What I have said does not begin to explain delinquency. I hope it will explain what the great majority of Puerto Ricans are going through. I hope it will help us realize that we can help the Puerto Ricans avoid delinquency but not by criticizing them. They do not need statistics to tell them about delinquency. They live in the face of it, they suffer from the behavior of delinquents much more than we do; they understand, much better than their middle and upper class American critics, the difficulties that many of their people face in disorganized family life, in poverty, in exploitation. But they also understand what I hope we will all come to understand, the greatness that lies in the hearts of so many of their people, their generosity and respect for friendship, their desire to become part of the life of New York.

In this regard, I could hardly exhort you to do anything better, as Catholic students, than to imitate the example of our spiritual leader, Cardinal Spellman. The public has not yet begun to realize or appreciate the extraordinary effort His Eminence is making to ensure that we will receive the Puerto Ricans as our brothers and sisters in Christ. At enormous expense in money and manpower, he has been sending large numbers of his priests and sisters to Puerto Rico for special training that will enable them to work more effectively with the Puerto Ricans in New York. Indeed, in the history of migrations, I know of no other instance where a receiving diocese has gone to such unusual lengths to prepare its priests and sisters to understand the culture and the background of the newcomers in order to receive them as our own. History will probably look upon this as a social miracle. What a pity it would be if, while His Eminence strives so hard to have the Puerto Ricans received with respect, we should alienate them by lack of understanding, discourtesy or prejudice.

I trust that my words have been of some guidance and some help. Perhaps, in the year 2059, when some Jesuit priest may be addressing Fordham students in the ancient halls of Lincoln Square, he may recall that in 1959, when Puerto Ricans were coming to New York, a group of

Fordham students met in Shealy Hall and decided to break the old tribal practice of blaming everything on the newcomers, and to receive the Puerto Ricans with understanding, dignity and respect, not as strangers, but as their own.

11

The Role of Language as
a Factor of Strength for the
Puerto Rican Community[1]

IN THE FIRST PLACE, LET ME IDENTIFY MY POSITION AS THAT OF A SOCIOLOGIST, interested more in the sociological and cultural rather than the psychological factors of the adjustment of Puerto Rican youth either on the Island or the Mainland. I have been interested mainly in those aspects of the child's experience which are related to rapid cultural and social change here on the Island, and to problems of cultural assimilation (or transculturation) on the Mainland. The major focus of my interest has been on the problem of identity, and the crucial role that community plays in the preservation of a sense of identity here, or in the reestablishment of identity on the Mainland. I have come to be particularly attracted in recent years to the significance of language in this process. It seems to me that on the Mainland, the Spanish language is the symbol for the identity of the Puerto Ricans as a distinct community; it is quite obvious that the Spanish language fulfills this same function on the Island. If this is true, the implications of it for education are rather obvious.

I doubt if there is any topic that has been discussed as much and as heatedly on the Island as the topic of language: whether Spanish or English should be the language of instruction; how the languages should be taught; and why they are not taught more effectively. This is not directly the object of my remarks. I am concerned with language as a symbol of identity, with its social and cultural function, with its function as the means whereby a person can define for himself "who he is," and

---

1. Address: Presented at "The Puerto Rican Child in His Cultural Context," Barranquitas, Puerto Rico, November 18-20, 1965.

with whom he belongs, and where he finds the social relationships on which he can firmly rely. Language as the symbol of that network of interaction which is the basis for security, is the sense in which I use it here.

The central role of the community (the immigrant community) in the process of transition from one culture to another has been abundantly documented in the studies of the experience of immigrants in the United States and elsewhere. The clustering together of immigrants had always been suspect, their persistence in using their Old World language, their perpetuation of Old World customs and values, these were considered to be a threat to the social and political institutions of the United States. This fear of the immigrant cultures finally led to the passage of restrictive immigration laws in 1924, laws which have just been abrogated in the new immigration legislation of 1965. In the perspective of the history of the immigrants, it is evident now that the strength of the immigrant community, far from hindering assimilation to American life and culture, actually fostered and promoted it. "One integrates from a position of strength" became a clearly recognized proposition. Just as it is very difficult to establish a friendship with an insecure person – he is suspicious, afraid, distrustful; so likewise if members of an immigrant group are weak, lack self-confidence, depreciate their own value, it is difficult for them to become part of the social and political life of a larger and active community. Whereas if the community is strong, self-confident, aware of its own values, secure, it moves strongly and consistently to take its place in the dynamic life of the larger community. From the classic study of the Polish peasant by W. I. Thomas and Florian Znaniecki through the study by Oscar Handlin of *Boston's Immigrants*, to the recent studies of Will Herbert (*Protestant, Catholic, Jew*), Glazer and Moynihan (*Beyond the Melting Pot*), to the most complete and detailed statement by Milton Gordon (*Assimilation in American Life*), it is clear that, when a community is really sure of itself, strong and self-confident, it takes its place quickly and confidently as part of the larger society.

This does not mean that its entire cultural heritage is lost. By no means. What has become clear in the studies of immigrant assimilation in recent years has been the theory proposed by S. M. Eisenstadt in his studies of the immigrants to Israel, that assimilation is a two pronged process. Immigrants assimilate culturally very quickly. They adopt those essential practices and values and customs without which they cannot function as members of a host society. (This Eisenstadt defines as cultural assimilation.) But they retain an identity of their own; a network of social relationships which gives then a specific identity, a strength, a security. When they lose this by absorption into the major society, Eisenstadt would say they have been assimilated socially as well as culturally. But in a pluralistic society, large numbers of social groupings can remain with an identity of their own, even though they all have adopted common patterns of behavior which enable them to function effectively in their new home. They have become culturally assimilated, but they remain socially distinct. Both Glazer and Moynihan, and Milton Gordon insist that this is the general characteristic of American society.

Therefore, as the Puerto Ricans have moved in large numbers to the new culture of the Mainland, we would expect two things to happen: they would quickly pass through a process of cultural assimilation, i.e., they would learn the language, adopt the essential values of the larger society, follow the behavior patterns which are required. At the same time, they would retain an identity of their own as a community (as a society, Eisenstadt would say; as a social structure, Gordon would say). They would be conscious of themselves as a people; be involved in extensive primary, face-to-face relationships with their own kind; preserve those particular values which distinguish them and which they cherish. Over the course of generations, if these particular characteristics were lost, they would become socially, as well as culturally, assimilated.

Central to this strength of the community, is the sense of identity among the members of the community. Who are we? And how do we and how does the larger community know who we are? To whom do I really belong and by what sign do I know it? The sense of identity among earlier immigrant groups was preserved and reinforced by a number of factors: for the Irish – years of suffering and persecution; for the Jews – their mysterious unity as a people and their history of oppression. But in general, conditions which helped to strengthen the immigrant community were: a) concentration of residence. You could tell what village in Italy a person was from simply by knowing where he lived in New York, b) the formation of immigrant associations to provide for their own welfare, c) religious identification with a parish that was their own, and, d) in many cases an important contributing factor was language. Note that in these cases, the function of language was not simply to be a means of personal communication. It was the symbol of social solidarity – language at once manifested the solidarity that existed and also reinforced it. So deep was the feeling of identification based on language that French Canadians, for example, feared that when their children stopped speaking French they would also lose their Catholic faith. Polish immigrants had difficulty with their early parochial schools. They wished to retain Polish as the ordinary language of instruction even in the parochial schools of the United States. Among Ukrainian Catholic groups of New York, language is the mediating instrument to retain the religious as well as the social solidarity of the Ukrainian community. In all these cases, however, the strength of the ethnic group has never hindered, it has always helped the newcomers to take their place strongly as members of the larger society.

When we examine the experience of the Puerto Ricans in New York, the first thing that strikes one is the fact that the circumstances which aided the earlier immigrant communities no longer exist to be of assistance to them. They are widely scattered throughout New York City. Despite a number of noticeable concentrations, it is doubtful that in any area they represent the strong concentration of people that was characteristic of the earlier immigrant groups. Nathan Glazer indicates, in his study of Puerto Rican housing, that concentration of the community becomes more evident the longer the Puerto Ricans live in New York. As they become more familiar with the City and as they move around seeking satisfactory dwellings, they find it possible to live in greater concentrations. But initially, they are widely scattered. The policy of integration in public housing also contributed to scatter. Earlier immigrants chose their place of residence and usually chose a place in the midst of their own people. With public housing, this is not possible. Organized welfare services make unnecessary extensive self-help associations for today's new arrivals. The institution, especially in the New York Archdiocese, of the integrated parish rather than separate churches and parishes for Puerto Ricans, means that religious identification will not be a strong factor in community. Finally, the Island is so close by: a Puerto Rican can travel from San Juan to New York faster than an Irishman could travel from Coney Island to Times Square a century ago. As one checks through this list and seeks the basis for identity among the Puerto Ricans, the one factor that looms large is language. I am not suggesting that the Puerto Ricans are not otherwise conspicuous. In many cases they are. But the use of the language is the key that opens the community to them, that immediately identifies them as "our own," that is evidence of the bond that binds them together in a common world.

Furthermore, the larger society in New York has responded to this. There are signs in Spanish in the New York subways and in other public places where Puerto Ricans congregate. (This appears to be eminently practical – but this practicality was neglected among the immigrant groups.) Thousands of teachers, public servants, clergy have learned Spanish in order to communicate. This also is eminently practical. One asks, in our puzzlement why it was never done before. Finally the recognition that literacy in Spanish is sufficient to enable one to vote in New York is most important. The Supreme Court has upheld the action of Congress in this matter. The fact that this political adjustment enabled the Puerto Ricans to elect a borough president (Herman Badillo, 1965) only serves to emphasize the significance of the language factor. It is an unusual public symbol of identity, of the solidarity of the Puerto Ricans in a group of their own kind – of the strength they can have if they remain together. In other words, when one searches in New York for a strong impressive sign of the unity of Puerto Ricans as a people, the only sign that stands out vividly is the sign of their Spanish language.

I wish to speculate a bit about some of the implications of this. Before I do so, let me say something about the relationship of this phenomenon to the Island itself. The Puerto Ricans on the Island have their own problem of identity quite apart from being newcomers to the Mainland. The problem of political status, the difficulties of rapid economic development and the social and cultural change which it has provoked, the ambiguity of the impressive development of Catholic life on the Island due to the fact that much of it has been associated with Mainland clergy who have given the Church a somewhat Mainland appearance. This may be modified with the rapid development of a native Puerto Rican hierarchy, but the ambiguity has been there. In the presence of uncertainties which have resulted from the above, it seems to me that on the Island also, language has become a sensitive symbol of identity.

In the hearings held last summer about the political status of the Island, attention was centered on the question of the culture of the Island. Repeatedly in the Hearings, the question of language became paramount. As I recall, some of the people who testified had no fear of Statehood endangering the identity of Puerto Rico provided statehood raised no threat to the Spanish language as the language native to the Island. Loss of language was represented very clearly as being a loss of self. You recall the heated controversy in 1963 between some of Puerto Rico's Catholics and the Bishops of the Island about the problem of Spanish in the Catholic schools. The complaint was voiced that lack of proper emphasis on Spanish frequently leaves the student in the Catholic school without an adequate formation in his traditional culture. The conviction was vigorously expressed that, among other things, religion could not be properly communicated to a child in Puerto Rico unless it was communicated in Spanish. In his excellent speech in New York last Spring (1964), the new Resident Commissioner, Santiago Polanco Abreu, sought to assert the particular identity of Puerto Ricans and he humorously quoted the popular song:

"Los que dicen Ai Bendito, esos si son de aqui."
(Those who say "Ai Bendito," they are the ones who come from here.)

It is not without significance that identity is revealed thus clearly by language.

I am aware of the danger of exaggerating the above evidence of the concern of Puerto Ricans for their traditional language. But I think it is clear that it is a sensitive point; and it is sensitive because the identity of the people of the Island depends on it. Renzo Sereno's interesting, if controversial, article, "Boricua, A Study of Language, Transculturation and Politics," probably exaggerates in his suggestion that language is the medium through which political powers dominate the culture of subordinate groups. But he does well to call attention to the important political relationships involved in language. It is a symbol of domination or subordination, however it may become that way. Therefore, vigorous efforts to retain a native language, proceeding from a self-consciousness that it is threatened, are indicative of a people seeking to hold on to their identity. O'Flannery's article, "Social and Cultural Assimilation," (*American Catholic Sociological Review* XXII:3, Fall, 1961, 195-207), is a study of second generation Puerto Rican girls in a religious society in the Bronx. Although all of these girls knew English well, they still insisted on having their own Spanish speaking association, not because they did not like the American girls in the English speaking association, but because they felt this way that they had an identity, and they clung to it.

We may now ask what has this to do with the Puerto Rican child. It is important for the identity of the Puerto Rican, whether here or in New York, to have a strong sense of identity – belonging – that he belongs to a Puerto Rican community that is strong, self-respecting and self-assured. And language evidently has a great deal to do with this kind of strength in the community. It is important to note that I am speaking here in a sociological context, not a psychological one. I am referring to the social group, the organization of their social life, the institutional framework which gives identity and strength. Actually, the importance of this context is becoming recognized increasingly at this time. The functioning community is the focus of the new direction being given to the identification and care of persons who are mentally ill and, in the Anti-Poverty Program, the community is the focus of the programs designed to enable the poor to prepare themselves to take advantage of the opportunities available in American society. Therefore, I would suggest that the Puerto Rican community as it functions to provide a basis for identity, must be an important focus of our attention in our concern for the education of the Puerto Rican child.

Let me take a few moments to clarify what I mean here. Let me refer for a moment to the Project, Mobilization for Youth. This is a massive community-based program initially conceived as a delinquency prevention project. The theoretical basis of the project is the theory of Cloward and Ohlin that a great deal of delinquency is not primarily a manifestation of personality maladjustment; it is the consequence of a social system which motivates youth to compete for the benefits of American society, and then effectively prevents these same youth from competing by blocking the channels to ordinarily expected opportunities for competition. The resulting frustrations, tension, aggravation, burst out in forms of delinquent behavior. In view of this, an effective program to prevent delinquency must address itself to social structures, to the community. In seeking to do this, Mobilization has found itself involved in a range of activity from counselling youth to community action pro- grams. It proceeds on the principle that psychological help or psychiat- ric treatment in many cases is of limited use unless the context of the youth's total life in the community enables him to develop strongly as a man in our American society.

This same principle has carried over into psychiatry. An excellent presentation of the situation can be found in the collection of readings, *Mental Health and the Poor*, edited by Frank Riessman, Jerome Cohen and Arthur Pearl. The authors insist that both diagnosis and therapy, par- ticularly rehabilitation, will become effective with the poor only when it involves itself more completely in the community of the poor, when it is "much more closely integrated with other institutions, such as the com- munity, the world of work and the church" (viii). The research and demonstration projects emerging from this theory seek to bring psychia- try into this close integration with the social life of the patient; and they seek to involve not only the patient, but the members of his own com- munity in the process of identifying mental illness and caring for it. An excellent popular review of these developments is found in the article by Maya Pines, "The Coming Upheaval in Psychiatry," in *Harpers*, Oct. 1965, p. 54ff.

Finally a word about the policy of the anti-poverty program in insisting that the poor be involved in defining their needs which must be satisfied, and the programs which are aimed at satisfying them. The presupposition here is that the poor have remarkable strengths which are continually overlooked; insights into the nature of their troubles, and a keen ability to do something about them if circumstances were created which would enable them to do so. The theory of the anti-poverty programs is that the kind of welfare service needed today cannot be provided effectively on a case work basis. It requires a community-wide program in which the poor are enabled to organize and exploit their own resources for coping with their own problems.

These three quick references to Mobilization, to the community orientation of psychiatry, to the anti-poverty program, are intended simply to illustrate the growing recognition today that the massive problems of the modern urban environment can be met effectively only on a community basis; that the role of the community is crucial in coping with such large problems as delinquency, mental illness and poverty.

In reference to the point of this paper, therefore, the importance of identity for Puerto Ricans; the crucial role of the community as the basis for identity; and the significance of language in this community process, can be seen as reflecting the major orientation of the social sciences today toward contemporary problems. In order to cope with the problems of the Puerto Rican child, we must look carefully to the situation of the Puerto Rican community.

My own research at the present time is guided by this orientation. For the past three years, we have been cooperating with a Training School for delinquent boys in a study of the assessment and treatment of delinquent behavior. When we began the study, we were somewhat dismayed as we read case history after case history, to discover that all the cases were being diagnosed with psychological and psychiatric concepts. In brief, the presumption seemed to be that the delinquency proceeded from some personality maladjustment of the child. We looked through the cases for some indication that the social and cultural dimensions of delinquent behavior had been taken into account. We rarely found them. For example, the cultural background of Puerto Rican children was not considered in diagnosis. Sex relations between boys and girls were consistently evaluated according to a single set of norms, with little or no attention being given to the variations between Mainland norms and those of Puerto Rico. In one case, a Puerto Rican boy was living with his boyfriend's sister. She was pregnant when the boy was arrested. To me this seemed to be an example of a rather ordinary and fairly common kind of consensual union. The case record indicated it as a manifestation of hostility against women on the part of the boy; he had a need to punish women and did this by making the girl pregnant.

What became clear to us as we proceeded was the fact that the social and cultural dimensions of delinquent behavior were rarely involved in the diagnosis or treatment of the delinquent person, whereas many cases of delinquency which we examined appeared to be quite clearly a reflection of the cultural patterns of the boys' lives, or an understandable response to the social situation in which they operated. In other words, in many cases, it is only in the entire social and cultural context that a reliable assessment of delinquency can be made. We are now engaged in a continuation of this research, in an effort to develop a method of accumulating information about the social and cultural dimensions of delinquent behavior. In the setting of a course for the training of probation workers, we are developing curriculum materials which hopefully will prepare the probation workers to be alert to the social and cultural aspects of delinquent behavior.

In relation to our present discussion, the significance of the research is as follows: once again it has highlighted for us the importance of studying a youth in a total social and cultural context. Much delinquency does not indicate that a boy is a maladjusted personality, but that he is well adjusted to a whole culture or way of life which is deviant from the major culture of the society. In this context, the correction of delinquency is not the adjustment of a personality, but rather a process of transculturation by which the boy is resocialized into the dominant culture of the society.

The research has led us back again to a recognition of the central role of the community in the experience of the Puerto Rican child. The strengths he has from his strong identity with the community are easily interpreted as weaknesses, or deviance, by ourselves. When seen in the context of the total community, they often begin to appear as strengths.

It is possible that language, particularly among Puerto Ricans on the Mainland, may appear as a weakness, a failure to master the language of our society. In many cases, I have no doubt it is. But from another point of view, the strong insistence on Spanish may be a manifestation of the strength of the Puerto Rican community, of a sense of clear identity. It is important to recognize it as such, if it is. I see no danger of this interfering with the learning and use of English.

Actually, this implies in a situation like New York, the ability to speak English also. Ability to function effectively in the world of a new culture ordinarily requires knowledge of a language. According to Eisenstadt, it is the basic step in cultural assimilation. But knowledge of Spanish in a situation like New York in no way implies an hindrance to the learning of English. In fact, confidence in the knowledge of the native language is a strong basis for the confident learning of English.

The methods or techniques for doing this are beyond the scope of this paper. A great deal of attention is being given to this in the experiments in teaching English as a second language. But I am convinced that if strong community support is present, the task of forming children well in both languages would be much more effectively carried out. I recall the Ukrainian community on the Lower East Side among whom the knowledge of both languages is admirable.

Let me add a final comment about the Island. If Sereno's thesis is correct that political changes, especially those implying subordination, operate through language to offer the integration of personality, it would seem that the security-strength of Puerto Ricans on the Island could be maintained by the strong emphasis on the Spanish language. If the theory of the strong community is valid, self-assurance or a sense of security symbolized in the Spanish language, would be the most effective way of encouraging knowledge of English. Knowledge of English would not be considered a threat. If language, therefore, is a symbol of identity, the stronger it is, the better. It means a strong community and it reinforces the strength of the community. In the long run this is healthy. One integrates from a position of strength, not from a position of weakness.

12

Oscar Lewis and
the Puerto Rican Family

A Noted Anthropologist Offers Controversial
Insights Into the Culture of Poverty[1]

PUERTO RICO HAS NEVER LACKED FOR SOCIOLOGICAL AND ANTHROPOLOGI-
cal inquiries. It is a well-studied island. With the publication of Oscar
Lewis' *La Vida: A Puerto Rican Family in the Culture of Poverty – San Juan
and New York* (Random House), another significant title is added to the
list.

La Vida is an extraordinary book: extraordinary as an anthropological achievement; extraordinary in its potential danger. It marks Oscar
Lewis once again as a creative innovator in anthropological method, an
artist of rare ability as well as a competent scientist. But it raises serious
questions about the discretion of allowing wide public circulation of
valuable anthropological material that is exposed to misinterpretation
and possible misuse. The Puerto Ricans in Puerto Rico and on the
Mainland have been waiting for *La Vida* with fearful expectation. They
are deeply frightened at the public image of the poor Puerto Rican that
may be created by the book. Nevertheless, to one who has the eyes to
see and the heart to appreciate, *La Vida* is a contribution of untold value
to the understanding of a segment of Puerto Rican life.

No priest, religious, teacher, social worker, or public official of any
kind who has occasion to deal with the type of Puerto Ricans described
in *La Vida* can afford to omit a careful reading of this document. It will
enable them to penetrate a way of life more deeply than any other
instrument I know. And it throws into remarkably meaningful perspec-

---

1. Review of *LaVida*, reprinted from *America*, Dec. 10, 1966. Reprinted with
   the permission of America Press, Inc., 106 West 56th Street, New York, NY
   10019. ©1966. All Rights Reserved.

tive, patterns of behavior that are not only misunderstood, but ordinarily judged as barbarous or revolting by the wider world of rich and poor to whom this way of life is foreign. As an eminent Puerto Rican educator remarked last year in a heated discussion about the potentially damaging consequences of Lewis' book: "The danger of over-generalization is great; but even more dangerous is the situation where teachers, social workers and others are dealing with this type of Puerto Rican people without the insights that Lewis' book can give."

Lewis is emphatic in explaining that the Ríos family in *La Vida* is not presented as a representative Puerto Rican family. The family was chosen because it represents a particular style of life, which Lewis calls the "culture of poverty." Neither is the Ríos family representative of the poor. Lewis insists that many people are poor without developing the culture of poverty. Lewis defines the culture of poverty as "both an adaptation and a reaction of the poor to their marginal position in a class-stratified, highly individuated, capitalistic society." "It represents," he says, "an effort to cope with feelings of hopelessness and despair which develop from the realization of the improbability of achieving success in terms of the values and goals of the larger society."

Lewis finds this adaptation both remarkably creative and reflective of great strengths, but also pathetic and filled with suffering and emptiness. He analyzes it according to four characteristics:

1) lack of effective participation of the poor in the major institutions of the larger society;

2) poor living conditions and a minimum of organization beyond the level of the nuclear or extended family;

3) absence of childhood, early initiation into sex, free unions and consensual marriages, high incidence of abandonment, female-centered families, authoritarianism, lack of privacy and lack of family stability;

4) a strong feeling of marginality, of helplessness, of dependence and inferiority.

The great value of the concept of the culture of poverty is the perspective it gives on the pressing problems of some segments of our contemporary poor. What we tend to identify as an American problem or a Negro problem now appears to have much wider dimensions and must be examined as a general reaction to particular social conditions anywhere throughout the world.

Lewis had explored this phenomenon in previous publications, particularly in *Five Families* and *Children of Sanchez* (Random House, 1959 and 1961). He is testing his theory in his present studies in Puerto Rico. *La Vida* is the first major publication of these studies. Its significance, therefore, is not what it tells us about Puerto Rico, but what it tells us about the culture of poverty. Nevertheless, it is the Puerto Rican details that will hold the center of the stage.

Lewis used every available source to assemble an enormous amount of information about the family he studies in a San Juan slum. He established a close friendship with the family over a long period of time; used a trained, competent Puerto Rican woman as a participant observer; and recorded on tape the life histories of his principal subjects. These he has skillfully edited to present the details of the way of life of the Ríos family.

The details are incredibly abundant and vivid. They range from the day-to-day struggle with poverty in a San Juan slum: for example, the reader cannot but be amazed at the capacity of Cruz, a crippled young mother abandoned by her husband, to cope with almost continuous destitution. The details range across the generosity and petty selfishness, the violence and cruelty, the loyalties and deceits, the intense activity, of the Ríos family. The contrast between Cruz's life in a public housing project and her life in the slum is a clear reflection of the vitality, the excitement, the human qualities of friendship and dependence of the slum, which its inhabitants evidently relish. And running through it all is the ever present involvement in sex, the reality that seems never to be missing from their lives or from their speech.

Their sex life is reported by Lewis in a surprising literalness of language and an unrestrained abundance of detail. Lewis insists that this is necessary; that the flavor of their lives would be missed if this exactness of language were omitted. Their language is earthy, simple and direct. "The description of the most intimate sexual scenes is so matter-of-fact that it soon loses the quality of obscenity and one comes to accept it as an intrinsic part of their everyday life." The book, however, is not a collection of dirty stories, as it will sometimes indignantly, sometimes facetiously, be described. It gets through to a way of life and can communicate to the reader the experience of people who seek to fulfill themselves in a world of severely limited resources; who succeed in surviving in a sea of human troubles, and reflect a vitality that often leaves the reader breathless.

Nevertheless, the very strengths of the book involve its dangers. It will be a best-seller, although its market performance will hardly be an indication of a sudden enthusiasm of the American people for anthropology. It is a brilliant portrayal, but a raw picture; it paints in bold, unmistakable lines the characteristics of the Ríos family, which have been the warp and woof of the damaging stereotypes that have made life difficult for the Puerto Ricans of our mainland cities. It will require a discreet reader to see this record of the Ríos family in its proper perspective, and it is doubtful how many people will read the lengthy introduction, which *must* be carefully read if the book is to be kept in its proper setting.

La Vida should be used in combination with other outstanding works on the Puerto Rican family. Sidney Mintz's *Worker in the Cane* (Yale University Press, 1960), the life history of a poor worker in Santa Isabel, on the south coast of the Island, is a remarkable portrayal of the deep human qualities, the dignity and self-respect in a different segment of Puerto Rican family life (see *America* September 3, 1960). Mintz's report is much more delicate and restrained than *La Vida*. It is interesting to note that Mintz could never get his principal informant to talk about sex. Yet Santa Isabel has always had one of the highest rates of consensual union on the island.

Julian Steward's *People of Puerto Rico* (University of Illinois Press, 1957) presents an excellent description of family life in two mountain areas, two coastal areas, and among the top four hundred families on the Island. The variety of these cultures is impressive, a variety that is a necessary backdrop for the portrayal of *La Vida*. In my own studies of the Island, I have never ceased to wonder at the amazing differences in Puerto Rican family life. Moca, a little town in the Northwest, which had the lowest rate of consensual unions in 1950, is only a few miles from Maricao, another little mountain town, which had one of the highest rates. And Aquada, which had the highest rate of Catholic marriages in 1960 (71.4 percent), is immediately next to Aquadilla, where 53 percent of the marriages were Protestant.

David Landy's study, *Tropical Childhood* (University of North Carolina Press, 1959), portrays a Puerto Rican family life that is much quieter and less active and exciting, where social controls over sexual behavior are much stricter than those found among the people of *La Vida*. On the other hand, much of the interview material in the study of mental illness among Puerto Rican families by Lloyd H. Rogler and August B. Hollingshead, *Trapped: Families in Schizophrenia* (Wiley, 1965), approaches the style and spontaneous earthiness of the people in *La Vida*.

The more serious difficulty, however, is the general problem of misunderstanding and possible misuse of the kind of data that Lewis makes available. The book rends the veil of the geographical and cultural segregation that ordinarily shields the people of *La Vida* from the eyes of curious and critical onlookers, and exposes them to a world that in large part is likely to judge their nakedness according to its own standards. Lewis published the study in an effort to uncover for the larger world the strengths and human qualities of these people, which often lie hidden beneath the emptiness, suffering and crudity that impress the outsider. It seems to me that this insight is not conveyed immediately by the book, but will depend upon the compassion and perception of the reader. In other words, only those who already love will have the vision to perceive the potential greatness that expresses itself in the life of the Ríos family. When the love is there – and may it be there often – it will profit abundantly by the record that Lewis has provided.

13

The Catholic School: Its Place in the Witness of the Church[1]

DURING THE SUMMER, I HAD OCCASION TO SPEAK TO A NUN IN PUERTO RICO who had just finished a Head Start program in her parish school. I have rarely in my life heard anyone more ecstatic. Description after description tumbled out with her words – of new experiences, challenging, humorous, pathetic. She capped them off with an emphatic gesture and a surprisingly emphatic remark: "Father, this as the first time I was the kind of a nun I had entered the convent to be."

I talked a while longer, trying to discover why she had said this. It seemed to come down to three things:

1. This was the first time in her religious life that she was up to her ears in the immediate experience of the life of the very poor. Through the back alleys, in the homes, on the street corners, she was, in a way that she had never been before, one of them, one of their own kind.

2. There was the satisfaction of being able to respond immediately to immediately evident needs. The needs were so numerous that anything she did seemed to help: a glass of milk in the mid-morning; some quick medical attention for a rash that wouldn't disappear; all the big or little lessons that opened the windows of a great world to the mind of a little child. Many of these children, who lived three miles from the Caribbean Sea, had never seen it. A ten minute drive in the station wagon quickly took care of that. Sister was aware of a mountain of needs that she could not begin to touch.

---

1. Address given at a workshop on inner city schools, sponsored by the Superintendent of Schools, Archdiocese of New York, Nov. 11, 1965. Reprinted in *Catholic Mind*, March 1966, pp. 28-35. Reprinted with the permission of America Press, Inc., 106 West 56th Street, New York, NY 10019. ©1966. All Rights Reserved.

But every time she turned around she was conscious of the immediate effectiveness of what she did.

3. She was aware that she was part of a great nationwide effort to meet the problems of poverty and deprivation in the United States.

I have since reflected a great deal on that conversation. Involvement, effectiveness and service to the total community, these were the three features of her experience that made the nun enthusiastic. It gradually dawned on me that each of these three things touched directly on the three most serious crises that are troubling us today. The first is the crisis of the relevance of our religious life, for those of us who are religious. Have we created a structure in our religious life that enables us to serve God, so to speak, only by neglecting our neighbor? The second is the crisis of effectiveness. To what extent is the Catholic school achieving the objectives for which alone it exists? The third is the crisis of responsibility to the total society, the crisis of our citizenship in the city, the nation and the world. This is our responsibility to use our resources not simply to protect or promote our isolated Catholic interests, but to help our total society meet the pressing problems it must meet if it is to be a society of men. Relevance and involvement; effectiveness; responsibility – it is a striking thing that the challenge of the inner city to the Church sharply defines the crisis we must face as Catholics in the world. In the providence of God, it may also be the occasion of our solving them.

I would like to frame my remarks around these three points. I do not intend these remarks as something that I am saying to you. I understand them as something I am saying with you. The problems that face us as Catholic educators have been as troublesome a preoccupation with me as they have been with you. I would like my words to give some expression to the spirit of inquiry and innovation that has inspired this meeting. Perhaps they will also give some perspective to the problems.

Let me take the topics I mentioned in reverse order: responsibility, effectiveness, involvement. I think this enables us to move into the problem more logically, from the definition of our responsibility for the great public issues of poverty, through a discussion of the effectiveness of the Catholic school in coping with it, to an examination of our involvement as Catholic educators and Catholic citizens in the process.

The Responsibility

The great public responsibility that we seem suddenly to have discovered is the problem of poverty in the world's most affluent society. What was the discovery? It was not the discovery that people were poor.

People were much poorer a century ago in New York than they are today; and there are many more poor in other parts of the world than there are here. It was not a discovery that people did not have enough to eat or enough to wear. Even the poor today have much more to eat and are better clothed than they were a century ago. The important discovery was the discovery that poverty in our kind of society is not a matter of material possessions, although the material dimension can never be avoided. Poverty is a cultural and a social quality. It is identified by the absence of those things that enable a person to participate fully as a man in our way of life.

About two centuries ago, when industry was beginning to grow up, men realized that a man could not participate in a world of industry, commerce and technology unless he could read and write. Until that time, a person could be a full-fledged citizen, possess great public responsibility, even though he was illiterate. This was not to continue. In a world of developed industry and commerce, a man would be helpless to participate unless he was literate. As a result, in the nations of developed economies, social institutions are geared to the task of making sure everyone can read and write. We are in the midst of a deeper discovery. Not only is literacy needed to participate in a world of electronics and automation; a high level of training, of skill, of sophistication are essential. Otherwise men cannot be men in our kind of technological world. They cannot even survive economically, much less politically or socially. Our society, therefore, has set out to make available to everyone this high level of training and skill.

But the great discovery went beyond this. Even when opportunity was made available, it became clear that people could not take advantage of it unless they were culturally and socially prepared. In other words, education is perceived today not as a simple matter of studying lessons or mastering a body of knowledge. Education is perceived more clearly as a response of the total person. He will not be able to respond to learning, knowledge and skill unless his cultural background, his social relationships and his personality enable him to do so. This is the poverty that we have suddenly discovered. Abruptly we have been shocked into realizing that we have created a set of institutions that have left a vast segment of our society deprived of the cultural background, the social relationships, the personality formation that are essential if one is to perform effectively in our kind of a world.

I cannot delay on a discussion as to how this happened. We simply excluded the Negro, for example, from our way of life, from social relations as an equal to ourselves, from access to cultural advantages.

As a result it was difficult for him to develop those qualities of inquiry, of aggressiveness in learning, of competitiveness that enable a person to perform in the educational structures of our world. We then routed him into a system geared to our kind of world, and instead of enabling him to take advantage of his own cultural and personality strengths, it tends to crush him.

This is the problem of poverty. It has revealed to us a massive educational challenge that at present we are seeking to meet. From an educational viewpoint there are two important characteristics of this challenge.

In the first place, we have come to realize that, in order to educate the poor, we must first know the poor, we must know them not in terms of acquaintanceship, but in terms of the values, the virtues, the loyalties as well as the problems and difficulties of their way of life. Like the Sister in Puerto Rico, we must in some way become "one of them." Otherwise our tendency will be to impose our way of life on them. When the native Americans sought to do this to the immigrant groups, the immigrants resisted fiercely. And the poor may well resist if we seek to make them over on the model of ourselves. They have virtues of which they are proud; they have loyalties to which they are deeply attached; they have strengths and ingenuities that amaze the people who have eyes to see them. What is more serious, our way of life often seems to them to be strange, inhuman, sometimes immoral. What they want is to share in the great society not by becoming someone else, but by fulfilling themselves. Surely they want to change. But they don't want us to be the ones to change them. They want a situation in which the virtues and strengths of their way of life will have a chance to develop, to come more fully alive and grow into the same world as ourselves.

To know and respect a way of life that is very different from our own is one of the most difficult of achievements; to sense the spirit of the Lord in a way of life that often appears to us as disorganized, possibly immoral, this is an extraordinary gift. But unless we achieve this, the possibility of meeting the challenge of the education of the poor for our society will be very slight A monsignor told me some weeks ago about a young priest, a friend of both of us, who spent the summer living in a store front in a slum area of the city. I remarked to him: "I suppose he did that in order to make Christ present to the poor." The monsignor replied: "No, he did it to find out how Christ was actually present to the poor." This is the task, and it is not an easy one.

In the second place we have come to realize that education of the poor demands the involvement of the whole person. It is not a matter of hours in a classroom, or school exercises performed, or routine teaching techniques. It demands a knowledge of the child in the entire context of his life, a perception of his position in a family and a sensitivity to the kind of family life he leads; an awareness of the meaning of sights and sounds for him, of the experience of touch and smell. It requires an ability on our part to sense the things that he respects; to know his definitions of honor or deceit; his reactions to excitement, to activity; to understand the way he expresses himself, not in words, but with the motions of his body, the glances of an eye, the idiom, the tone of voice.

But you know this much better than I do. Our education is abstract; the experience of the poor child is concrete. We communicate by words; the poor child communicates by physical movement. Evidently what is needed to reach him effectively is innovation, imaginative experimentation; a willingness to seek the things that will be meaningful to him rather than simply to run him through routines that we have followed perhaps for generations.

In any event, this educational task, requiring a deep and perceptive understanding of the life of the poor, and an adjustment of teaching method to reach the poor child in the context of his whole life, this is now recognized as an enormous national task. It is a responsibility of the nation, the city, the neighborhood. And, as citizens, we must share that task. It is our task as well as that of the state or the government. It does not seem possible anymore to say: "What is good for the Catholic Church is good for the nation." It is possible to press our parochial interests to the neglect of more critical needs of the common welfare. There are millions of the poor who need the special kind of educational research I mentioned above. And we simply cannot say: "Let the State see to it." We must see to it also. And the most difficult problem we have to face is the relationship of our Catholic interests to the responsibilities we have as citizens to meet the challenge of the education of the poor. As the Sister said in Puerto Rico; "I felt I was involved in a great national effort to teach the poor."

Effectiveness: The Catholic School

In order to meet this responsibility, primarily an educational one, we have one enormous resource, our Catholic school system. How effectively will it help us?

The controversy over the effectiveness of Catholic schools, which has been current the past few years, is concerned with one particular type of effectiveness, the effectiveness of the Catholic school in forming intelligent, alert, committed Catholics who bring the power of their Catholic faith and ideals to bear upon the life of the nation and the world. I do not wish to enter into this particular controversy now. My present concern is the fact that we have an enormous resource in our hands, in fact, so enormous that the Church has often been called a vast school system accompanied by a number of churches. In terms of financial investment, human investment and object of interest, Catholicism in the United States is predominantly the Catholic school.

To what extent is it effective, or does it enable us to be effective in the great social responsibility I have just described? The picture is rather upsetting.

The basic policy of the Catholic school is that it exists for Catholic children. There are a number of exceptions, particularly where Negroes are involved. But by and large, the school population of the parochial school consists of Catholic children. In maintaining this type of institution, we have created a structure that does not permit us to become seriously involved in the educational challenge of the inner city. The statistics are eloquent. Last year in New York City, there were 115,000 Negro children in the public schools of Manhattan and the Bronx. There were 6,640 in the Catholic schools of Manhattan and the Bronx. It is clear why there are so few. Negroes, for the most part, are not Catholics. But the Negroes constitute the crucial problem of the education of the poor in the inner city. If the Church is to bear witness to our brothers in need, it must involve itself in this pressing problem But institutionally, we have excluded ourselves from it. I am not speaking here of personal involvement; I'll speak about that later. I am speaking about the involvement of the Catholic school. You asked me to speak about the role of the school in the witness of the Church in the inner city. As long as the policy remains that the Catholic school is for Catholic children, it cannot have more than a negligible role. We are out of the combat.

I am not suggesting here that we turn white children out and fill the schools tomorrow with Negroes. But if we are going to talk seriously about the witness of the Catholic school in the inner city, we have to talk seriously about this problem. Surely there must be something that we could do, more imaginative than what we are doing. Are there no more extensive experiments that we could try? Is it really a problem of Catholicism? I am beginning to doubt it. Catholicism is not the problem in the case of the Puerto Rican, the second large segment of the poor and deprived in the inner city of New York. The great majority of the Puerto Ricans are baptized Catholics. But last year, there were 111,000 Puerto Ricans in the public schools of Manhattan and the Bronx; 14,646 in the

Catholic schools of Manhattan and the Bronx, about 12 percent of all Puerto Rican school children living in these two boroughs.

There is nobody in this auditorium who knows better than I do the enormous effort of the New York Archdiocese to prepare for the apostolate among the Spanish speaking. It will go down in history. But if the school is going to be an effective witness in the apostolate of the inner city, I am afraid it will be a very limited witness if we cannot do better than 12 percent. In some cases, I know there is a problem of overcrowding. One parish in the Bronx just opened its second school. I know that often there is the poor response of Puerto Rican parents to the Catholic schools. But I think we should give some serious thought to this problem of the small numbers of Puerto Ricans in the Catholic schools. In this massive public responsibility for the education of the poor, our Catholic schools are not only out of action in the case of Protestant Negroes; they are almost out of action in the case of Catholic Puerto Ricans. Whatever else this may be, it is hardly being relevant.

The problem is not lack of zeal or dedication or good will. The great mystery of our lives is why these priceless qualities, which we have in abundance, are not more effective in reaching the problem. And we have incredible talent, also. One of the government officials of Puerto Rico told me he never saw anything like the ability of some of the Sisters in dealing with the poor. And one of the officials of the Board of Education here in New York frankly admitted to me that his lifelong stereotypes about Catholic Sisters were blasted to pieces when he saw the skill with which some of them handled the summer programs. I think the problem is fairly obvious. We have been maintaining the traditional routines of the system, and expecting the Puerto Ricans to adjust to it, instead of adjusting the system to meet the needs of the Puerto Ricans. By the system, I mean the system as a whole, not only certain routines such as testing methods or admissions procedures. There is obvious need for imaginative adjustment, experimentation, continued evaluation. This is why we are here today. God speed your work. The day is already far spent, and if we cannot find an effective method by which to gather the harvest, we may lose it.

And when the child is in the school, can we not hope that workshops like this will prepare you to have the contact, the understanding, the insight into his life that I have spoken about? If the child could only be aware that we want him as part of our way of life because of the values that are part of his way of life. I have been with many of you at the Institute in Ponce, and I was conscious of the enthusiasm that you had for the background of the Puerto Rican people. I hope this will communicate itself to the child and his parents and help them realize that it is they whom we respect and whom we want. If this same enthusiasm and respect could be developed toward the Negro background and way of life, the school would provide the experience that the poor need in order to take their places confidently in our world.

Personal Involvement

I now come, finally, to the most important of the three topics of my talk, that is you. You are the great resource. Without you, the Catholic school is a pile of brick and concrete, a mute pile with neither heart nor tongue. You are the one that gives it life, that makes it a human thing.

If you are going to bear witness to the Church and to Christ in the inner city, you have to be involved. This involvement may take place in the school, if the school numbers the poor among its students. Or it may take place in the school but outside of the context of the regular school day, in tutoring programs, in CCD, in group work with children or adults. Finally, involvement may take you out of the school into the street, the tenement, the boys' club, the playground.

The single point that must guide anyone in the inner city apostolate is this: we must adjust the structure of our lives to the demands of the apostolate; we cannot insist that the poor structure their lives to fit into our regulations and schedules. This is a simple technical point that is elementary. Yet it is the point that has regularly isolated religious from the challenge of modern life. Secondly, we do not seek the poor simply in order to be engaged in doing good. Recall St. Vincent DePaul's remark: "We must ask the pardon of the poor for the bread we must give them." Nothing can be more humiliating to a poor person, to any person in fact, than to feel he is the object of charity. Only love can prevent this, a love for the deep values and merits of the life of the poor; an awareness, on their part always, that we recognize the greatness and the value of the person we serve, and that we accept him as our equal. Finally, a recognition on our part that, in the apostolate to the poor, we are not going to them to make Christ present to them, but to discover how Christ is already present in their lives. In order to make the poor one with us, we must first make ourselves one with them. This is involvement; this is relevance.

Let me end with a brief and well known story. When a young man asked Our Lord how he could gain eternal life, Our Lord answered: "Love the Lord thy God, and love thy neighbor as thyself." And the young man questioned Him again: "But who is my neighbor?" and Our Lord answered him by telling him a little story. And I can never read or hear that story without a terrible uneasiness coming over me. "A man was going from Jerusalem to Jericho," Our Lord began, "and he fell among robbers who robbed him, beat him and left him injured by the roadside." And a priest passed by (that's me) and seeing the man, he continued on his way. (He was probably rushing to evening devotions or a meeting of the Holy Name Society; maybe to a golf date or his favorite TV show.) In any event he passed the poor man by. Then a Levite came along (that's you, the one who was chosen to serve in the temple) and seeing the poor man, he also passed by. (Probably had to get the church door open or get the incense ready for benediction; or maybe his superiors would not permit him to speak with strangers on the road.) Finally a Samaritan came by. You know what Samaritans were! They were the enemies of the Jewish people, the ones who had broken centuries before with the Judeans. This poor fellow was really an enemy of the true faith. He probably never had the opportunity to go to Catholic schools; he had never had a chance to study ethics at Fordham; he never learned the principles of right morality. He was just a Samaritan. And what did he do? He bound up the man's wounds and comforted him; he himself went on foot so that the injured man could ride; he put the injured man up in a hotel, paid for his lodging, and left word with the manager that, if there were any other expenses, he should send the bill to him. And Our Lord asked the young man "Which of the three was the neighbor of the injured man?" And the young man answered: "He who befriended him." And Our Lord said: "Go thou and do likewise."

To be a neighbor is to be Christ. But how shall I be a neighbor in the inner city? This is not easy to answer. There are many ways of being a neighbor. I could have assisted the man on the way from Jerusalem to Jericho by making sure no robbers were on the road in the first place; I could have given him a horse that could have outrun any robbers; I could have given him weapons to protect himself. Each of these can be different levels of Christliness. Father Dowling, the founder of the Cana conference movement used to say: "I have always wanted to be the water commissioner of a great city like New York. Because, if Our Lord promised a reward in heaven for a cup of cold water given in His name, think of the millions of cups the water commissioner provides every day." Charity can be indirect as well as direct; complicated as well as simple. But the impressive thing about the Samaritan is that he had time for the injured man; he took time in order to befriend him. I do not know how the parable should be applied to our lives, but Our Lord was evidently trying to tell us something: that personal involvement is the way of becoming a neighbor to my fellow men. I think that in our classrooms, underneath the crucifix, we might tack up a picture of the Good Samaritan so that for God's sake, and for the sake of our neighbor, and for our own sakes, He might teach us how to be a neighbor in the inner city, and teach us soon.

14

The Role of the Parish in the Spiritual Care of Puerto Ricans[1]

THE PROBLEM OF NUMEROUS LANGUAGE AND ETHNIC GROUPS HAS CHARAC-
terized the New York Archdiocese since the beginning of its history. The
first Church in the City, Saint Peter's on Barclay Street, was established
in 1785 and provided services in four different languages, English,
French, German and Spanish, for its varied congregation. The second
Church established in the City in 1809 was the original Saint Patrick's
Cathedral on the lower east side. The third Church established in the City
in 1825 had a Spaniard as its Pastor, although it apparently served a
multi-lingual congregation. Two other Churches, predominantly Irish,
were soon founded and, in 1833, the founding of the first Church to serve
a predominantly German population gave evidence of the increase in the
number of German immigrants coming into the City. This was the
Church of Saint Nicholas on East 2nd Street.

The presence of Spaniards in the early years of the Diocese is quite
striking. The first Church established in 1839 on Staten Island, now the
borough of Richmond of New York City, was Saint Peter's Church. Its
founder and first rector was a Spaniard, Father Ildefonso Medrano. It is
not clear whether this Church ministered to a predominantly Spanish
congregation. It was not long before it was predominantly an Irish
parish.

In 1840 the Church of Saint Vincent de Paul was established to
minister to the French speaking people of the City. By the year 1855,
when the population of the City totalled 623,000, of whom 28 percent
were Irish and 16 percent were German,[2] there were 31 Catholic
Churches in what is now the New York Archdiocese. Five of these were

---

1. *Studi Emigrazione*, October 1966, Anno. III-N.7.
2. Robert Ernst, *Immigrant Life in New York City, 1825-63*, New York: Columbia
   University Press, 1949. Table 14, p. 193.

German parishes; one was French. The character of New York as a mosaic of language and ethnic groups was very evident.

The problems of a diocese of many nationalities also began to appear in these early years. The Diocese had been established in 1808, at a time when immigration, particularly from Ireland, was beginning to attain considerable proportions. By the year 1826, the Irish constituted the largest group of Catholics in the Diocese and when a Frenchman, John Dubois, was appointed as Bishop of the See of New York, the resentment of the Irish was serious, and a coldness marked the introduction of the Bishop to his flock.[3]

Bishop Dubois was succeeded by Bishop John Hughes in 1842[4] and it was during the administration of Bishop Hughes that the principle of the national parish was firmly established, especially for the Germans. However, apart from the French Church and the German Churches, the multiplication of nationalities had not become serious. It was during the administration of Cardinal McClosky (1865-85) and particularly during that of Archbishop Corrigan (1885-1902) that national parishes increased rapidly and the underlying problem of nationality became acute. By the end of Archbishop Corrigan's administration in 1902, the Diocese of New York counted thirteen German Churches, two French, one Bohemian, four Polish, one Maronite, two Slovak, one Hungarian, one Spanish, eleven Italian, and two for the Colored. The significant activity was in the foundation of the Italian Churches. Ten of these were established in the eighteen years between 1884-1902.[5] It was an impressive response to the need of the Italian immigrants who were coming in numbers that made earlier immigrations look small. The impressive effort was to continue during the period of large-scale Italian migration. Nine more churches were to be established between 1902-1915.

During the administration of Archbishop Corrigan, the Third Plenary Council of Baltimore meeting in 1884, discussed the problem of the

---

3. Rumors apparently were widespread that Bishop Dubois had used influence to gain the New York post. The Bishop felt it necessary to deal with these rumors in his first pastoral letter. *The Truth Teller*, the Catholic paper of the Diocese at that time, refused to print the letter. Cf. J. T. Smith, *History of the Catholic Church in New York (1905)*, Vol. I, pp. 74-5.

4. He had actually become administrator of the Diocese some years earlier.

5. In 1880, according to the United States Census, there were 12,000 Italians in New York City. The number increased to 115,000 in 1890; 220,000 in 1900. One can see immediately the dimensions of the problem Archbishop Corrigan had to cope with. The increase was to continue after Corrigan's time. It was 341,000 in 1910. If persons born in New York City of Italian parentage are added, the total Italian population in 1910 was 545,000.

spiritual care of the newly arrived. It was evident from Archbishop Corrigan's remarks at the Council that Italians could not be attracted to the existing Churches staffed by Irish or German priests. He expressed his doubts whether they would be responsive to Italian parishes staffed by Italian priests. Corrigan was very pessimistic about the Italian apostolate.[6] In 1888 Pope Leo XIII addressed a letter to the Hierarchy of the United States, emphasizing the spiritual need of the immigrants, particularly the Italian immigrants.[7]

Archbishop Corrigan, however, was deeply concerned about the possible unfortunate consequences of national parishes. During his administration, a movement began among the German Catholics of the United States led by Peter Paul Cahensly, demanding that the Germans have not only German national parishes, but that Germans have their own national bishop. Corrigan saw clearly the chaotic possibilities in this kind of a policy. If every language group was to have its own diocese and its own national and language bishop, in a city of so many nationalities such as New York, the life of the Church would be hopelessly fragmented. Corrigan's struggle against Cahenslyism carried over into

---

6. The Coadjutor Archbishop of New York related how the head of the Salesians had told him personally that he would not be able to spare priests for the American missions until 1886. Then he described at length the recent census of Italian Catholics taken in New York City and vicinity at the request of Propaganda. His report had not even been acknowledged. In brief, it told of 50,000 Italians in New York, of whom all but 1200 neglected the opportunities given them to go to Mass and the sacraments. Besides this, about 200 had been confirmed by an heretical bishop, ten of the twelve priests in charge of them had been expelled from Italy for crimes, and the religious ignorance of the peasants, especially from the south of Italy, was abominable. He considered all the efforts of the Province of New York in their behalf a failure. Cf. *Acta et Decreta Concilii Plenarii Baltimorensis Tertii* (Baltimore, 1884), (private edition), pp. LXXI-LXXII. Quoted almost verbatim in Frederick J. Zwierlein, *The Life and Letters of Bishop McQuaid*, (Rochester, 1926), II, 333-334. Also quoted in Browne, Rev. Henry J., "'The Italian Problem' in the Catholic Church of the United States, 1880-1900," *Historical Records and Studies*, Vol. XXXV, p. 58, New York: United States Catholic Historical Society, 1946.

7. The Letter, *Quam Aerumnosa*, (Dec. 10, 1888). *Leonis XIII Pontificis Maximi Acta*, (Rome: Vatican Press, 1889) VIII, 383. It seems that Bishop McQuaid of Rochester, New York, did not think the letter was intended for the United States. He wrote to Archbishop Corrigan: "They say now here that the Pope's letter for the Italians was intended for South America. Monsignor Jacobini authorized Miss E. to say so. The harm however is done all the same. Everyone believes that it was intended for us." (Quoted in Henry J. Browne, *Op.Cit.*, p. 66).

his attitude toward national parishes. He was to accept their necessity for newcomers such as the Italians, but he exhorted his people against an emphasis on nationalism which would be internally divisive, and would hinder the development of a strong united Catholicism in the United States.[8] This may explain why Corrigan was not impressed by the extraordinary development of the Italian parishes during his administration. It was certainly one of the most striking religious achievements of the period. Like many Americans he favored the use of Italian speaking priests in the existing parishes.[9]

In the perspective of history, it is now evident that Archbishop Corrigan's fears about the national parish were unfounded. Far from hindering the assimilation of the Italians into American life, the national parish assisted it. The parish became the focus of a strong sense of identity and of community solidarity which protected the Italians against the social disorganization which generally affects newly arrived immigrants. Studies of migration and assimilation have indicated that "one integrates from a position of strength, not from a position of weakness." It is widely recognized today that, if the Italian parish had not given the strength and solidarity which it did give to the Italian immigrants, their lives would have been seriously disorganized and their assimilation into American life much more difficult.[10]

By the time the New York Archdiocese became aware of the challenge of a new group of migrants, the Puerto Ricans, the real problem of national parishes which Corrigan had not foreseen had already begun to manifest itself. The process of assimilation moved along relentlessly and the evidence of history revealed that it was generally a three generation process. The grandchildren of the immigrants no longer spoke the language of their grandparents; old world customs and cultures had given way to the American way of life; the mobility characteristic of American people showed itself in a pattern of movement in which the children, and especially the grandchildren, of immigrants left the area of residence of the older folks and moved to the suburbs where they could find better housing, more open land, and enjoy a sense of prestige in their conviction that they had bettered themselves and their families. This

8. Cf. Browne, *Op.Cit.*, p. 63.

9. *Ibid.*, pp. 55-56.

10. For a discussion of the process of assimilation and the role of national parishes in providing a sense of solidarity, cf. Jos. P. Fitzpatrick, "The Integration of Puerto Ricans," *Thought* (Autumn 1955) XXX: 402-20. Cf. also Milton Gordon, *Assimilation in American Life* (New York: Oxford Univ. Press, 1964).

meant that, by the third generation, usually thirty to forty years after the immigrants had arrived, the national parish faced a rapid decline in parishioners, a loss of function, and often the challenge of a new language and ethnic group in the area vacated by the earlier immigrants. . . .

After the passage of restrictive immigration laws in 1924, immigration from foreign countries dropped sharply. However two other internal migrations began to bring people in large numbers to New York City; one was the migration of Negroes from the American South. These were predominantly Protestant. The other was the migration of Puerto Ricans who, as citizens of the United States, faced no restriction in their movement to the mainland. These were predominantly Catholic. . . . The New York Archdiocese responded to this new challenge in the traditional way by establishing language parishes.[11] Two parishes for the Spanish speaking already existed in the City. . . . By the late 1920's it became evident that some special attention had to be given to the increasing number of Puerto Ricans in the City. Consequently the Archdiocese established... [two churches] in or near the East Harlem area of the City where the Puerto Ricans had begun to cluster. By 1940, the number of people born in Puerto Rico who were living in New York had increased to 61,000. It was at this moment, shortly after Cardinal Spellman had been appointed Archbishop of New York that a new direction of the Puerto Rican apostolate became evident. The circumstances of this new migration were different in many ways from those of previous migrations. These changing circumstances had to be given careful consideration if the kind of spiritual care suggested by Leo XIII for immigrants was to be given to the Puerto Ricans.

In the first place, the migration was to reach unusually large proportions after the termination of World War II. . . . This meant that, in twenty years, a number of Catholics greater in size than that of most dioceses in the United States, had appeared in the midst of this already large and complicated Archdiocese.

Secondly, they came into a city which was completely built up, not only in terms of homes but also, in terms of Churches and parochial schools. In other words, when the Italians, for example, came to New York City, many of them moved into crowded areas of the City which older residents were leaving. But large numbers moved into areas where there was vacant land, where the neighborhoods were not yet developed, and where Churches either did not exist or existed in small numbers.

---

11. It must be noted that not all of New York City is in the New York Archdiocese. Two large sections of the City, Brooklyn and Queens, are in the Brooklyn Diocese. . . .

This was not the case when the Puerto Ricans arrived. The City was crowded; had little empty land; and the Archdiocese was highly developed with parish churches and parochial schools in almost every corner of the City. In the dynamic movement that had been characteristic of the City between older residents who leave as the new immigrants come in, the Puerto Ricans found themselves inheriting territory where valuable and extensive Church properties already existed, and where organized parish life was already in force. . . .

. . . An effort to cope with this [large and rapid population change] by the method of the traditional national or language parish would have two consequences: the existing parish facilities would rapidly decay; enormous expense would be involved in establishing special parishes for the Puerto Ricans; and it is possible that these parishes would lose large numbers of their Puerto Rican parishioners in programs of urban redevelopment and slum clearance.

Finally, the Puerto Ricans were not in a position to bring their own clergy with them. Since the turn of the century the Island had suffered from a shortage of native born priests and religious, and religious orders from the United States and Europe were sending personnel to Puerto Rico. In 1940 the majority of the priests on the Island came from outside.

These circumstances were evidently very influential in the new orientation which appeared in the Puerto Rican apostolate. This new direction was apparently considered necessary if the Archdiocese was to provide the kind of care which Leo XIII had requested for migrating peoples. The effort was aimed at using the existing parish facilities, staffing them with priests who spoke Spanish and who had some familiarity with the culture of the Puerto Ricans, and who could assist the Puerto Ricans through the difficulties of adjustment to the American way of life. This would be called the "integrated parish" rather than the national or language parish. . . .

A number of practical pastoral problems are obviously involved in the "integrated parish," such as the problem of dual parish organizations, one in each language, location of services (upper church or lower church), etc. These were extensively discussed at a number of meetings of the clergy of the New York Archdiocese and of many other dioceses.[12]

The major problem of the integrated parish, however, was not the question of practical pastoral arrangements. It was the danger that it

---

12. *Report of the First Conference on the Spiritual Care of Puerto Rican Migrants,* edited by William Ferree, J. P. Fitzpatrick, Ivan Illich. (New York: Office of the Coordinator of Spanish Catholic Action, 451 Madison Avenue, New York, NY 10022, 1956).

would give the impression to the Puerto Ricans that an effort was being made to get them to become Americans as quickly as possible. There was abundant evidence in the experience of the immigrants to the United States that, when efforts were made to "Americanize" them quickly, the immigrants resisted strongly. They struggled always to retain a sense of identity and a strength of community. . . . There is little doubt that this hasty Americanization was also a danger in the parishes. Given the general attitudes at the time, there is little doubt that many American priests, referred to above were opposed to Italian parishes because they sincerely felt that integrated parishes would help them to become Americans more quickly. The same sentiments have been voiced by some modern pastors in reference to the Puerto Ricans.

A number of things worked to minimize the possibility of excessive Americanization. In 1953, the Archdiocese established an office of Co-ordinator of Spanish Catholic Action, and through the agency of this Office, it began a systematic program for training of young priests for work in parishes into which Puerto Ricans were moving. . . .

Together with intensive work in Spanish, [the program at] the Institute of Intercultural Communication has emphasized the need for a knowledge and understanding of the culture of the Puerto Ricans, a sensitivity to the Puerto Rican style of Catholicism, an awareness of the values involved in their way of life which often contrast with those of our own. The spirit which the Institute seeks to inculcate is one of respect for the valuable aspects of Puerto Rican Catholicism, and a willingness to work with Puerto Ricans so that their life may express itself in a richer Catholicism, rather than seek to impose an American style of Catholicism on them. Secondly, the Institute seeks to give its students an understanding of the process of transition from one culture to another which is involved in the assimilation of Puerto Ricans into American life. Hopefully, with an awareness of what is involved, the student is prepared to make the transition a little easier for the Puerto Rican migrants. As a result, many of the parishes of the New York Archdiocese are staffed by priests who have learned Spanish, have a deep insight and appreciation of the culture of the Puerto Ricans, and who provide spiritual care with a sensitivity to the values of Spanish culture and to the problems of cultural transition to an American way of life.

It is too early yet in the experience of the Puerto Ricans to ask how successfully this program has been. A number of questions will be answered only in the course of history.

1. To what extent does the integrated parish enable the Church to establish effective contact with Puerto Rican migrants. Rough es-

timates suggest that the Church is now in effective contact with about one third of them. It is certainly true that, by the time of the third generation, the problem of language parishes which have lost their purpose will not arise. What remains to be seen is the extent to which the Puerto Ricans have integrated strongly, without the strengths which earlier immigrants derived from the national or language parish.

2. One strong argument in favor of the integrated parish is the advantage of existing facilities, particularly the parochial schools, which are available to Puerto Rican children. There seems to be some difficulty here. In 1965, the Office of the Superintendent of Schools for the Archdiocese published the information that, . . . only 12% of all Puerto Rican school children were in Catholic schools. In view of the extensive facilities available, it is still puzzling why such a small percentage of Puerto Ricans are being reached by the Catholic school.

3. The problem of the parish and the Puerto Ricans, particularly in a City like New York, is being studied increasingly not so much in reference to migrant or immigrant groups, but in reference to the question of the role of the parish in the rapidly changing city. The problem of the newcomer is seen not only in terms of spiritual care for people who are in a process of cultural uprooting and cultural transition, but in terms of the need of people of any culture to cope with the problems of the emerging city. The effort of involvement on the part of the Church in the lives of the poor of great cities will have its application to the lives of poor migrants or immigrants. It is likely that this will be marked not by the continuation of traditional methods, but by imaginative innovations in the Liturgy, and in the methods of spiritual and religious formation of the people.[13]

---

13. Cf. *Proceedings of the CARA Conference on the Church and the Inner City*, November 1965. Available through CARA (Center for Applied Research for the Apostolate) 3620 Twelfth Street, N.E., Washington, D.C. 20017.

15

The Hispanic Poor
in the American Catholic
Middle-Class Church[1]

HISTORIANS GENERALLY REFER TO THE CATHOLIC CHURCH OF THE UNITED states in the nineteenth century as "The Church of the Immigrants." And indeed it was![2] A small number of Catholics were scattered around the nation before the Revolutionary War, some of them wealthy and distinguished. But what is known as the American Catholic Church came out of the immigrant ships of the last century when millions of poor, many of them Catholics, poured out onto the shores of the nation. Between 1820-1920, 40 million people arrived. Thousands of priests, religious sisters, and brothers came with them. They established parishes, organized dioceses, built and manned thousands of Catholic schools. It was an extraordinary achievement. Because of the Church, the leadership of the clergy, the influence of the parish, and the identification of the Church with the poor as their advocate and defender, the poor moved into the mainstream of American life and brought the Church with them. Now well established, the Catholic Church is one of the major institutions of American society. The immigrants of the nineteenth century have generally moved into the American middle class. The Church has moved with them. Its organizational characteristics, its activities, its style of life are typically American; it shares the middle-class charac-

---

1. Reprinted by permission of the publisher from *Thought*, 63, No. 249 (June 1988), pp. 189-200. Copyright© 1988 by Fordham University Press.

2. Hennessey and Dolan provide excellent histories of the Catholic Church in the United States in recent years. Both books have numerous chapters about the experiences of the immigrant Church. The intimate involvement of the Church and its religious leaders in the total experience of their people is made abundantly clear.

teristics of the third- and fourth-generation Irish, German, Italian, Polish, and others. It came, poverty stricken and persecuted. It struggled like the immigrants, took advantage of the opportunities of life in America and "moved ahead." As we say of the immigrants themselves, we can also say that the Church "made it."[3]

However, at the very moment when the Church seeks to relax in comfortable middle-class status, millions of new immigrants and refugees are arriving, flocking into parishes abandoned by sons and grandsons of European immigrants. Of the new population, most of them are Catholic, most of them are very poor. Once again the Church is being challenged to be "The Immigrant Church" for the newcomers, to do for the Spanish-speaking, the Haitians, and the Southeast Asians what it did for the poor and persecuted immigrants of the last century. But the scene has shifted. The Church is not coming out of the boats with the boat people, nor is it crossing the Mexican border with the so-called "illegals," nor is it identified with the poor as it was with the European immigrants. As a middle-class Church, it faces the task of ministering to a new and increasing group of the very poor. Can a middle-class Church do for the poor of this century what "The Immigrant Church" did for the poor a century ago? This will be the challenge to the Church during the next two generations.

The Hispanic Poor

Who are the newcomers? This paper will concentrate on the Spanish-speaking, since they are the largest and most important part of the challenge. A U.S. Census Report for 1985 reported 16,900,000 persons of Hispanic origin in the United States, a substantial increase of 2,300,000 (16%) over the 1980 census figure of 14,600,000 (U.S. Department of Commerce No. 403). The Catholic population of the U.S.A. is estimated at 50,000,000. That makes Hispanics more than one-third of the entire Catholic population. However, there are millions of so-called "illegals," persons in the United States with no documents, who live in the shadows, in constant fear of being apprehended and deported, often ex-

---

3. The massive movement of the Catholic middle class to the suburbs is evident in the census reports. To take New York City as only one example, according to the 1980 Census, between 1970-80, New York City lost 1,750,000 citizens of white, European background, a population twice the size of the city of Buffalo. These were the grandchildren of the Irish, Italian, Jewish, Polish, etc., newcomers of the last century. They are replaced by Asians, large numbers of Hispanics, and blacks from the American South and the Caribbean.

ploited in housing and employment. Their numbers are estimated between three and five million. It is doubtful that many of them allowed
themselves to be counted in the census. If these are added, the Hispanic
population may be closer to 20 million, 40 percent of the Catholic population of the United States.

However, this is not the whole story. Hispanics are a much
younger population. According to the 1985 Census Report, the median
age of Hispanics (half above, half below) is 25; the median age of the U.S.
population is 31.9. Hispanics have larger families: 28.7 percent according to the census had five persons or more; only 14.9 percent of all U.S.
families had five persons or more. An examination of the Hispanics
reveals a very large, young, rapidly growing population, many of whom
have not yet reached marriageable age. If this trend continues, by the
middle of the next century, they may constitute the majority of the
Catholic population of the U.S.

But that is not all. The largest number of legal immigrants is now
coming from Central and South America and the Spanish-speaking islands of the Caribbean. This trend will very likely continue and increase.
Puerto Ricans are citizens and need no visa. They keep coming and
going. According to the 1985 Census Report, Puerto Ricans numbered
2,600,000 in the continental United States, an increase of 500,000 since
1980. With reference to noncitizens, our present immigration laws provide up to a total of 270,000 visas for legal entry, a maximum of 20,000
visas per year for any nation whose residents can qualify and request
them. This figure does not include about 100,000 per year who are
admitted legally as unnumbered immigrants – parents or children of
American citizens, for example – or about 100,000 refugees per year who
eventually are granted the status of legal aliens. Given the economic
distress and political turmoil of many of the Hispanic nations and the
fact that they already have numerous relatives and friends in the United
States, the flow of legal immigrants from the Spanish-speaking world
will continue to be high. Add these to the population already here and
it is clear why Hispanics will be for the Church and nation in the next
century what the European immigrants were for the Church and nation
in the present century.

It important to remember that the Catholic Church in what is now
the geographical area of the United States was originally Spanish. The
entire Southwest that was annexed after the Mexican-American War of
1848 was heavily populated by persons of Spanish background. The first
Mass on what is now United States soil was celebrated at Saint
Augustine, Florida, in 1565. The first Vicar General of the New York

Archdiocese was a Cuban, Father Félix Varela; and the first Catholic Church in New York City, Saint Peter's on Barclay Street, was built with the help of money from Spain and dedicated in the presence of the Spanish Ambassador.

Therefore, not all Hispanics are newcomers. Many of them have been here for a long time. In fact, those who lived in the Mexican territory annexed by the United States after the Mexican War were here before the United States became a nation. But the great majority are relatively new and their numbers are increasing every day.

What is particularly significant, however, is the fact that many of the Hispanics are among the poorest people in the United States. The Puerto Ricans – who are born American citizens – are one of the poorest populations in the United States. According to the 1985 Census Report, 42 percent of all Puerto Rican families in the continental United States were living below the poverty level. Only 30 percent of the blacks were then living in poverty. For all Hispanics the figure came to about 25 percent; for non-Hispanics in the nation, it was 11 percent.

The third draft of the Bishops' Letter on the American Economy, *Economic Justice for All: Catholic Social Teaching and the United States Economy*, has a powerful statement about poverty in the United States (National Conference #167-212). The Bishops' document the increase and the extent of poverty in the U.S., calling attention to the desperately poor (the homeless), the one out of every three blacks and one out of every four Hispanics who live in poverty. They emphasize the plight of the children, one in every four children under six in the entire population living in poverty; among blacks, it is one out of two. They are emphatic about the need to enable these marginalized citizens to become part of the mainstream of American political, economic, and social life. They point very clearly to the problems of doing this, namely the vested interest and control of power in the hands of the more affluent members of American society. Somewhat hidden in the powerful statement is the particularly Catholic challenge: a large percentage of these poor persons are Catholics; a large percentage of the affluent are also Catholic. The Letter discusses the issue in economic and political terms, in a context of moral imperatives. But the social and cultural dimensions are even more difficult, namely, bridging the gap between middle and poorer classes. This is the problem of middle-class and upper-class citizens making common cause with the poor, becoming their advocates in a way that enjoys credibility among the poor, employing a preferential option that is neither patronizing nor manipulative but that succeeds in "empowering" the poor, placing in the hands of the poor the capacity to demand their rights and privileges instead of having them given to them.

Poverty and Female-Headed Families

The poverty of Hispanics is impacted in female-headed families. In 1985, for example, 25 percent of all Hispanic families were living in poverty; more than half of these were headed by a woman. It is becoming clear that if something is not done to correct the problem of female-headed families, there will be little success in correcting the poverty of Hispanics. Senator Daniel Patrick Moynihan has repeatedly called for an adequate "family policy" in the United States, to the extent that women, especially women as single parents with children, should be guaranteed an income that brings them at least above the poverty level.[4] Welfare payments in New York State, in the form of Aid to Families with Dependent Children, provide an income 33 percent below the poverty level. And New York State has the best welfare rates in the nation. The Bishops' Letter on the U.S. Economy attributes some of the poverty of women to prevailing discrimination against women at all levels of employment. Only a substantial increase in women's wages can correct this serious flaw. Finally, serious efforts to train both youths and adults in responsible parenthood are needed to enable them both to fulfill the values of Christian family life.[5]

Poverty and Economic Change

Some of the poverty is explained by large-scale shifts in the economy. For example, between 1970-80 New York City lost 600,000 jobs at unskilled or semiskilled levels, many of which were occupied by Hispanic men and women. Largely poorly educated, they are not prepared to take the white collar jobs that are developing in New York City.[6] As a result, unemployment rates are high: in 1985, 15 percent of Puerto Rican men in the United States and 13.5 percent of Puerto Rican women, in

---

4. For an excellent analysis of the problem of family policy, see Moynihan, *Family and Nation*. He points out that the perpetuation of poverty, especially among children, is a result of unfair tax structures of the U.S. government.

5. Black leaders have finally begun to speak openly about the need to help black families to return to the basic values of family life. See, for example, Joint Center, "The Black Family," and Height. See also Norton for an excellent discussion of the issue. Hispanic leaders should follow their example.

6. For an analysis of the changing economy of New York City and its impact on the jobs of the poor, see Ehrenhalt.

contrast to 7.8 percent for men in the total population, 7.4 percent for women. The unemployment rate for all Hispanic men in the United States was 11.8 percent, for Hispanic women, 10.5 percent, lower than the rate for Puerto Ricans but still considerably higher than the rate for the total population (U.S. Department of Commerce Table 6). There have been substantial socioeconomic gains for Hispanics of the second generation (born in the United States of parents who were born abroad) but in general, Hispanics are a poor and economically depressed population.

The above details describe the newcomers, a rapidly increasing population likely to become the dominant population in the Catholic Church in two or three generations. Large numbers of them are living in poverty. Where then does the Church come in? It would indeed be a great blessing if the Church were in the same position to the Hispanic newcomers that it was to the immigrants of the last century as the "Church of the Immigrant." This is not the case. And this is the enormous challenge that God has given to the Church at the present time. What are the dimensions of the problem? In the first place, the Hispanics are the first large-scale immigration of Catholics who have not brought their own clergy with them. This problem is rooted in the history of Spanish colonization – too much to go into here. Secondly, the relationship of the Church to the continuity of their culture and the stability of their neighborhoods is, for many reasons, very different. This will be explained later. Finally and most seriously, the Hispanic poor find themselves dependent for pastoral care and spiritual ministry on a predominantly middle-class clergy and middle-class Church. Notwithstanding the enormous generosity in the efforts being made to respond to the newcomers, the class difference is an extremely difficult gap to bridge. Wonderful things are happening in many places, but the problem is enormous.

The Earlier Immigrant Church

The Hispanics' lack of their own clergy is critical. In the last century the clergy came out of the desperately poor families to which they later returned to minister. They were Irish or German priests out of a poor Irish or German background. Later it was Italian priests or Polish or Lithuanian or another nationality. They were identified with the people they served. They knew the way their people felt, the sufferings they endured, the values they cherished, the practices that meant loyalty or generosity or devotion to the faith. They had a keen sense of the interests and needs of their people, not only spiritual but economic, social, and political. Many a rectory kitchen served as a political club.

They vibrated with sensitivity to the joys and sorrows, the frustrations or satisfactions of their people. Because the poor were *their* people, there was an identity between them that was deep and strong.[7] This is not the situation of the clergy with Hispanics in many cases today. To a large extent, American bishops, priests, religious, and lay personnel of a variety of European ancestries are trying to minister to increasing millions of a different cultural background and in most cases, of a different social class. Many of these persons have made remarkable efforts to prepare themselves for this ministry. Before describing the response of American clergy to the challenge, the nature of the challenge must be described in more detail. One aspect of the challenge is the cultural difference between the clergy and the Hispanic newcomers. This aspect is coming to be understood more clearly, and many efforts are being made to prepare both clergy and faithful to deal with it. The second aspect of the challenge, namely, the class difference between clergy and the Hispanic poor, is much more subtle. Many of the clergy are not aware of this and are not prepared for it.

Cultural Differences

A word must first be said about *culture*. Persons from a Latin culture see the world in very different ways than North Americans. Their sense of the sacred, their concept of the Church, their sense of the primacy of family loyalty rather than self-advancement, their sense of *personalismo*, the primacy of personal relationships rather than competition for personal gain, are very different from the lifestyle of the people of the United States. Hispanics feel a relationship to Saints as if they are members of the family: patrons, advocates, *compadres*, as they say in Spanish. They have a different perception of the relationship of men to women, the authority of the father, the protection of wife and daughter. Everything from the tone of voice, the way one walks, the embrace or the kiss rather than a handshake, the profound sense of mutual obligation, is part of the Hispanic, not the American, world view. Briefly, the whole world of meanings is different. Persons of one culture can develop a keen sensitivity to persons of another culture; thousands of American priests and Church personnel have sought to do this through language training and courses in intercultural communication. There is a lot of love between Hispanics and "Gringos" in many parishes of this

---

7. See Shaw for a remarkable description of the political and social as well as religious leadership that Hughes gave as an immigrant bishop to his immigrant people.

land. But sensitivity to people of other cultures requires enormous effort and not everyone who tries to cross cultural barriers succeeds.

The Problem of Social Class

Differences in *social class* are more difficult. It is true that a social class involves a culture of its own, a way of life that is taken for granted and which provides a sense of identity, of psychosocial satisfaction. But class becomes much more immediately involved with economic and political interests, with patterns of behavior and tensions which can become irritating. Class in the United States touches issues of power, wealth, and education. These are all interrelated. The indicators generally used to identify class are education, occupation, and income. What is striking about the United States is the fact that, unlike Latin America, it is predominantly a middle-class society. But at the same time, large pockets of poverty exist which cut across racial and ethnic differences. Poor educational achievement, lack of skills, inability to compete economically or politically, unemployment, and reliance on public welfare are some of the features of the poorer class. In any event, even for middle-class persons with great intercultural sensitivity, it is difficult to identify with the poor and to have a sure sense of the way the poor perceive their needs. However adaptable they may be to the cultural differences of Hispanics, sincere middle-class Americans will generally make an aggressive effort to get the poor to adopt the skills and styles that will enable them to "make it" into the middle class. But note, it is not one of their own who is urging the poor to move as a group into the mainstream and who is working with them from within the whole world of meanings that they share together. It is a person of the middle class telling the poor to "be like us," to become different. Life is not "of one piece," as we would say. The problem of the poor then becomes the problem of achieving and maintaining a deep sense of identity, of being themselves with a mastery over their own lives, within a Church whose ministers view the world as a place where everyone should be middle class.

The Role of the Parish

An important related issue here is the function of the parish. In the last century the parish became the heart of the immigrant neighborhood. People of the same nationality clustered together in "little Dublins" and "little Italies" and "Germantowns." The Church came with the people. If they were Italian they started an Italian parish; if they were Irish they started what the Irish called the Catholic parish. Clustering in those days was possible. People could choose to live where they wanted. All dwellings were privately owned and rentals were within the reach of a poor workingman's income. Thus, in the last century and in the early years of this century immigrants clustered in immigrant communities, and among Catholics, the parish or Church played a central role. The Church was the one institution where everything was the same as in the old country: language, religious services, feast days and celebrations, practices that lit the meaning of birth, marriage, illness, death. The cycle of life proceeded through the year as it did before they came. In a strange world the Church gave them a continuing identity, a sense of security and stability. It is still common for Irish people in New York, if asked where they live, to answer according to which parish they belong to. These "national" or language parishes were sharply criticized by many Americans as being divisive, as perpetuating old world cultures in a world where people should be seeking to become American as quickly as possible. Actually, far from hindering adjustment to American life, the immigrant community and the immigrant church gave the immigrants a sense of stability and strength that enabled them to move gradually but persistently into the mainstream of American life.

There are numerous reasons why bishops are reluctant to form national parishes for Hispanics. The official statement of the Church indicates that ideally, a ministry should be provided to newcomers in their own language, in their own style of Catholicism, by clergy and religious of their own background. This was done for the earlier immigrants through the national parish. The absence of Hispanic clergy and religious is only one reason for the decision of many bishops not to establish national parishes for Hispanics. Some fear that such a parish may later become obsolete. By the third generation, many of the national parishes of the earlier immigrants had lost their flocks to the suburbs. Grandchildren no longer spoke the language, had adopted a largely American style of life, and had moved out of the area of the national parish. Church, school, and convent lost their functions. I served as a consultant to one bishop who was trying to cope with the numerous national Churches in his diocese. On the block where we met there were four Catholic churches, one Polish, one Slovak, one Italian, and the geographical parish, Saint Mary's. The entire neighborhood was black and Puerto Rican. In view of this, many bishops opt to fulfill the Church's instructions by providing services in Spanish in established parishes rather than by opening a separate Church.

It is true that many Hispanic neighborhoods slowly form over a period of time, like *El Barrio* (the neighborhood) in East Harlem, New

York. But for many reasons it is much more difficult today to form an immigrant community. Hispanics cannot easily move to where their brothers or sisters or cousins live. Decent private rentals are beyond the reach of the poor; and for public housing, one must put up with applications and waiting lists. In New York City, 18,000 families are on the waiting list for public housing. You cannot move in where you want to. Added to this, the Hispanics face a parish staffed by American priests – who may or may not have learned their language or developed a sensitive understanding of their Hispanic culture. For Hispanics the parish is not "theirs" in the way Saint Anthony's was the Italian parish, or Saint Stanislaus' the Polish parish, or Saint Mary's the Irish parish. It does not give the neighborhood the sense of identity as an immigrant community; it is not the continuation of religious practices and celebrations, a small oasis of their old cultural world in the midst of a strange land. And for the most part, the style, the organization, the institutional framework of the Catholic world to which the Hispanic newcomer seeks to relate is middle-class American, highly organized, bureaucratic at many levels, with a style and expectations quite different from the ones with which Hispanics are familiar. They often find it difficult to feel *en su casa*, "at home" in this environment. Many of them shift to the storefront Pentecostal Church on the corner where everything makes sense to them in a style which makes them feel they are among their "own."[8]

This should not be over exaggerated. Many of the old territorial or national parishes have, over time, become completely "Hispanic" and operate very much like the old "national" parish. But for the most part, Hispanics do not feel the deep identity with the Church that was felt by immigrants of the past century.

The Response of the Church

The response of the Church to the challenge presented it has been enormous. To take the New York Archdiocese alone, in 1957 Cardinal Spellman sponsored the founding of the Center of Intercultural Communication in Ponce, Puerto Rico, where over a period of 15 years, thousands of priests, religious, and Catholic lay persons were trained in the language, Puerto Rican culture, and the problems of adjustment to the Mainland. In San Antonio, Texas, the Mexican American Cultural Center fulfills the same function. There probably has never been a time in the history of the Church when host dioceses went to such great efforts

---

8. The best study of a Pentecostal congregation (and the reasons Puerto Ricans and other Hispanics are attracted to them) is found in Poblete and O'Dea.

to receive newcomers of different language and cultural backgrounds. The Church has sought to institutionalize this apostolate. The American Bishops have established a Secretariat for Hispanics in the U.S. Catholic Conference, and regional centers exist in various parts of the nation. Most dioceses where Hispanics are numerous have established "Offices for the Apostolate to the Hispanics." It would seem that this effort would have resulted in great gains. But the gains have been far fewer than one would expect. The theme of this paper identifies the basic problem as class. The generous efforts at evangelization and an understanding of culture have been complicated by the difficulty of middle-class Catholics in identifying with the poor.

At their national meeting in Washington in November 1983, the Bishops of the United States issued a pastoral letter on the Church's responsibility to Hispanic newcomers: *The Hispanic Presence: Challenge and Commitment.* The letter focuses largely on the apostolic response. But it describes the condition of poverty and exploitation of many Hispanics and calls the members of the Church to a commitment to social justice and a "preferential option for the poor." If this can actually be achieved, if the gap between the classes can be bridged as effectively as the gap between the cultures, the efforts of the Church are likely to be more effective.

The letter reflects an awareness of the difficulties involved in Hispanic ministry. It calls for new and creative efforts to meet the adjustments which will be necessary if Hispanics are to be received into the mainstream of Catholic life.

> We in our turn pledge to raise our voices and go on raising them as leaders in defense of the human dignity of Hispanics. We remind our pastoral associates that their work includes the effort to gain for Hispanics participation in the benefits of our society. We call all U.S. Catholics to work not just for Hispanics but with them, in order to secure their empowerment in our democracy and the political participation which is their right and duty. In this way we deepen our preferential option for the poor which, according to Jesus' example and the Church's tradition, must always be a hallmark of our apostolate. (National Conference #15)

The Letter speaks of the presence of Hispanics as "a gift"; "it is a prophetic presence to be encouraged and needed." The ideal is there. Its fulfillment, bridging the gap between a middle-class institution and a poor population, requires more than an official statement. When it occurs, wonderful things can happen. In recent years the priests of the

South Bronx and the Northwest Bronx, New York, have become very active with the poor populations in the deteriorated sections of the Bronx. The two community districts in the South Bronx lost 57 percent of their housing units between 1970-80 in an epidemic of neighborhood fires which are a scandal to the city. The rebuilding of the Bronx, the resurrection of viable communities among the poor, the "empowerment" that the Letter speaks of, have been taking place. It is described in detail in a recent book for which Senator Daniel Patrick Moynihan wrote the foreword. He concludes: "After much travail and much failure, and much avoidance of the obvious, the people of the South Bronx and the Catholic Church got together and have set to work. And the Lord's work it is. . . . And more, it is news. *Good News.*" (xxiv).

Meantime the great promise has been the assertiveness of the Hispanics themselves. Long before the first national Assembly of Catholics, the "Call to Action" in Detroit in 1976, the Hispanics had already organized two national assemblies, *Encuentros* as they are called. They celebrated a third one in Washington, D.C., in August 1985, as a follow-up to the Bishops' Letter. At the "Call to Action" assembly in Detroit in 1976, the Hispanics, to everyone's amazement, were the best organized and most aggressive participants. They have developed their own style of religious practice in the *Cursillos*, a short retreat with intense follow-up which has had an unusual influence on the religious life of Hispanics. The charismatic movement flourishes in many Hispanic parishes as do activities such as "Marriage Encounters" for the strengthening of Catholic family life.

The Letter calls for the involvement of *comunidades eclesiales de base*, the remarkable grass-roots small Christian communities that have helped to revolutionize the life of the Church in Central and South America. If the spirit of these basic Christian communities can come alive in the United States, they will go far to enable the Church to become identified with the life of the poor. But there are many concerns about the *comunidades de base* which reflect the anxieties of a middle-class church when the poor begin to assert political power in their own right.

There is also resistance to a concept of "assimilation" which appears to seek an involvement of the poor in the American middle class in a process in which their language and culture would be lost. Actually this is what happened to the earlier immigrants. The Bishops' Letter makes a plea for "cultural pluralism" in which the poor could become empowered and could participate in the mainstream of American politics and economics without the loss of their language or the loss of values and ideals of their cultural background.[9] If the Hispanics succeed in achieving this, they will write a new chapter in the history of the American Catholic experience. The proximity of Hispanics to the lands of their origin and the strong efforts toward bilingualism and bicultural education are part of the Hispanic effort to create a cultural pluralism in the nation. It will be another generation or two before the success or failure of this effort will become clear.

Nevertheless, all these activities and processes continue to flourish among the Hispanic poor, and American bishops, clergy, and religious are deeply involved in them. Many Americans have remarked that their own faith has become more vital in their associations with Hispanics. There is indeed a vitality to Catholic life in many of the Hispanic parishes that is not often found in middle-class Catholic parishes. There are signs that the influence of Hispanics may be significant in giving the Church a new vision, a new life. In doing so, it will be converting the Church again into an Immigrant Church of a different kind, a collaboration of middle-class Americans and poor Hispanics in an effort to respond to the increasing millions on whom the future of the Church will depend in the next century.

References

Dolan, J. *The American Catholic Experience: A History from Colonial Times to the Present*. New York: Doubleday, 1985.

Ehrenhalt, Samuel M. *Key to New York Trends and Puerto Rican Prospects*. U.S. Department of Labor, Bureau of Labor Statistics, Washington, D.C.: U.S. Government Printing Office. 1986.

Gordon, Milton. *Assimilation in American Life*. New York: Oxford University Press. 1964.

Height, Dorothy I. "What Must be Done about Children Having Children?" *Ebony* Mar. 1985: pp. 76-83.

Hennessey, James J. *American Catholics: A History of the Roman Catholic Community in the United States*. New York: Oxford University Press. 1981.

Joint Center for Political Studies. "The Black Family." *A Policy for Racial Justice*. Washington, D.C. 1983.

Jonnes, Jill. *We're Still Here: The Rise, Fall, and Resurrection of the South Bronx*. New York: Atlantic Monthly. 1986.

Moynihan, Daniel Patrick. *Family and Nation*. New York: Harcourt. 1986.

_____. Foreword. *We're Still Here: The Rise, Fall, and Resurrection of the South Bronx*. By Jill Jonnes. New York: Atlantic Monthly. 1986. pp. i-xxvi.

---

9. The best discussion of these processes can be found in Gordon, Chapters 3-6.

National Conference of Catholic Bishops. *Economic Justice for All: Catholic Social Teaching and the United States Economy.* Third Draft. Washington, D.C. 1986.

_____. *The Hispanic Presence: Challenge and Commitment, A Pastoral Letter on Hispanic Ministry.* Washington, D.C.: Dec. 12, 1983.

Norton, Eleanor Holmes. "Restoring the Traditional Black Family," *New York Times Magazine,* June 2, 1985.

Poblete, Renato, and Thomas F. O'Dea. "Anomie and the Quest for Community: The Formation of Sects among Puerto Ricans in New York." *American Catholic Sociological Review* 21 (Spring 1960): pp. 18-36.

Shaw, Bernard. *Dagger John: The Unique Life and Times of Archbishop John Hughes of New York.* New York: Paulist, 1977.

U.S. Department of Commerce. Bureau of the Census. *Current Population Reports, Population Characteristics:* "Persons of Spanish Origin in the United States." Series P-20. Washington, D.C., U.S. Government Printing Office. Dec. 1985 (Advance Report: March 1985).

16

Hispanics in New York: An Archdiocesan Survey[1]

A three year study based on in-depth interviews with a sample of 1,000 subjects confirms the achievements of past pastoral efforts and identifies new resources and challenges for the church.

On the feast of Epiphany this year (*Los Tres Reyes* – or Three Kings Day among Hispanics), the New York Archdiocese released its extensive study and survey of Hispanics in the New York Archdiocese. This had been in the making for almost three years and now appears as the first survey of its kind, a document that promises to be a significant influence on the response of the New York Archdiocese to Hispanics in the years to come. Indeed, it is valuable not only for New York but wherever the Church in the United States faces the task of ministering to Hispanics.

The heart of the study is a scientifically executed survey of a sample of 1,000 Hispanics from the four counties of the Archdiocese in which the Hispanics are concentrated: Manhattan, Bronx, Richmond and Westchester. (Two large boroughs of New York City, Brooklyn and Queens, are not in the New York Archdiocese and are not included in the study.) The survey consists of a one-hour interview on the basis of a bilingual interview schedule, carefully planned and tested in advance.

There are three other components to the study: 1) a demographic profile, 2) some case studies to provide a more concrete illustration of the religious experience of Hispanics and 3) a series of background papers ("Popular Religiosity," by Jaime R. Vidal; "Cultural Change and Cultural Continuity: Pluralism and Hispanic Americans," by Joseph P. Fitzpatrick; "The Social and Economic Situation of Hispanics," by

---

1. *America*, March 12, 1983, pp. 185-187. Reprinted with the permission of America Press, Inc., 106 West 56th Street, New York, NY 10019. ©1983. All Rights Reserved.

Douglas Gurak; "The Hispanic Family," by Dorothy M. Dohen, Ruth T. Doyle, Olga Scarpetta and Patricia Pessar; "Hispanic Vocations," by Rutilio del Riego, and "The Evolution of Hispanic Ministry in the New York Archdiocese," by Robert L. Stern). The background papers are bound in a separate volume and constitute a unit in themselves.

The study was commissioned by Cardinal Terence Cooke, who wrote the Foreword. Requests for the study had come from the Ad Hoc Committee for Hispanic Evangelization and the Liturgical Commission of the New York Archdiocese. It was under the general direction of Ruth T. Doyle, director of the Office of Pastoral Research of the New York Archdiocese. She was assisted by a large steering committee under the direction of the Rev. Raoul del Valle as chairperson and a technical committee of sociologists with Dr. William C. McCready of the National Opinion Research Center as chairperson. The field study was directed by Olga Scarpetta.

As always the hard demographic data are impressive. According to the 1980 census, there are 835,000 Hispanics in the New York Archdiocese, 17 percent of the total population. Most of these are Puerto Ricans, 537,000 or about 65 percent of all Hispanics; about 200,000 or roughly 25 percent of all Hispanics are Dominicans, the rest are from Cuba and a wide variety of Central and South American nations. The Office of Pastoral Research estimates that 35 percent of all Catholics in the Archdiocese are Hispanic. More significant than the numbers is the age profile: 28 percent of all Hispanics are under five years of age; more than 50 percent are under seventeen years of age. The future is already here, and it is decidedly Hispanic.

Strong Faith, Weak Practice

Probably the most important finding of the survey was the strong adherence of Hispanics to the basic truths of the Catholic faith, despite the fact that 36 percent said they never go to Mass and another 24 percent said they went sporadically (anything from monthly to once a year). The majority, however stated that the local church and Catholic school were important to them. This is not surprising in view of the fact that the norm of identification as Catholics in Latin America is not attendance at Mass. It is rather the awareness that they are members of a Catholic "pueblo," or Catholic community that celebrates its faith in public festivities such as processions, fiestas and important commemorative events. Regular attendance at Mass and participation in parish organizations are cultural adjustments the Hispanics face. There is also the fact that many Hispanics come from areas where few priests were available and where formation in the faith was limited, especially among the poor. And the Hispanics of New York City are to a large extent a poor population. The census indicates that Puerto Ricans are the poorest population in the city.

Popular Religiosity

Folk religious practices still abound among Hispanics: candles, incense, shrines in the home, the rosary, wearing medals, blessings, prayer at meals, sprinkling holy water, especially on the newborn child, reading the Bible. These are found more frequently among the churchgoers than among others, but they are still surprisingly alive among those who never attend Mass. They evidently represent an elemental response to the sacred and constitute a basic religious experience that could develop into a mature Catholicism. Occasionally they are diverted into magical or superstitious practices (putting a curse on others) that may be harmful. Dealing with these practices presents a challenge to pastors. It involves the ability to cultivate the basic religious response to the sacred, which is evident in the rites, without appearing to sanction those practices that are not compatible with Catholic faith and practice. The background paper, "Popular Religiosity" provides some insight to assist in this process.

These practices show a noticeable decline from the generation of parents to the children. They also decrease as education increases.

Familiarity Only with Local Issues

There is a surprising lack of familiarity among the Hispanics with significant events even in the Latin American church. Very few had ever heard of Medellin or Puebla, the great and revolutionary conferences of the Latin American bishops. Sixty percent never heard of Vatican II. For most the visit of the Pope was the one event that stood out in their memory. Very few (14 percent) had heard of the two national congresses (*Encuentro* 1 and 2) of Hispanic Catholics, nationwide congresses of Hispanics that antedated the "Call to Action" Congress of American Catholics that took place in Detroit in 1976. There was a greater familiarity with the activities that touched the people more directly on the local level, such as the *Cursillo*, a short intensive retreat with follow-up that has played a major role in the religious life of Hispanics. The importance of parish councils rated fairly high (41 percent) as did religious education (34 percent), family prayer groups promoted by *Luz y Vida* (33 percent), and charismatic renewal (29 percent).

Language and Culture

One central concern of Hispanics has been the continuity of their culture and the continuity of the great symbol of culture, their language. More than any previous group of newcomers, they have consciously pursued a permanence of culture and language. The programs of intercultural understanding, such as the Institute of Intercultural Communication, which flourished for 15 years at the Catholic University of Puerto Rico in Ponce, or the Mexican American Cultural Center (MACC) in San Antonio, TX, never existed for previous immigrants. And the bilingual/bicultural educational programs in the schools that have been promoted by Hispanics have been a controversial innovation. In view of this, the study searched out the reaction of the Hispanics of the New York Archdiocese to both these issues.

A large majority of respondents (71 percent) are bilingual; 26 percent speak only Spanish; 56 percent speak only Spanish at home. Despite bilingual ability, Spanish is still the language of religion. About 75 percent pray only in Spanish, and 75 percent of most recent baptisms were in Spanish. Those who speak only Spanish consider themselves more religious, but as bilingualism increases religious practice decreases. The theory that language is associated with preservation of the faith has some support from the study.

The positive response to the church, which is evident in more than half of the respondents, does not seem to be related to language or culture as much as their "feeling welcomed" by priests and ministers who had a warm and friendly attitude. Among those who found fault with the church, a very small percentage mentioned lack of Spanish language services (4 percent) or lack of sensitivity to Hispanic culture (5 percent) as the source of their complaints. Coldness and lack of concern on the part of priests and ministers were the most frequent complaints (15 percent).

Positive Attitude Toward the Church

The strong positive attitude toward the Church came as a surprise to many people in view of a popular impression that Hispanics were largely "alienated" from the Church. An enormous task of evangelization and ministry is certainly indicated by the study, but half the respondents said they "felt welcome." This evidently reflects the great effort the archdiocese has made over the years to respond to the spiritual and religious needs of the Hispanic people. The background paper, "The Evolution of Hispanic Ministry in the New York Archdiocese," provides a record of the impressive struggle of people at all levels of the archdiocese to minister to the newcomers. The Hispanics, unlike any previous Catholic group, came without their own clergy to minister to them. They depended on an American clergy of different language and cultural background to provide spiritual care to hundreds of thousands who were pouring into a large and complicated city. Although many priests from Spain were recruited to assist and served well, the major task fell to American bishops and clergy. Certainly the program of the New York Archdiocese for the apostolate to the Hispanics must stand as a rare event in the history of the Church. Its significance has not received the recognition that it deserves. The positive response in the survey is one of the few emphatic signs that the effort was more effective than is generally believed.

Some commentators attributed the favorable response to the fact that the interviews identified the study as a study of the Catholic Church. The directors of the study have dealt with this issue openly and well. Hispanics are so suspicious of any stranger as a possible government investigator that interviewers would not have been received had they not identified themselves as workers with the church. The confidence of the Hispanics in "church" people results in a ready welcome and willingness to participate. The "debriefing" sessions with the interviewers contributed their own insights into the character of the study. Whatever bias may have colored the study presented as a "Catholic study," the over-all impression reported by the interviewers was one of seriousness, interest and credibility.

Cultural Assimilation or Cultural Pluralism?

The challenge of the next generation is brought to light sharply in the study. If present trends continue, the New York Archdiocese in the next century will be predominantly Hispanic. The largest segments of this population are Puerto Ricans and Dominicans. They are also the poorest in terms of socioeconomic status. Briefly, the church now faces, more so than ever before, a ministry to the poor. This is complicated by the fact that, institutionally, the church has become decidedly middle class. Probably the most serious aspect of ministry will be the problem of a middle class church ministering to a predominantly poor population. In the last century the clergy came from the poor families to whom they later ministered. Unless a clergy emerges from the Hispanic population, this will not be repeated. An important background paper, "Promotion of Hispanic Vocations and the Formation of Hispanic Seminarians," calls attention to this: Hispanic seminarians feel out of place in the American style seminary; and the lifestyle of American seminarians makes it difficult for them to minister to the poor. Nevertheless, Hispanics are beginning to be noticeably present. In the academic year 1979-80, there were 190 Hispanic seminarians in the seminaries of the United States.

The survey reflects the relentless impact of American culture. As length of time in the United States increases, and as education increases, use of language lessens, deeply rooted religious sentiments and attitudes are lost, acceptance of traditional moral values diminishes. In brief, the process of assimilation moves forward, and it appears to have a negative effect on religious beliefs and practice. Furthermore as the background papers on "The Hispanic Family" show, traditional family values and practices are shaken by the impact of life in the United States, and evidences of serious problems appear such as the high level of out of wedlock children (46 percent of all births to Puerto Rican women in New York City in 1980) and the high level of abortions (60 percent of all pregnancies among Puerto Rican women in New York City in 1980). Some crisis intervention is indicated as well as long range planning.

Ministry to a people facing this cultural turmoil, especially second generation people (and more than 400,000 Puerto Ricans in New York City now are second generation), will continue to be a complicated challenge. A sense of identity, rooted in one's cultural background, has been a critical factor in the smooth adjustment of previous immigrants to American life. An effort will have to be made to help Hispanics to retain this as they become increasingly bilingual and run the risk of the attrition of their religious life as they become more educated and feel the impact of American culture. The background paper, "Cultural Change or Cultural Continuity: Pluralism and Hispanic Americans," examines this issue at great length, namely, the importance of retaining a strong sense of Hispanic identity as a position of strength from which one moves into the mainstream of American life. At the same time, an overemphasis on culture may create the danger of ministering to youth in a cultural style that they have already left behind.

Nevertheless, there are signs of promise and hope. There is a much more favorable "climate" in the United States around the issue of cultural pluralism. There is a greater understanding of and sensitivity to cultural differences and a more favorable attitude toward newcomers. This is reflected at the level of national policy in the changes toward more favorable immigration legislation since World War II. There is a crisis about immigration legislation at the present moment, but the trend over the years has been favorable. Likewise the proximity of Hispanics to their native lands, the ease of communication and the constant travel back and forth may enable the Hispanics to retain a cultural base and a sense of identity that earlier immigrants did not enjoy.

Ministry to Hispanics will not be an easy task. Yet the future depends on it. However, the paper cited above, "The Evolution of Hispanic Ministry . . . " describes the New York Archdiocese as in a process of constant experimentation, struggling through successes and failures to assist the Hispanics to retain their faith and cultural values. There is every reason to expect that the archdiocese will continue to struggle, to experiment, to innovate, trusting that the Lord will give the increase. The Hispanic study ("Hispanics in New York: Religious, Cultural and Social Experiences," New York Archdiocese, Office of Pastoral Research, 1011 First Avenue, New York, NY, 10022, $15.00) is one more significant step in the process, and one which anyone dealing with Hispanics, religiously or not, can use with great profit.

Chronology[1]

1913: Born, 2nd of 5 sons to Anna and Patrick Fitzpatrick of Bayonne, NJ (Feb. 22)

1930: Graduated, Saint Peter's Prep, Jersey City, NJ

1930: Entered the Society of Jesus, Saint Isaac Jogues Novitiate, Wernersville, PA

1934-37: Studied for Bachelor of Arts Degree, Woodstock College, Woodstock, MD

1937-38: Studied for Master of Arts Degree in Philosophy, Fordham University, Bronx, NY

1938-40: Assistant Director then Director, Xavier Labor School, NYC

1938-40: Instructor in English, Latin and Social Studies, Xavier High School, NYC

1940-44: Studied for Licentiate in Sacred Theology, Woodstock College

1943: Ordained at St. Ignatius Loyola Church, New York City (June 24)

1943-44: Auxiliary Chaplain, US Coast Guard Training Station, Curtis Bay, MD and Marine Hospital, Baltimore, MD

1945-48: Graduate Studies in Sociology, Harvard University; Ph.D. March 1949; Delancey K. Jay Prize for best thesis of the year in American Institutions (*White Collar Worker on Wall Street*)

1949-95: Fordham University; From Instructor to Professor of Sociology (1949-83), Founding Chair of the Department of Sociol-

---

1. This notes only a few of the highlights in Father Fitzpatrick's life. It completely omits the 14 research projects which he directed or co-directed, as well as his numerous articles, chapters of books, addresses, and homilies. He served as a consultant to many parishes, dioceses, schools, police departments, departments of health, social welfare agencies and courts whose names have been omitted for purposes of brevity. Finally, the chronology only hints at the lengthy list of awards that were presented to him.

ogy and Anthropology, 1959-64 and 1970-72; Director, Institute for Social Research 1976-95; Professor Emeritus, 1983-95

1953-95: Consultant on Spanish-speaking Affairs, Archdiocese of New York

1953-93: Editorial Advisory Board, *Thought*, the Fordham University Quarterly

1953-57: Advisory Committee, Puerto Rican Study, New York: City Board of Education

1955: 1st Conference on the Spiritual Care of Puerto Rican Migrants, San Juan and Ponce

1955: with W. Ferre and I. Illich, published *Spiritual Care of Puerto Rican Migrants* (2nd ed. pudished in 1981)[2]

1955: Award of Merit, Council of Spanish-speaking Organizations of Greater New York, "For Distinguished Scholarly Contribution to the Understanding of the Puerto Rican People of New York City"

1957-71: Lecturer, Summers, Institute of Intercultural Communication, Catholic University of Puerto Rico

1961-71: Lecturer, Summers, Center of Intercultural Documentation, Cuernavaca, Mexico

1962-64: Lecturer, Summers, Center of Intercultural Formation, Petropolis, Brazil

1963-95: Board of Directors, Puerto Rican Family Institute

1964: Board of Directors, American Council for Nationality Services; US Committee for Refugees

1964: with J.M. Martin, published *Delinquent Behavior:A Redefinition of the Problem*

1966-76: Board of Directors, Center of Intercultural Formation (later Center of Intercultural Documentation), Cuernavaca, Mexico; President of the Board, 1968-76

1967: Edited *Educational Planning and Socio-economic Development in Latin America*

1967: "Operation 'Friend' Award for Promoting Better Understanding Between NYC Police and Our Spanish Speaking Community," Conferred by Radio Station WBNX

---

2. Complete citations for Father Fitzpatrick's books may be found in Part I of this memoir.

1969: with J. M. Martin and R.E. Gould, published *The Analysis of Delinquent Behavior: A Structural Approach*

1969-95: Founder then Chairman of the Board, Neighborhood Youth and Family Services

1969-95: Founding Consultant, sometime Board member, Centro Isolina Ferré, Ponce Playa, PR; Edificio Padre José Fitzpatrick (Father Joseph Fitzpatrick Building) dedicated in 1991

1969-88: Board of Directors American Immigration and Citizenship conference (later renamed National Immigration, Refugee and Citizenship Forum)

1969-94: Faculty/Student Committee on Puerto Rican Studies, Fordham University

1970-95: Board of Directors, Neighborhood Youth and Family Services; Chairman of the Board, 1982-95.

1971: Publication of *Puerto Rican Americans*

1971-75: Chairman, Board of Trustees, LeMoyne College, Syracuse, NY

1972-90: with Rabbi Louis Finkelstein, established the seminar, "The Enhancement of Civilization" at the Institute of Religious and Social Studies, Jewish Theological Seminary

1973-95: Board of Directors, Puerto Rican Legal Defense and Education Fund

1974: Honorary Chairman Award, First Diocesan Congress for the Spanish Speaking of the United States, Diocese of Brooklyn

1974-85: Board of Directors, Group Living in Experience (GLIE) – small group homes for children in the Bronx

1974: Catholic University of Puerto Rico, Honorary Degree, Doctor of Humane Letters

1975: Loyola University Chicago, Honorary Degree, Doctor of Humane Letters

1975-95: Board of Directors, American Council for Nationalities Services

1977-80: Research Advisory Committee, Aspira

1979: Named "Puerto Rican Man of the Year" at the San Juan Fiesta

1979: with D. Gurak, published *Hispanic Intermarriage in New York City*

1979-83: Consultant to the New York Provincial, Society of Jesus, on issues relating to justice, peace and faith

1980-92: Public Policy Committee, New York State Catholic Conference

1983: Fordham University, Honorary Degree, Doctor of Laws

1983: John Jay College of Criminal Justice, Honorary Degree, Doctor of Law

1983: Special Award for Service to the Puerto Rican Community, Puerto Rican Family Institute

1984: Manhattan College, Honorary Degree, Doctor of Humane Letters

1985-94: Board of Directors, Thorpe Family Residence

1986: Special Award, Puerto Rico Chamber of Commerce of New York

1987: Special Award for Service to the Puerto Rican Community, Puerto Rican Bar Association

1987: Publication of *One Church, Many Cultures: The Challenge of Diversity*

1987: Publication of *Puerto Rican Americans*, 2nd ed.

1987-89: Director, Institute of Dominican Small Business, Fordham University

1987-90: Advisory Committee to the Chancellor on "School Related Health Clinics," Board of Education of the City of New York

1988-95: Advisory Committee to the President, Hostos Community College, City University of New York

1989: Fullbright Lecturer, Montevideo, Uruguay

1990: Jesuit School of Theology at Berkeley, Honorary Degree, Doctor of Divinity

1990: Published *Paul: Saint of the Inner City*

1991-95: President, Puerto Rican Foundation

1993: Celebrated Golden Jubilee – Fifty Years of Priesthood

1994: completed manuscript with Greta Gilbertson, *The Effects of Intermarriage on Hispanic Ministry*, (publication forthcoming)

1995: Died at the age of 82 (March 15)

1996: Posthumous publication of *The Stranger Is Our Own: Reflections on the Journey of Puerto Rican Migrants*